the series on school reform

Patricia A. Wasley
Coalition of
Essential Schools

Ann Lieberman
NCREST

Joseph P. McDonald
Annenberg Institute
for School Reform

SERIES EDITORS

This series also incorporates earlier titles in the
Professional Development and Practice Series

MAKING
PROFESSIONAL
DEVELOPMENT
SCHOOLS
WORK

POLITICS
PRACTICE
AND POLICY

MARSHA LEVINE
ROBERTA TRACHTMAN

EDITORS

TEACHERS COLLEGE
COLUMBIA UNIVERSITY
NEW YORK AND LONDON

Published by Teachers College Press, 1234 Amsterdam Avenue, New York, NY
10027

Library of Congress Cataloging-in-Publication Data

Making professional development schools work: politics,
    practice, and policy / Marsha Levine, Roberta Trachtman, editors.
        p.   cm. — (The series on school reform)
    Includes bibliographical references and index.
    ISBN 0-8077-3634-1 (cloth : alk. paper). — ISBN 0-8077-3633-3
(pbk. : alk. paper)
    1. Laboratory schools—United States.   I. Levine, Marsha.
II. Trachtman, Roberta.   III. Series.
    LB2154.A3S87   1997
    370′.7—dc21   97-1604

ISBN 0-8077-3633-3 (paper)
ISBN 0-8077-3634-1 (cloth)

Printed on acid-free paper
Manufactured in the United States of America

04   03   02   01   00   99   98   97   8   7   6   5   4   3   2   1

Contents

Acknowledgments

We would like to acknowledge the people who are doing the hard work of building Professional Development Schools in sites all over the country; and we thank the contributing authors who have written about this work. We would also like to thank Wendy Schwartz, a talented editor, for her assistance in preparing the manuscript.

M.L. would like to thank the Exxon Education Foundation for their support, over several years, of her work in the design and development of Professional Development Schools. An early grant supported the creation of a national task force at the American Federation of Teachers. This task force focused on the relationship between restructuring schools and teacher education. The work of the task force resulted in the publication in 1992 of *Professional Practice Schools: Linking Teacher Education and School Reform*. The Foundation's continued funding created three Professional Development School pilot projects, whose experiences offer important insights into the challenges of building these unique partnership institutions. Exxon's funding has supported the development of this volume, which brings together the stories of these pilot projects with the contributions of expert practitioners, researchers, scholars, and analysts who have been building Professional Development Schools and studying the work that goes on in them. Neither the Exxon Education Foundation nor the AFT are responsible for the views expressed in this volume.

M.L. and R.T.

Introduction

MARSHA LEVINE

The basic concept underlying the Professional Development School (PDS) — that is, an elementary or secondary school where teachers learn and research is a part of practice — is not a new idea. PDSs are rooted philosophically in the progressive education movement (Levine, 1992). Antecedents of the PDS are found in John Dewey's Laboratory School, in the work of Lucy Sprague Mitchell (1950), and in Schaefer's "schools of inquiry" (Schaefer, 1967).

Education reform and school restructuring of the 1980s and 1990s have rekindled interest in this concept. In 1986, the Carnegie Forum on Education and the Economy called for the establishment of clinical schools where new teachers would learn to work in collegial, performance-oriented environments. In 1990, the Holmes Group called for a major restructuring of teacher education in which Professional Development Schools played a central role. These influential reports, together with a significant grassroots effort to restructure schools, have resulted in a movement to create a new institution that is specifically designed to link teacher education and school reform.

In the past decade, university–school partnerships have created Professional Development Schools in over 250 locations around the country (Abdal-Haaq, 1995). They bring together university and school-based faculty to share responsibility for the clinical preparation of new teachers, the professional development of experienced faculty, the support of research directed at improving practice, and enhanced student learning. Several national networks have supported their development, including the Holmes Group (now the Holmes Partnership), the National Network for Educational Renewal initiated by John Goodlad, and the PDS Network begun by the National Center for Restructuring Education, Schools, and Teaching at Teachers College. Statewide initiatives and district networks also have been developed.

The best PDSs are imbued with a vision of teaching as professional practice — knowledge-based, collegial, and inquiry-oriented. Work in PDSs is guided by a commitment to a set of principles that include a student-centered approach to teaching and learning; the sharing of responsibilities between the partnering institutions; the simultaneous renewal of school and university; and a commitment to provide equal opportunity for all participants.

We believe PDSs are important for two major reasons. In their most developed state, they embody fundamental changes in the basic assumptions about knowledge, teaching, and learning, and they support these new assumptions with organization, roles, and relationships. More generally, they are important because of the key role they have to play in enabling several other major reform strategies to have an impact.

MAKING CHANGES AT THE CORE

PDSs challenge the traditional assumptions about core elements of schooling: What is knowledge? Who has it? How is it developed? These are questions raised and answered differently in the PDS than in the traditional school setting. Several critically important assumptions underlie the PDS.

- There is a knowledge base about teaching that resides among practitioners.
- Knowledge about teaching is created in school settings.
- Teaching and learning are ineluctably tied together; teaching is learning.
- Teachers' learning needs to be contextualized if teachers are to be oriented to continuous learning in practice.
- Teachers' learning needs to be collegial to generate more knowledge and to produce comfort with public practice and habits of conferral.
- Teachers' learning needs to be problem-based in order to develop a problem-solving orientation toward practice.

These assumptions about teacher learning are also assumptions about student learning in the PDS. Professional Development Schools thus seek to create an environment in which both adult and student learning are supported. This is why PDS work is so difficult. We are accustomed to thinking about teacher education, student learning, and staff development as three very different enterprises — with different individuals being the teachers, different goals, and different contexts. Thinking about a school setting as an environment that supports learning across participants, that creates new roles in which university and school-based faculty share responsibility for student and adult learning, is thinking very differently indeed. Similarly, emphasizing teachers as researchers who are focused on how their students learn best, represents a radically different view of the teacher's role than that traditionally held by most educators.

Getting to the core, however, requires a level of understanding and communication that the dailiness of schooling typically does not support. One needs space and time to think at the core level, and one needs colleagues willing and prepared to discuss these issues. There is little about the traditional organization of schools to encourage this kind of activity.

An additional obstacle to creating changes at the core comes from the realities of interinstitutional collaboration. Partners who work across cultures to build a new institution blur the boundaries and create wholly new roles for people. But these institution builders have to change their "home" institution as well. Otherwise, their work is vulnerable; their status is in jeopardy, they operate on the margins, and they never are more than a "project."

ENABLING KEY REFORM STRATEGIES

The landscape of education reform in the 1990s is dotted with many approaches to addressing the major problem of America's schools—not enough children are learning, and what they are learning is not enough. Anyone acquainted with the issues recognizes that although it may be stated simply, it is a very complex problem and requires a comprehensive solution. A portfolio of many approaches is necessary; indeed, some reform efforts depend on other reform efforts for their success. Professional Development Schools are one part of the solution (Levine, 1994, p. 1). They cut across several other approaches, both supporting and being supported by them. A brief summary of the major approaches will help the reader identify how PDSs are uniquely related to them—both relying on them and necessary to their success.

The first group of reform strategies focuses on curriculum and pedagogy. These reforms include the development of standards for what students need to know and need to be able to do in the many content areas. Such curriculum standards are being created by professional groups and associations representing scholars and teachers in the various subject areas taught in schools. This category also includes those reforms that promote specific pedagogical approaches to content, such as whole language instruction, or more generic teaching methods, such as cooperative learning. For these reformers, setting high expectations for student outcomes and promoting specific pedagogical approaches are central to improving schools. Professional Development Schools, as exemplary schools, ought to serve as models of exemplary practice and uphold the curriculum standards mandated in their states and localities. In this way they can serve as "standard bearers" in the education community.

A second group of reform initiatives is school-centered and has focused on developing new organizational models that restructure what Seymour Sarason has called the regularities of schooling—time, space, resources, roles, and relationships. These initiatives operate from two assumptions—that change needs to take place at the school-building level and that the conditions for teaching and learning in the school are the key elements in improving student outcomes. PDSs restructure these elements in order to support both student and adult learning, and clearly they overlap with these initiatives as well.

Another important strand of reform activity is motivated by a drive to provide equity in opportunities to learn, particularly for poor, minority students in mostly urban areas who are at risk of failure for many reasons. While motivated by a common concern, these initiatives take different forms. Programmatic efforts of this kind typically focus on building individual students' skills, as in Chapter 1 programs, or in keeping students from dropping out of school, as in many local dropout prevention programs. Additionally, there has been some attention to institutional and structural issues associated with these inequalities. The School Development Project headed by James Comer and the Accelerated Schools Program developed by Henry Levin are examples of such institutional approaches. Professional Development Schools are intertwined with this strand of reform as well. Some analysts view PDSs as being a double-edged sword in this regard. Locating PDSs in settings in which there is the greatest student need will ensure that those students benefit from the presence of the best teachers, those who qualify to be teachers of teachers. Second, by ensuring that new teachers develop the skills and knowledge they need to be effective practitioners in the most challenging settings, PDSs contribute to the establishment of a well-prepared professional cadre of teachers, available to all children.

Finally, PDSs are directly related to professionalization, the reform strategy that is fueled by the belief that professional teachers are the key to school improvement. Characteristic of professional teaching practice is a strong knowledge base, collegiality, and a commitment to continuous improvement. Teachers need the knowledge, skills, and dispositions to make professional judgments about what their students need. They also must be able to implement an instructional program that will help their students learn. Most important, teachers need to work together in pursuit of best practices. This kind of practice, as in all professions (including medicine, law, and architecture), requires intensive clinical education and a deliberately structured induction into practice. Professional Development Schools are designed to support the development of these characteristics and to provide these experiences (Levine, 1992). They are schools designed for building a profession (Darling-Hammond, 1994).

Among the strategic approaches to professionalizing teaching are policies altering state licensure requirements, innovations in teacher education and staff development programs, and policies and practices affecting teacher evaluation and career development. In addition, a critical role is played by the development of standards and assessments to accredit teacher education (NCATE, 1995), to establish initial teacher requirements (INTASC, 1991), and to provide advanced certification for teachers (National Board for Professional Teaching Standards, 1991). Underlying each of these initiatives is a shared vision of professional teaching as knowledge-based, collegial, and inquiry-oriented. Together, they create a continuum of professional development extending throughout the professional career of the teacher from initial preparation through advanced certification. The PDS is designed to play a unique role in that continuum as the site in which clinical preparation, induction, and professional development occur, under the collaborative governance of school and university. To the extent that PDSs share this vision of teaching and are linked to these policy initiatives, they can play an integral role in the creation of a professional teaching force.

A FRAGILE INSTITUTION

In the course of building Professional Development Schools, we are learning a great deal about developing new school cultures, and we are learning what it means to think differently about teaching, learning, and learning to teach. Working together, university and school-based faculties, administration, districts, and unions have confronted the frustrations and the satisfactions of being change makers in their own worlds and in each other's worlds. Several of the chapters in this volume, including the three case studies, provide windows into the lives of these leaders and the worlds they are trying to create. New roles are being developed as boundaries blur and educators struggle to work differently and to do different work. Such efforts sometimes meet with dramatic resistance, casting in high relief the deeply ingrained expectations that guide the behaviors of educators who work in schools and universities.

It is clear that important work is being done in Professional Development Schools. It is also clear that PDSs have a unique role to play in leveraging other critical reform strategies. However important they may be, PDSs are extremely vulnerable institutions. Threats to their survival come from two directions. The first concern comes from the nature of the work. PDSs are high-stakes partnerships that involve building trust, learning to share responsibility, and identifying common goals. Building PDSs also involves changing people's minds about ideas and beliefs that are closely held. The politics of reform are another cause for concern. PDSs have, for the most part, flourished on the margins of their partnering institutions. They struggle for support and compete with other programs. Universities and schools are slow to change; PDSs call for change in both institutions simultaneously! School districts, with some important exceptions, continue to ignore the potential impact that PDSs can have in terms of professional development, recruitment, and new teacher induction. Furthermore, PDSs often are initiated in urban districts that present challenging environments for growing a new institution. Teacher shortages, inadequate facilities, large numbers of at-risk students, and high turnover among district leaders threaten the fragility of these partnerships.

While we cannot change the difficulty of the work of the PDS, there are some directions in which we can move to begin to build an infrastructure to support these institutions. Most PDSs are supported by external funds, largely foundation grants. Just how much PDSs cost is still an open question. What is clear, however, is that a new funding strategy needs to be developed that will be consistent with the concept of linking teacher education and school reform. Existing funds, now separated by sector and function, need to be reallocated in ways that reflect the functions of the PDS. Governance for Professional Development Schools needs to be worked out: How are decisions made? How is responsibility shared? Finally, the question of standards for Professional Development Schools has been raised. How can standards help safeguard the concept of the PDS and at the same time support its development?

GOALS FOR THIS VOLUME

We have two main goals for this volume. First, we want to move beyond the rhetoric about what PDSs should be like, to see what it is really like trying to make changes at the core, sometimes with great success and sometimes not. We want to explore the deep nature of the changes that people are trying to make—changes in how people learn, what they learn, the nature of leadership, and the quality of institutional change. Second, we want to move the conversation forward to address what needs to be done in order to ensure that Professional Development Schools do not remain the exception, but really exercise their leverage and become the expectation. This requires that we start to think about issues like standards, finance, and governance of PDSs.

All the contributors to this volume have been directly involved in the design and development of PDSs, or in the study and evaluation of them. They are well acquainted with the politics, policy, and practice of education reform. The authors draw on their experiences in different initiatives to offer the reader a thoughtful consideration of the issues involved in building Professional Development Schools.

ORGANIZATION OF THE BOOK

In Part I, "Making Changes at the Core," we explore some of the fundamental changes that are taking place within Professional Development Schools. These represent changes at the core of schooling, teaching, learning, and learning how to teach. Here authors address areas underrepresented in the PDS literature—how student teacher roles are changing; how teachers are learning from colleagues; how the PDS is giving rise to new definitions of teacher leadership; and how PDSs call for new roles for traditional leaders. Changes are occurring among faculty in schools of education. PDS partnerships are precipitating new definitions of knowledge, and ideas about the relationships between teaching and learning, and theory and practice are changing. It is difficult, slow work, but in success these changes can be powerful forces for fundamental education reform.

Student teacher learning looks different in Ken Zeichner and Maurine Miller's description of changes occurring in the PDS setting in which they work. They place these changes in the context of research on learning to teach and site-based teacher education, providing the reader with a way of looking at what is happening in PDSs from a developmental perspective.

Kathy Beasley, Deborah Corbin, Sharon Feiman-Nemser, and Carole Shank look very closely at colleagues struggling to change their practice and to learn from each other. They are supported by various structural elements of a Professional Development School. Based on research in a PDS site, the authors talk about what teachers learn when time is restructured and communication is encouraged. The relationship between school-based faculty and university faculty, which is encouraged by the PDS, is powerful.

A core element that often is overlooked in PDS work is leadership. This concept takes on new meaning and definition in the PDS setting. Katherine Boles and Vivian Troen are two classroom teachers who founded the Learning/Teaching Collaborative in 1987. Based on their research in their PDS, the authors develop a new definition of teacher leadership and describe the characteristics of such leadership in a learner-centered school.

The Professional Development School also makes demands on traditional leadership roles. Most literature about PDSs focuses on the changing role of teachers in school–university collaboration or on the characteristics of a new school culture. In fact, PDSs typically are thought of as teacher-centered projects. Too little attention has been paid to those in formal organizational leadership positions — deans, school principals, superintendents, union leaders, and building representatives — with respect to PDS leadership. Based on observations made in PDS sites and on the literature on organizational change, authors Roberta Trachtman and Marsha Levine develop metaphors for PDS leaders that mirror the restructuring of teacher roles, student roles, and schools as organizations.

In some settings, university faculty are beginning to think differently, changing their minds about long-held beliefs about research, teacher roles, learning to teach, and how students learn. Nona Lyons, Beth Stroble, and John Fischetti describe these changes in two institutions. One setting is in a rural area where the university works with both rural and suburban school districts. The other operates largely in an urban context. Both have managed significant restructuring in their programs. These authors are able to describe the outward changes, but also get beneath them to reveal the necessary shifts in expectations and beliefs that have to support real reform of the programs.

In Part II, "Building Professional Development Schools in the Context of Education Reform," we consider Professional Development Schools within the context of school reform. It is our intention here to ratchet up the conversation about PDSs on the basis of several years of experience in implementation and to deal with some hard policy issues. If Professional Development Schools are to move from being the exception to the expectation for how teachers are prepared, we need to deal with some critical issues: for example, financing, standards, and governance. These are the subjects of chapters in Part II.

Lee Teitel, author of a number of articles and studies on PDSs, has written here about the various ways in which PDSs have dealt with the question of governance. This issue goes to the heart of the Professional Development School and pushes its participants to deal with the challenges of new roles, relationships, and responsibilities. Traditional roles are challenged, as is the conception of the larger institutions from which the partners emerge. In addition to providing models of how various PDSs have organized themselves and how they make decisions, Teitel offers an interpretation of institutionalization and suggests a web of connections as an alternative to narrow collaborative linkages.

With few notable exceptions, funding for PDSs has come from outside sources — foundations and government grants. The range in budgets is enormous. There are so-called PDSs that have little or no additional funding and others that have as much as $100,000 a year. How much does a PDS cost? Where should or could the money come from? These are the questions that frame Richard Clark and Margaret Plecki's chapter on costs and financing of PDSs. They examine several models of PDSs and identify the costs associated with each one. One of the difficulties encountered in that exercise, which the authors address, is the lack of an accepted framework for the essential characteristics of a Professional Development School. It is daunting to try to address the question of funding if one cannot identify the costs readily. This leads us directly to the final chapter in this section of the book.

The question of standards for Professional Development Schools is complex and critical. What are the necessary ingredients that a school-university partnership must have in order to call itself a PDS? This question is dealt with in a thorough and practical manner by Gary Sykes. On the one hand, the absence of some agreed-upon set of characteristics endangers the concept; any group can say they are a PDS. On the other hand, it is difficult to mandate what is important in a PDS—trust, communication, and mutual respect. Furthermore, PDSs are by definition continuously developing institutions. Sykes lays out the challenge—to construct standards as a learning system, standards that will protect the concept but also support continuous improvement. He offers a proposal for how this can be achieved.

Finally, in Part III, "Stories from the Field," we conclude the volume with insiders' tales about the work of creating Professional Development Schools. The three cases in this volume provide insights into just how difficult this process can be, as well as how motivating and sustaining the promise of real change is, even in the most challenging circumstances. In these cases we hear the voices of insiders giving their perspectives on the work of invention, collaboration, and school reform. The cases serve to illustrate both the successes and failures of efforts to create a new institution. They give life to the struggle for changes at the core and they show us what it is like to work to change schools in highly political and sometimes tumultuous contexts. Further, they point to the need for developing an infrastructure of the kind addressed in Part II. The stories are told by the participants, and the cases are themselves an example of practitioner research. The importance of the major themes of this volume—learning, leadership, change, inter- and intrainstitutional relationships, governance, standards, funding—often are richly illustrated through either their presence or their absence.

Jean King's story is about a relationship between a school of education in a large public university and an urban high school. In the past the school of education prepared teachers for largely white rural and suburban schools. It now needs and wants to learn how to prepare teachers for multicultural schools in the inner city. The school of education views the Professional Development School as a vehicle for learning to do this. The high school it partners with is the least chosen school in a school district where choice is the policy. The school views the PDS as a way to distinguish itself, attract students, and retain good faculty. The teacher's union facilitates the relationship. Administrative leadership becomes a key factor in this story.

Rita Lancy's story is partly about trying to make deep changes in a small urban school district. While faculties from the high school and two partnering universities (an additional level of complexity) struggled to figure out what it was they wanted to do together, the school and district context in which they worked radically changed around them. The school was engulfed in racial tension, administrative turnover made the school setting very unstable, and the district, while superficially acknowledging the significance of the PDS, never really acted on its self-interest with respect to the PDS's development. The tenacity of the teachers in this project, in spite of the considerable turmoil that surrounded them, is impressive. They saw in the concept an opportunity to enhance their professional roles through close work with colleagues and sharing responsibility for teacher education. They saw in it the possibility of meeting their students' needs.

Finally, Jon Snyder's story about a large elementary school in a large school district working with a local university is in part a story about teacher empowerment. The PDS experience is a source of significant teacher growth. It is also a story about the importance of a shared vision. This story raises important questions about how PDSs could and should be initiated, and illustrates the high-risk nature of these cross-sector partnerships.

All of the cases show how difficult it is for people to change their minds about core elements of schooling and how hard it is to question assumptions about relationships between universities and schools, about who has knowledge, and about what knowledge counts. But most important, these cases are testimony to how powerful it can be when teachers in schools and universities are given permission to think about those things that are most important to them.

These stories will be of interest to practitioners, researchers, and policy makers alike. Readers may choose to read them as individual cases or in relation to the discussion chapters.

CONCLUSION

We hope this book will be helpful to those who work in schools, those who prepare them to do so, and those who provide the financial and policy support to make their work possible. While Professional Development

Schools typically have been thought of as teacher projects or teacher education projects, it is clear in these chapters that many others are instrumental to their success. Furthermore, the potential of Professional Development Schools will be reached only if decision makers understand the relationship these institutions have to broader initiatives in education reform, and act positively to support them in their efforts.

REFERENCES

Abdal-Haaq, I. (1995). *Professional development schools directory*. Washington, DC: Clinical Schools Clearinghouse, American Association of Colleges of Teacher Education.

Carnegie Forum on Education and the Economy. (1986). *A nation prepared: Teachers for the twenty first century*. Washington, DC: Author.

Darling-Hammond, L. (1994). *Professional development schools: Schools for developing a profession*. New York: Teachers College Press.

Holmes Group. (1990). *Tomorrow's schools: A report of the Holmes Group*. East Lansing, MI: Author.

Interstate New Teacher Assessment and Support Consortium. (1991). *Model standards for beginning teacher licensing and developing: A resource for state dialogue* (working draft). Washington, DC: Council of Chief State School Officers.

Levine, M. (1992). A conceptual framework for professional practice schools. In M. Levine (Ed.), *Professional practice schools: Linking teacher education and school reform* (pp. 8–24). New York: Teachers College Press.

Levine, M. (1994). Visions of teaching in education reform. National Board for Professional Teaching Standards. Unpublished paper.

Mitchell, L. S. (1950). *Our children and our schools*. New York: Simon & Schuster.

National Board for Professional Teaching Standards. (1991). *Toward high and rigorous standards for the teaching profession: Initial policies and perspectives*. Detroit: Author.

National Council for Accreditation of Teacher Education. (1995). *Standards, procedures, and policies for the accreditation of professional education units*. Washington, DC: Author.

Schaefer, R. J. (1967). *The school as a center of inquiry*. New York: Harper & Row.

Part I

Making Changes at the Core

Chapter 1

Learning to Teach in Professional Development Schools

KENNETH ZEICHNER AND MAURINE MILLER

In the past decade, teacher educators across the United States have attempted to alter the nature and structure of school-based studies (SBS) in preservice teacher education by situating them in public schools that are, or are becoming, Professional Development Schools (PDS). SBS include observational and teaching experiences in a preservice teacher education program that take place in a school, such as practicums, student teaching, internships, or early field experiences. This chapter, based primarily on a case study of one PDS in Madison, Wisconsin, examines the kinds of changes in the conduct of SBS that have been associated with this shift to Professional Development Schools, and the ways that the shift has affected the character and quality of student teacher learning. Specifically, it covers the degree to which the location of SBS in PDSs addresses obstacles to teacher learning long associated with school-based studies, whether the use of the PDS in preservice teacher education affects the preparation of teachers to teach all students to the same high academic standards, and how PDSs affect the long-standing gap between what teacher educators hope their students learn about teaching and what they actually learn.

OBSTACLES TO TEACHER LEARNING IN SCHOOL-BASED STUDIES

There is much evidence that school-based studies as they traditionally have been conducted in the education of teachers in the United States interfere with the ability of prospective teachers to learn all that their teacher educators hope they will learn (Goodlad, 1990; Guyton & McIntyre,

1990; Richardson, 1988; Zeichner, 1980, 1986, 1990, 1992, 1996a). The underlying problem seems to be that SBS are not a priority concern in either the college and university or in the schools. The low status of SBS in the college and university often has resulted in inadequate allocation of resources that translates into a lack of a planned and purposeful curriculum, and poor articulation of SBS with the rest of the teacher education program; an uneven quality of mentoring and evaluation of the work of student teachers; a focus on the classroom but neglect of the school and community domains of the teacher's work; and a lack of placements in geographically, socioeconomically, and culturally different schools. This apprenticeship-oriented approach to the conduct of SBS has encouraged the observation and imitation of practice rather than the thoughtful analysis of practice.

BENEFITS OF SCHOOL-BASED STUDIES
IN PROFESSIONAL DEVELOPMENT SCHOOLS

Newly emerging Professional Development School partnerships in many different parts of the United States are beginning to reshape school-based studies, and several major trends, many of them encouraging, are associated with situating SBS in Professional Development Schools.

First, in many places, the location of SBS in the PDS has resulted in increased time spent in schools by prospective teachers during their preservice education. In some programs, a semester of student teaching has been changed to a full-year internship experience, and in most programs the initiation of a PDS partnership has resulted in some increase in school-based work (e.g., Haymore-Sandholz & Finan, 1995; Neufeld & Haavend, 1988; Snyder, 1994; Worth, 1990). This increased time allocated to SBS in the PDS is believed to have resulted in a greater commitment by school staff to student teachers and in more opportunities for responsibility and risk taking by student teachers as a result of the trust that develops between mentors and student teachers in a longer experience (Troen, Boles, & Larkin, 1995; Worth, 1990).

A second trend associated with the PDS is the emergence of a greater number of workshops and seminars to prepare and support cooperating school personnel in their mentoring of prospective teachers. Although some states, like Wisconsin, have long required those who work with student teachers to complete coursework in mentoring, most cooperating school personnel did not participate in mentoring seminars prior to the advent of the PDS (Guyton & McIntyre, 1990).

The structure for the mentoring and evaluation of student teachers also appears to be changing in the PDS. There has been an increase in the use of school-based college and university supervisors in PDSs (Anderson & Boles, 1995; Kroll, Rutherford, Bowyer, & Hauben, 1990; Yerian & Grossman, 1993). Instead of the typical pattern of a college/university representative coming to a school on a periodic basis to observe and confer with prospective teachers about their teaching, the university supervisor either is located in the school on a full-time basis or works with a given school over a number of years and spends more time there than under the old model.

The idea of a single cooperating teacher for a student teacher's experience also is beginning to change. In the PDS, it is becoming more common for prospective teachers to be placed with several teachers or on teaching teams during a given experience (e.g., Anderson, 1993; Barnhart, Cole, Hansell, Mathies, Smith, & Black, 1995; Berry & Catoe, 1994; Teitel, 1992). This has resulted in student teachers being exposed to a variety of teaching models and in an increased emphasis on collaboration among teachers and other student teachers. Moreover, the whole school, rather than an individual cooperating teacher's classroom, generally is viewed as the site for an SBS in a PDS.

There is also some evidence that the role of school personnel in the SBS and in relation to the entire preservice teacher education program is beginning to change. School staff members are beginning to play a role in screening applicants for SBS (Teitel, 1992; Walters, 1995) and are increasingly involved in designing teacher education program features, including, but also going beyond, SBS (Barnhart et al., 1995; Haymore-Sandholz & Finan, 1995). Many more college and university teacher education courses now are being offered on site in the schools (e.g., Pasch & Pugach, 1990; Stallings, 1991; Walters, 1995; Whitford, 1994), and school staff are assuming greater instructional roles in program courses and SBS seminars (e.g., Anderson & Boles, 1995; Yerian & Grossman, 1993).

THE LINCOLN PROFESSIONAL
DEVELOPMENT SCHOOL PARTNERSHIP

To illustrate the experiences of participants in an urban PDS, we next examine a case study of a PDS in Madison, Wisconsin, in which both of us work. Maurine is the school-based university supervisor and Ken is the university liaison to the school. This case also will demonstrate some of the changes that have taken place in SBS in PDSs.

Lincoln Elementary School in Madison, Wisconsin, is a grade 3–5 elementary school of about 350 students, 54% of whom come from very low-income families and about 57% of whom are of color. The Lincoln

Professional Development School partnership, involving the Madison Metropolitan School District and the School of Education at the University of Wisconsin–Madison, has been in existence for the past 8 years, although it is only in the past year-and-one-half that the PDS has become involved with a new graduate teacher education program, "Teach for Diversity" (TFD), at the UW–Madison emphasizing issues of culture, teaching, and learning. There is a strong focus in Lincoln Elementary School on the continuing professional development of staff. One example of this is the fact that over two-thirds of the staff have participated in the school district's action research staff development program (Caro-Bruce & McReadie, 1995), the highest participation rate for a school in the city. Several of the current teachers student taught there as part of previous PDS cohorts. Around 60 students in the school are part of a district-wide open classroom program that is based on the British infant school model. While there is some variation in instructional styles in the school, the Lincoln classrooms generally are oriented toward the active engagement of students in learning and a constructivist approach to teaching. One example of this constructivist orientation is the widespread use of the Cognitively Guided Instruction in Mathematics approach that was initiated by faculty at UW–Madison (Carpenter & Fennema, 1992). Lincoln volunteered and was then selected for involvement in the TFD program because of the strong commitment of its staff to multicultural education and the academic success of all children, as well as its success with previous cohorts of undergraduate student teachers.

Student teachers who enroll in TFD spend two summers and an academic year completing university courses and school-based studies. At the end of the program, they receive a Master's Degree in Elementary Education and teaching certification in grades 1–6. Seven TFD teacher education students worked in Lincoln from August 1994 to June 1995, spending five mornings a week in the school from August to January, and full time from February until early June. The university supervisor's role was carried out by Maurine, who is the school's instructional resource teacher (IRT). She spends about one-half of her time working with the TFD student teachers and the other half providing support to the Lincoln staff and children. Ken serves as the university liaison to the school. He team taught the weekly SBS seminar with Maurine, advised TFD students on the completion of their master's projects, co-led with Maurine a study group on school reform for staff and parents, and occasionally observed and conferred with TFD students about their teaching.

The Lincoln PDS includes many of the characteristics associated with the restructuring of SBS in the PDS movement.

- An increase in the amount of time spent by student teachers in schools
- A broader scope for SBS as student teachers are placed for periods of time throughout the school and in the community rather than just in individual classrooms
- A peer supervision component for student teachers
- Increased decision-making roles for school staff in screening applicants and placing student teachers, as well as in designing the new integrated methods courses in the program
- School-based university supervision
- Team teaching of the weekly SBS seminar by university and school staff.

The following report on experiences by participants illustrates some of the key elements of the Lincoln PDS program and their influence on student teacher learning.

Strategic Placement of Student Teachers

The IRT enters a third-grade classroom to observe Trent during his lead teaching and is greeted by a buzz of activity. In one corner, pairs of children are creating their own flash card games; several other students are working independently at their desks on math activities; still others are at a table working on some problems together. Trent is offering words of encouragement to one African American boy who seldom engages in whole-group instruction, and restates his expectations for quality work with the math activities. Simultaneously, he is recording on a class list which activity other students began during this math workshop and which children have already completed some of the choices. One pair of students invites the supervisor to participate in their game and still others call to her for assistance. Trent's smile to his supervisor confirms his pleasure with this trial run as he quickly turns to confer with another student while giving a friendly nod to a girl who is placing her papers on his desk.

What is significant about this situation is the chain of events that led to it and how it represents a major shift in Trent's thinking about effective teaching practices. Trent is a 30-year-old African American male who has enjoyed a successful career as a fire fighter and paramedic. The pull to give something back to his community and particularly to influence the educational and social development of young African American males motivated him to apply to the Teach for Diversity program. He was placed with six other TFD students in Lincoln during the 1994–95 school year.

During the postobservation conference on the above observation, Trent and the IRT discussed the journey that he had taken during the past 9 months that helped him re-examine the assumptions he brought to the program about promoting student success through a "teaching as telling" approach, and that enabled him to introduce the idea of the math workshop into his cooperating teacher's classroom. Trent attributed his change to a variety of factors, including coursework and extensive outside reading, but he gave the most credit to what he labeled "strategic placements" provided by the IRT over the year.

In the regular teacher education programs at UW–Madison, practicum students are given one placement for the entire semester by someone at the university, based on a list of staff volunteers provided by the schools. In the regular elementary education program, students complete two semesters of practicum work and one semester of student teaching, and there is typically little communication among the three different supervisors who mentor and evaluate the prospective teachers. More than likely, the university supervisors, who are graduate students, do not know their students' particular strengths and needs as they begin work with them.

Here, the IRT, who is based in Lincoln full time, has firsthand knowledge of both the evolving perspectives and capabilities of student teachers and the particular characteristics of the various classrooms available for placements, including detailed knowledge of the pupils and families.

The wide range of experiences that Trent has had as a TFD student are a result of a "customized" plan for placements developed by the Lincoln PDS staff, IRT, and university liaison, during the summer before Trent began his SBS. This group attempted to develop a plan for placements that would make the expertise in the whole school available to TFD student teachers.

Whole School Focus

The plan for Trent and the other student teachers included beginning the fall semester with one-week observation/participation placements in three different classrooms in order to get a feel for Lincoln School, followed by two 8-week practicum placements for 4 half days per week. Throughout the semester, a unique "fifth-day" experience was completed by TFD students that took them to various parts of the school beyond their "base" classroom. Here TFD student teachers spent about one-half day per week either observing another program that involved their pupils (e.g., English as a Second Language [ESL], Chapter 1 compensatory education) or shadowing a support staff member, such as the social worker or speech and language clinician. Conversations during the weekly SBS seminar about these fifth-day experiences became a collective source of knowledge about the school and the families and communities it served. TFD students also engaged in required peer supervision experiences that took them into several additional classrooms.

The result of this new placement configuration was that student teachers became contributing members of the school community more quickly than had student teacher cohorts in the past, and that more Lincoln staff became actively involved with teacher education students. During the second semester student teachers were placed in one classroom for the whole semester, but unlike student teachers in the regular program, they often had prior knowledge of the classroom either from their own observations or a peer's involvement in it. The fifth-day experiences and peer supervision continued throughout the second semester.

Moving Toward Learner-Centered Teaching

Trent began the semester believing that a traditional classroom centered on "teaching as telling" and pupil respect for the teacher were the keys to academic success. He spent his first one-week placement in a team taught, inclusive classroom comprising students identified as having emotional disturbances and/or learning disabilities and a group of "regular" education students. Trent was distressed about the apparent disrespect toward the teachers shown by several students who previously had been involved in "pull-out" programs.

During his second and third one-week placements, Trent worked in third- and fourth-grade classrooms where the students participated in several pull-out programs such as Chapter 1 reading instruction and ESL. Here Trent was upset about the burden placed on the children who moved in and out of their classroom on a daily basis and about the behavior problems created by several students in each class.

For his first 8-week practicum, the IRT purposefully placed Trent in a grade 4–5 open classroom. This placement not only provided an inclusive program for all students, but also challenged Trent's ideas about effective instruction and gave him experiences with students who were given a lot of responsibility and who often were actively engaged in constructing their own knowledge.

After spending 2 weeks in this classroom, Trent was astounded. Seldom was the issue of respect on his mind, and when asked to reflect about that by the IRT, he began to talk about the relationship between how children are organized to learn and how they behave. His dream of a classroom where the teacher stands at the front all day dispensing knowledge and allowing only one person to speak at a time began to give way to the challenge of learning how to facilitate students' ongoing work on self-designed projects that allowed each child to demonstrate individual talents and knowledge for at least part of the school day.

The IRT placed Trent in a more traditional setting for his second 8-week practicum and semester of student teaching. The purpose was for him to be able to compare and contrast the open and more traditional settings, and also for him to get a chance to work with an African American teacher, which was important to him. Most of the instruction in this classroom took place in a whole-group format with a strong academic focus. There was also a strong sense of family in this room that was highly valued by the pupils. During these later placements Trent worked on trying to develop a personal resolution of the tensions between his entering and emerging perspectives that took advantage of the strengths of both the traditional and more open settings. With the encouragement of his peers, an important part of this resolution became the introduction of some of the ideas he learned about in his open classroom placement into the more traditional classroom setting.

Learning in a Cohort

Trent greatly valued the many conversations that he had with the other members of his cohort during the year, both in the weekly seminars and in many discussions concerning peer observations of each other's teaching. This support that he regularly experienced was instrumental in helping him take the step of introducing the math workshop into his classroom. During one seminar, Trent revealed his desire to move to more of an open classroom format, similar to his previous placement. He did not wish, however, to appear disrespectful to his cooperating teacher by greatly altering the classroom routine. The TFD students in the seminar were collectively challenged by Trent's dilemma and brainstormed a list of possibilities for what he might do. Eventually the group, including Trent, reached a consensus around the idea of opening up a portion of the school day while maintaining the overall classroom routines. This conversation in the seminar helped equip Trent with the resolve to introduce the math workshop into his classroom.

School-Based Seminars

The setting for the seminar moved periodically, with meetings sometimes held in an unused classroom and other times in the IRT and university liaison's office, which was just large enough to hold 10 chairs. Space at Lincoln School was at a premium, but having the seminar in the school instead of at the university allowed Lincoln staff to participate in the sessions more readily, and the university liaison to spend more time in the building.

The school's math specialist participated in one of our seminars. The TFD students were enrolled at that time in an integrated math/science methods course and were in a state of great confusion about Cognitively Guided Instruction in Mathematics (CGI), a constructivist approach to teaching math that clashed drastically with their memories of how they learned math in elementary school. Because of the desire of the IRT and university liaison to draw as much as possible on the expertise of practicing teachers, this pattern of involving staff in instructional roles in the weekly seminar was repeated several times during the semester with regard to such issues as integrated curriculum, building a teaching portfolio, and the first years of teaching.

The seminar revolved around the specialist's efforts to relax the student teachers and literally to give them permission to be frustrated. She assured them that it has taken veteran teachers 2 to 3 years to make the transition to CGI. She encouraged them to let the children teach them, to listen carefully as their pupils explain their strategies for solving story problems, and to open their minds to multiple ways to solve any problem. At the end of the seminar each TFD student vowed independently to facilitate a CGI lesson, although they made arrangements to supervise each other and draw support and affirmation from each other's experiences. Student teachers from all of the cohorts that worked at Lincoln School over the past 8 years found peer supervision to be a valuable part of their experience, especially as a tool for reflection. Spending a year or more working in the same school with the same group of peers enables a level of trust to develop in the cohort that is necessary for student teachers to engage each other in an authentic manner.

On a very practical note, the IRT noted that the initiation of peer supervision with earlier student teacher cohorts contributed to increased interest in working with preservice teachers by the Lincoln staff. As student teachers visited different classrooms to observe their peers, teachers became more accustomed to having observers there, got to know several student teachers, and frequently were pleasantly surprised by the quality of conversations they had with student teachers about teaching. At present, although the primary focus of the Lincoln PDS remains on pupil learning, the teachers and staff share a collective concern and responsibility for student teacher learning. Over time, staff language has changed from *my* student teacher to *our* student teachers.

A Social Action Project

One of the requirements for the TFD student teachers at Lincoln was to engage their pupils in a social action project, providing the children with an opportunity to make a difference in their own lives and communities. This learning-centered teaching can permit deeper and more powerful pupil learning than is available only within classrooms. The following vignette concerning Marissa's social action project demonstrates how having the university supervisor on site and knowledgeable about the curriculum in each classroom, provides many opportunities to take advantage of critical moments for student teacher learning. The IRT wrote in her journal:

> I literally bumped into Shannon [Marissa's cooperating teacher] at the copy machine this morning as she was photocopying a newspaper article explaining that MacKenzie Center might be being defunded by the state. I had read the same article over my morning coffee and immediately thought of Marissa since her class recently experienced a two-night winter camping stay at this environmental center. I suggested to Shannon that this issue had great potential for a social action project. Later in the day Marissa came back to me and said, "Shannon has turned the MacKenzie project over to me."

At the time that she made the suggestion about the social action project to Shannon, the IRT had no idea about the depth of learning that her capitalizing on this "teachable moment" would have for Marissa, for Shannon, for the pupils in their classroom, for two other classrooms of students who shared the camping experience at the MacKenzie Center, and for Marissa's peers. During the first observation when Marissa introduced the newspaper article, the IRT noticed that the children became enraged and focused on fund raising as an immediate means to save the center. After this was discussed at the postobservation conference, Marissa thought about how best to facilitate students' thinking in broader and more political terms, and she prepared a chart that illustrated the state legislative process regarding budgetary considerations.

The students then invited a state senator supportive of the center to come to their school and speak to all three classes regarding the center and the decision-making process. Students, wanting to make a difference, responded by dividing themselves into committees. Several prepared a petition for all Lincoln students and staff to sign and developed the explanations and arguments in support of their position. They went to the other classrooms and made presentations about the MacKenzie issue and their petition. Three other students wrote a letter to the editor of the local newspaper. Still others created posters to place in the school and community. Two students who rarely participated in class discussions wrote and practiced speeches in preparation for an upcoming legislative hearing at which they would testify.

During the 3 weeks of intensive work on this project, Marissa commented in her journal:

> Enticing curriculum can really give students no choice but to participate and learn. That seems to be the case with the MacKenzie Center. Today without any instruction, E and M sat together and wrote out what they are going to say when they visit the different classrooms next week with their petitions. . . . This is amazing when you think about who I'm talking about. All the more proof to show that E is capable of doing work. We need to find ways to get her hooked . . . creating curriculum that is relevant to the students and allowing her to shine with her talents and experiences.

In her teaching portfolio, Marissa discussed a shift in her perceptions of the teacher from merely being a facilitator of learning to also being a talent scout who creates opportunities for all students to show what they know and what they can do.

> With a deficit model in mind, it is difficult for particular students to be successful for the teacher and for themselves. Teachers must rethink the deficit model and look for student strengths. . . . We need to create a curriculum and an atmosphere that allow all students to feel that they belong, that they are valued just because of who they are. . . . The result of culturally relevant teaching was more enthusiasm, more participation, and more success.

Marissa's peers were noticeably impressed by her classroom social action project as she reported on its progress during the weekly seminars. Finding a similar powerful opening for a project was proving to be difficult for some of the other student teachers. Having a supervisor on site with an intimate knowledge of the school and the community and of the student teachers makes it more likely, in our view, that these openings for deep and powerful learning will be found.

OVERVIEW

These brief vignettes have illustrated a few of the key elements of the Lincoln Professional Development School's role in preparing preservice elementary teachers enrolled in the Teach for Diversity program. They include the presence of a school-based university supervisor who is able to strategically place student teachers in different parts of the school to address their learning needs at particular times and to capitalize on teachable moments for student teachers because of her intimate knowledge of the setting and her constant availability. They also include the use of the whole school as the placement site for student teachers, and many efforts to draw upon the expertise of Lincoln staff and to foster collegial support among cohorts of student teachers. There are several other aspects of this program not described here, such as the community field experiences engaged in by student teachers throughout the year, the construction of a teaching portfolio and keeping a teaching journal, and student teacher participation in a study group focused on current education reforms that was co-led by the IRT and university liaison and involved staff and parents. This study group is just one example of the overall climate of inquiry and focus on professional development among staff in the building.

Our discussion in this chapter has suggested certain links between the characteristics of preservice teacher education in the Lincoln PDS and the character and quality of student teacher learning. The vignettes, which reveal brief slices of the student teaching experiences of a few students, suggest some movement during the year toward a more learner-centered and learning-centered kind of teaching. It is our belief that this shift, which characterized the experience of all our student teachers to some degree, was related to the overall climate of inquiry and reflection that existed in the school; to the student teacher group culture that we were able to establish, which encouraged supportive collegial interactions among student teachers; and to the constant presence of the university supervisor in the school. We also made efforts to integrate learner-centered and learning-centered instruction into the entire Teach for Diversity curriculum and to select students for the program with consideration of their potential to teach in this way. Any movement toward learner-centered and learning-centered instruction that was evident among Lincoln School student teachers must be attributed to the entire constellation of these factors rather than to the PDS alone.

STUDENT TEACHER LEARNING IN
PROFESSIONAL DEVELOPMENT SCHOOLS

The existing literature on SBS in PDSs has made it fairly clear that the experience at Lincoln was not anomalous; several significant changes are occurring in SBS as they become situated in Professional Development Schools around the country. These include:

- An increase in the amount of time spent by preservice teachers in schools
- More planned and purposeful experiences for student teachers
- A greater focus on the whole school as the placement site
- An increased emphasis on collaboration among teachers and peers
- Greater access to university supervisors
- A greater respect for teacher knowledge and more decision making about the program by school staff
- More access to workshops and seminars on mentoring student teachers for school staff.

It is also clear that several aspects of SBS have not changed all that much with the advent of PDSs. For example, although the PDS has focused more attention on the purpose and content of SBS, there do not appear to be major changes in the institutional incentives for high-quality work in SBS by schools and universities. Many of the existing PDSs are supported on a temporary basis by grants from foundations, but even with this outside support, the staffing ratio does not appear to be improving. There are many reports of college and university faculty providing work in PDSs on an overload basis.

Also, despite the clear intent of many teacher educators to locate PDSs in a broad range of schools, including those primarily serving poor students of color, there is little or no discussion in the literature of how the scope of SBS has been broadened to include student teacher work with parents and in the community. There is much evidence available that placing student teachers in schools that provide them with culturally diverse experiences without also extending the placement into the community is insufficient for enabling the kinds of personal transformations that are needed to prepare them to successfully teach all children (Zeichner, 1996b).

The question now is how all of the changes that have taken place in SBS in PDSs have affected the learning of student teachers. How have these changes helped better prepare teachers to teach everybody's children to the same high standards? How have these changes affected what student teachers learn about teaching in SBS, where they choose to teach, and how they teach?

Despite all of the evidence available about more time spent in schools, more collaboration, greater access to university supervisors, and so on, there is very little information reported about how the quality of student teacher learning has been affected by the changes. Neufeld and Boris-Schacter (1991), in their analysis of several PDSs in Massachusetts, are two of the few even to comment at all on the issue of the substance of student teacher learning. They make several comments about how the PDSs have influenced the learning and teaching of both student teachers and teachers.

> The collaborations are too new to have demonstrated that they lead to better teaching . . . and enhanced learning for children. (p. 4)

> At this point, we are unable to draw conclusions about whether, in what ways, and to what extent future teachers are better prepared in PDS sites. (p. 49)

A fundamental element of the PDS with regard to preservice teacher education is the assumption that preservice teachers are immersed in schools that are committed to the process of reform (Darling-Hammond, 1994). In the PDS, student teachers are supposed to get the idea that changing teaching and schools is part of the work of teaching (Pasch & Pugach, 1990). As a student teacher in a Massachusetts PDS reports, "The training at Devotion gives you a sense of what is possible. It helps you push for what can be. I don't forget. I know it's happening someplace. It has encouraged me to push for it" (quoted in Worth, 1990, p. 20), rather than focus on what has been.

There are also several reports in the literature of student teachers' exposure to new interdisciplinary and collaborative teaching opportunities as a result of work in a PDS (e.g., Berry & Catoe, 1994; Haymore-Sandholz & Finan, 1995; Lythcott & Schwartz, 1994), and claims have been made about the anticipated impact of these experiences.

> As a consequence of this model, student teachers acquired entirely new frames for thinking about their teaching, frames that include professional collaboration and collegial problem solving, interdisciplinary and whole child perspectives upon which to build their future. (Darling-Hammond, 1994, p. 13)

There has been little direct study, though, of the degree to which these and other anticipated consequences of completing SBS in a PDS actually have been realized. Stallings, Bossung, and Martin (1990) and Stallings and Kowalski (1990) conducted several analyses that compared the teaching of student teachers in an inner-city PDS (the Houston Teaching Academy) with the teaching of student teachers who taught in non-PDS settings. They found through observations and interviews that the PDS student teachers had a greater academic focus in their classes and less off-task behavior by pupils. They also found that the PDS student teachers chose to work after graduation in schools serving low-income families from a variety of cultural groups at a higher rate than students from the regular program, and that after their first year of teaching they left teaching at a lower rate than other beginning teachers in the Houston School District.

What Stallings and her colleagues did not report, however, was information about the specific nature of the tasks that pupils engaged in and the quality of their learning. To say that there was more of a focus on academic tasks and less disengagement, without describing the tasks themselves, does not say much about the quality of student teacher learning.

Similarly, to say that student teachers are spending more time in schools and receiving more mentoring from cooperating teachers who receive more supervisory training and support, also does not indicate anything about the quality of student teacher learning. Although there appears to be more reflective analysis of teaching and collaboration going on in PDSs than in other schools, convincing evidence has not been presented to date that this reflection and collaboration have resulted in the more learner-centered and learning-centered teaching that is claimed to be an essential part of PDSs. More reflective teaching is not necessarily good teaching that enables all children to be educated to the same high academic standards (Zeichner, 1993).

We must be very cautious at this early point in the evolution of Professional Development Schools about uncritically embracing the PDS as a panacea for the ills of teacher education. It is very important that the focus of future analysis of student teacher learning in PDSs go beyond statements of the general processes that are fostered by PDSs, such as reflection and collaboration, and illuminate the specific quality of student teacher learning and teaching that emerge in these schools. The literature thus far has not demonstrated a link between the establishment of Professional Development School partnerships in teacher education and the development of the kind of teaching by prospective teachers that will lead to the education of all students to high academic standards. Nor has much attention been paid in the PDS literature to issues of culturally relevant and multicultural teaching (Wilder, 1995).

Regardless of the specific quality of student teacher learning and teaching that PDSs are able to promote at a given time, it is critical that greater institutional support be provided for the teacher education that takes place in PDSs. At this time, it does not appear that the fundamental obstacle to teacher learning in SBS — the low institutional status of preservice teacher learning in both the schools and universities — has been addressed. As has been pointed out above, classroom teachers in PDSs are still struggling to find the time to mentor student teachers, and college and university faculty often are still pursuing their work in SBS as overload and underreward systems that place little value on this work. Unless the marginal status of SBS is dealt with, and ways are devised to develop PDSs after the grant money runs out, any gains in student teacher learning that are achieved in the PDS will be short-lived.

REFERENCES

Anderson, C. R. (Ed.). (1993). *Voices of change: A report of the clinical schools project*. Washington, DC: American Association of Colleges for Teacher Education.

Anderson, M., & Boles, K. (1995, April). *The reflective mentoring seminar: Providing a means for teachers to cross boundaries in a professional development school*. Paper presented at the annual meeting of the American Educational Research Association, San Francisco.

Barnhart, R., Cole, D., Hansell, S., Mathies, B., Smith, W., & Black, S. (1995). Strengthening teacher education. In R. Osguthorpe, R. Carl Harris, M. Fox Harris, & S. Black (Eds.), *Partner schools: Centers for educational renewal* (pp. 45–72). San Francisco: Jossey-Bass.

Berry, B., & Catoe, S. (1994). Creating professional development schools: Policy and practice in South Carolina's PDS initiatives. In L. Darling-Hammond (Ed.), *Professional development schools: Schools for developing a profession* (pp. 176–202). New York: Teachers College Press.

Caro-Bruce, C., & McReadie, J. (1995). Establishing an action research program in one school district. In S. Noffke & R. Stevenson (Eds.), *Educational action research* (pp. 154–164). New York: Teachers College Press.

Carpenter, T., & Fennema, E. (1992). Cognitively guided instruction: Building on the knowledge of students and teachers. In W. Secada (Ed.), *Curriculum reform: The case of mathematics in the U.S.* [Special Issue of the *International Journal of Educational Research*] (pp. 457–470). Elmsford, NY: Pergamon Press.

Darling-Hammond, L. (1994). Developing professional development schools: Early lessons, challenge and promise. In L. Darling-Hammond (Ed.), *Professional development schools: Schools for developing a profession* (pp. 1–27). New York: Teachers College Press.

Goodlad, J. (1990). *Teachers for our nation's schools*. San Francisco: Jossey-Bass.

Guyton, E., & McIntyre, D. J. (1990). Student teaching and school experiences. In W. R. Houston (Ed.), *Handbook of research in teacher education* (pp. 514–534). New York: Macmillan.

Haymore-Sandholz, J., & Finan, E. (1995, April). *Blurring the boundaries to promote school/university relationships*. Paper presented at the annual meeting of the American Educational Research Association, San Francisco.

Kroll, L., Rutherford, M., Bowyer, J., & Hauben, M. (1990, April). *The effect of a school–university partnership on the student teaching experience*. Paper presented at the annual meeting of the American Educational Research Association, Boston.

Lythcott, J., & Schwartz, F. (1994). Professional development in action. In L. Darling-Hammond (Ed.), *Professional development schools: Schools for developing a profession* (pp. 126–155). New York: Teachers College Press.

Neufeld, B., & Boris-Schacter, S. (1991). *Professional development schools in Mas-

sachusetts: Maintenance and growth. Boston: Massachusetts Center for Teaching and Learning.

Neufeld, B., & Haavend, S. (1988). *Professional development schools in Massachusetts: Beginning the process.* Boston: Massachusetts Center for Teaching and Learning.

Pasch, S., & Pugach, M. (1990). Collaborative planning for urban professional development schools. *Contemporary Education, 61*(3), 135–143.

Richardson, V. (1988). Barriers to the effective supervision of student teaching: A field study. *Journal of Teacher Education, 39*(2), 28–34.

Snyder, J. (1994). Perils and potentials: A tale of two professional development schools. In L. Darling-Hammond (Ed.), *Professional development schools: Schools for developing a profession* (pp. 98–125). New York: Teachers College Press.

Stallings, J. A. (1991, April). Connecting preservice teacher education and inservice professional development: A professional development school. Paper presented at the annual meeting of the American Educational Research Association, Chicago.

Stallings, J. A., Bossung, J., & Martin, A. (1990). Houston Teaching Academy: Partnership in developing teachers. *Teaching and Teacher Education, 6*(4), 355–365.

Stallings, J. A., & Kowalski, T. (1990). Research on professional development schools. In W. R. Houston (Ed.), *Handbook of research on teacher education* (pp. 251–266). New York: Macmillan.

Teitel, L. (1992). The impact of professional development school partnerships on the preparation of teachers. *Teaching Education, 4*(2), 77–85.

Troen, V., Boles, K., & Larkin, E. (1995, April). *Boundary spanners in professional development schools.* Paper presented at the annual meeting of the American Educational Research Association, San Francisco.

Walters, S. (1995, April). *Walking the fault-line: Boundary spanning in professional development schools.* Paper presented at the annual meeting of the American Educational Research Association, San Francisco.

Whitford, B. L. (1994). Permission, persistence, and resistance: Linking high school restructuring with teacher education reform. In L. Darling-Hammond (Ed.), *Professional development schools: Schools for developing a profession* (pp. 74–97). New York: Teachers College Press.

Wilder, M. (1995). Professional development schools: Restructuring teacher education programs and hierarchies. In H. Petrie (Ed.), *Professionalization, partnership, and power: Building professional development schools* (pp. 253–268). Albany: State University of New York Press.

Worth, K. (1990, April). *The Wheelock/Brookline collaborative internship program.* Paper presented at the annual meeting of the American Educational Research Association, Boston.

Yerian, S., & Grossman, P. (1993, April). *Emerging themes on the effectiveness of teacher preparation through professional development schools.* Paper presented at the annual meeting of the American Educational Research Association, Atlanta.

Zeichner, K. (1980). Myths and realities: Field experiences in preservice teacher education. *Journal of Teacher Education, 31*, 45–55.

Zeichner, K. (1986). The practicum as an occasion for learning to teach. *South Pacific Journal of Teacher Education, 4*(2), 11–27.

Zeichner, K. (1990). Changing directions in the practicum: Looking ahead to the 1990's. *Journal of Education for Teaching, 16*(2), 105–132.

Zeichner, K. (1992). Rethinking the practicum in the professional development school partnership. *Journal of Teacher Education, 43*(4), 296–307.

Zeichner, K. (1993). Traditions of practice in U.S. preservice teacher education programs. *Teaching and Teacher Education, 9*, 1–13.

Zeichner, K. (1996a). Designing educative practicum experiences for prospective teachers. In K. Zeichner, S. Melnick, & M. Gomez (Eds.), *Currents of reform in preservice teacher education* (pp. 215–234). New York: Teachers College Press.

Zeichner, K. (1996b). Educating teachers for cultural diversity. In K. Zeichner, S. Melnick, & M. Gomez (Eds.), *Currents of reform in preservice teacher education* (pp. 133–175). New York: Teachers College Press.

Zeichner, K., & Melnick, S. (1995). *The role of community experiences in preparing teachers for cultural diversity*. East Lansing, MI: National Center for Research on Teacher Learning.

Chapter 2

"Making It Happen": Creating a Subculture of Mentoring in a Professional Development School

KATHY BEASLEY, DEBORAH CORBIN, SHARON FEIMAN-NEMSER, AND CAROLE SHANK

Kathy is a real risk-taker. She entered a very traditional school and started making changes for herself and her classroom and her kids. What she was doing fascinated me. When I got to know more about her thinking through our long conversations at management team meetings, I knew in my soul that I was connected to someone who knew something that I didn't and I wanted to know what she knew.

Carole Shank, 1993

Averill Elementary School, an urban elementary school in Lansing, Michigan, became a Professional Development School (PDS) in 1989 and created a management team consisting of the principal, three teachers, and two teacher educators from Michigan State University. Serving together on the management team in 1991 with Kathy Beasley, Carole Shank formed a view of her colleague as someone with valuable knowledge about teaching. Despite the fact that Carole had taught for 20 years and Kathy for 8, Carole felt that Kathy could help her transform her classroom into a caring learning community where differences were valued and all students could succeed as learners.

What did Kathy know about teaching that Carole wanted to learn? What did Carole learn from working with Kathy and how did this change

Carole's teaching practice? What PDS opportunities and resources made it possible for these experienced teachers to create a subculture of mentoring where Carole could be guided and supported by two less experienced colleagues? How did the professional culture of the school support and constrain this collaboration? These questions frame this story about a unique "peer mentoring" project carried out by three second/third-grade teachers and a university teacher educator in a Professional Development School. We could have disguised the asymmetry in this project by calling it "peer collaboration." Instead, we deliberately use the mentoring label to highlight the fact that a veteran teacher sought help from two colleagues and that they took responsibility for helping her make fundamental changes in her teaching.

LAUNCHING THE MENTORING PROJECT

Our current project builds on an inquiry about mentoring, teaching, and learning to teach that began in 1991. At the PDS Summer Institute, Kathy Beasley approached Sharon Feiman-Nemser to ask for help with her "problem." After working hard all year to develop a classroom learning community, Kathy was tired of watching everything fall apart when her student teacher took over the classroom. Unless she could find a better way to work with student teachers, one that did not disrupt the classroom learning community so completely, she would have to stop taking them. Sharon wondered about a student teaching program that expected cooperating teachers to step aside prematurely. She suspected that there were more productive ways to induct a novice into the intellectual and practical work of teaching. Interested in exploring new possibilities, she arranged to spend one day a week at Averill with Kathy and her student teacher, Debi Corbin. Instead of focusing on Kathy's so-called problem, Sharon reframed their inquiry around the following question: How can we use observation, conversation, and writing to learn about teaching and learning to teach?

Sometimes Sharon and Debi would observe Kathy teaching, then talk about the questions they would ask her later. Sometimes Kathy and Sharon would observe Debi teaching and talk about the questions and issues that Kathy would raise with Debi later. Often Sharon sat in on planning sessions, raising questions, sharing observations, and supporting both teachers in their desire to develop a more responsive curriculum. Writing and responding to journals was a regular feature of the work for all three participants. Over the course of the year, Kathy discovered how much practical knowledge she had. She also developed new ways to share her knowledge with Debi through co-planning and co-teaching. In the process, Kathy reconceptualized her role as a school-based teacher educator. Kathy and Debi formed a strong bond based on mutual respect and a shared vision of good teaching. Sharon refined and extended her thinking about learning to teach in the context of teaching and the contributions that experienced teachers can make to novices' learning. (For a more detailed account of this first year of work together, see Feiman-Nemser & Beasley, 1993.)

The following year, Kathy and Sharon initiated a new PDS project at Averill, the Teacher Education Circle, a forum for interested teachers to explore new ways of working with student teachers. Six teachers, including Kathy, Debi, and Carole, worked closely with Sharon and a doctoral student from Michigan State to design an experimental student teaching program that fit the contours of the school calendar and highlighted teachers' knowledge and ways of knowing. Debi had been hired as one of three "co-teachers" at Averill. Supported by PDS funding, co-teachers provided 2 hours of reallocated time a week for regular teachers involved in various PDS projects. Debi worked with the four second- and third-grade teachers, including Kathy and Carole. She had her own classroom across the hall from their classroom, where she brought the different groups of children assigned to her.

That year Kathy decided to follow her second graders into third grade. She persuaded Carole to move back to second grade and follow her students on to third grade the following year. Teaching many of the same students, working in the same wing of the building, and sharing a similar vision of good teaching set the stage for Kathy, Debi, and Carole to launch their peer mentoring project.

The year that Kathy, Carole, and Debi started working together marked an important turning point in Carole's teaching career. For 20 years, she had been team teaching third grade with the same partner. Although they had begun to make some changes in their teaching, their practice was still fairly traditional. Now Carole was not only teaching a new grade level (second), but she was also teaching on her own for the first time. Debi, Kathy, and Carole began having lunch together on a regular basis. They joined a math study group for teachers that was starting at the University. Carole's head was filled with new ideas about teaching and learning that she was hearing about for the first time since Averill became a PDS, and she determined to become a different kind of teacher.

As Debi and Kathy became more aware of Carole's practice, they realized that she was really struggling. Kathy heard it through the movable wall that divided her classroom from Carole's. Debi saw it when she went to pick up Carole's students. Sharon saw it when she worked with Carole's student teacher. Carole talked about it when the three teachers ate lunch together in Debi's room. The more we heard, the more concerned we became for Carole and her students. Sharon encouraged Kathy to think about how she and Debi might take advantage of the co-teaching structure and their developing friendship to help Carole sort out some of the difficulties she was experiencing.

To get to know each other better, Kathy and Debi invited Carole to lunch one Saturday. Away from school, the three teachers talked quite personally about themselves and their teaching. At one point in the discussion, the question of how to teach tolerance came up. Kathy said that she did not know how to do that. "Yes you do," Carole responded, "and I want you to tell me how to do it!" Looking back, all three teachers cited this lunch as the formal beginning of their work together.

The three teachers made a workplan that included meeting once a week after school, keeping journals and sharing them with each other and with Sharon, and observing in each other's classrooms. They also continued their conversations over lunch, and Sharon joined them on a weekly basis.

Kathy was unsure about her mentoring role and about the prospects for success in helping Carole. Close-to-the-classroom work among teachers is close to the bone. Kathy and Debi sought reassurances from Carole that their presence was welcome and their feedback helpful. Carole vacillated between feeling supported and feeling overwhelmed by what was happening in her classroom. She tried to assure her colleagues that she was serious about working on her teaching but she did not always know how to focus the work. It took a while to reach the point where we were ready for what Little (1987) calls "joint work" — rigorous and enduring interactions that "induce mutual obligation, expose the work of each person to the scrutiny of others, and call for initiative and leadership in matters of curriculum and instruction" (p. 512).

DOCUMENTING AND ANALYZING THE PROJECT

The data for this chapter consist primarily of journals that the three teachers kept and shared with each other and with Sharon, their university colleague, between 1993 and 1995. Over the 2-and-a-half years of working together, the teachers made approximately 70 journal entries, averaging between three and five single-spaced typed pages. Sharon read the journals and responded with questions and ideas they raised for her. She also met with the teachers at least once a month to talk about the themes and issues characterizing the entries. Through this ongoing data analysis, we developed some initial insights about what we were doing and learning, how Carole's practice was changing, and how our relationship and ways of working were evolving.

The ongoing data analysis also gave us ideas about how to conceptualize what we were doing and why it was both unique and important. At the most basic level, we recognized that this was a special case of collaboration among teachers and between teachers and a university colleague. Our use of the term *peer mentoring* highlights the giving and receiving of help among teachers and the ways in which the project challenges the norms of privacy, autonomy, and equality that shape the culture of teaching (Little, 1990). More specifically, the project is a case of professional development—three teachers and a university researcher/teacher educator learning about a new kind of teaching though observation, conversation, and writing. Carole's story alone is a dramatic case of teacher learning and change, and Kathy and Debi's initiative reflects a rare kind of teacher leadership.

The project also can be viewed as a case of teacher research (Cochran-Smith & Lytle, 1993). Helping Carole develop her practice involved all of us in a practical inquiry—framing problems, generating alternative solutions, trying out ideas, assessing the consequences. In the process, we generated knowledge about the teacher's role in a learner-centered classroom. Grounded in the particulars of our own practice, this practical or "insider" knowledge illuminates a familiar question in progressive education about what the teacher is supposed to do once she rejects a more traditional role in favor of a kind of teaching that honors both students and subject matter.

The prospect of talking and writing about the project for a broader audience precipitated a more systematic analysis of the data. We began by reading through all the journals with the following questions in mind: (1) What activities and moves characterize our ways of working together? (2) How can we document the impact of the work on Carole's thinking and practice? (3) What are we learning about teaching, mentoring, and teacher development? Based on our notes, we created a set of categories that we then used to code the journals.

One major theme that emerged from the data analysis and that integrates the different facets of the project is captured by the phrase "making it happen." Although Carole had a vision of the kind of classroom learning community she wanted to create, she did not know how to bring this into reality. Discovering what making it happen entails and figuring out how to help Carole make it happen in her classroom framed much of our work together.

Studying the journals, we identified four aspects of making it happen.

- Getting clear about the teacher's role in a learner-centered classroom
- Developing a repertoire of things to say and do that fit with one's beliefs

- Forming personal relationships with students
- Managing a responsive curriculum

In this chapter, we focus on the issues of role, repertoire, and relationship that dominated the talk and writing. To convey a sense of what we were thinking, feeling, and doing and how the teachers' discourse and Carole's practice changed over time, we assembled a set of journal entries that bear on the theme of making it happen. We augment the entries with jointly written commentaries that flesh out the story and highlight important aspects of the mentoring. Together they show how the threads of mentoring and professional development, teacher learning, and teacher research come together. We conclude the chapter by reflecting on how the PDS context both supported and constrained our project—a question we posed to our colleagues after making a presentation to them about the work.

LEARNING TO MAKE IT HAPPEN

We begin with excerpts from two of Kathy's journals where the idea of making it happen first appears. We all knew that things were not going smoothly in Carole's room, but we did not know exactly where the problems lay or what Carole might do about them.

Kathy, January 12, 1993
Carole and I have started working together. I am not sure that what I am doing is helpful. Carole has questions about her classroom. . . . I went in and observed but I wasn't sure what to observe. . . . I don't think Carole lacks a clear understanding of her vision. I think she is having trouble making it happen in her classroom. I think I could help maybe just by listening and letting Carole sort through her ideas and problems. . . . I know I have a tendency to back away from difficult situations, but there is not enough time to be cautious.

Kathy, March 20, 1993
It feels like Carole and I are talking more concretely. Clearly Carole is deeply upset about what is going on in her classroom. We can't seem to focus on specific instances with specific children or specific issues. I don't want to come off too critical. I want to focus on Carole's role, the part she plays in shaping her classroom. As I think about it,

Carole wants to focus more on the children and the part they play. . . .
We have to talk about this if we are going to work together.

Here Kathy is proposing a beginning focus for the work – the teacher's role. She wonders whether she and Carole have different notions about who is responsible for making it happen – the teacher or the students. Kathy's insights grow out of her own efforts to change her teaching the year she worked with Debi and Sharon. She, too, used to set things in motion and then expect the children to know what to do. Having discovered that the teacher needs to teach children how to participate appropriately in a learner-centered classroom, she wonders whether this insight may be useful to Carole. Since there are no precedents for sharing knowledge with a fellow teacher, Kathy worries about how to help Carole develop her practice without hurting her feelings.

These journal entries illustrate the tools of our work. Kathy is writing to Carole, sharing her questions about where she fits in and her thoughts about what Carole needs to work on. Writing helps us clarify our own thinking, document our experiences, and communicate difficult thoughts and powerful insights. Also, the journal is based on an observation in Carole's classroom. Watching each other teach is essential – not only Kathy and Debi watching Carole, but Carole watching both of them as well.

Kathy also writes about the need to deal in the particulars of teaching – specific children, specific incidents, specific problems. From their previous work with Sharon, Kathy and Debi had experienced the power of working through the particulars to new insights about teaching and learning. Through her questions and her modeling, Sharon promoted a way of talking about teaching that depended on knowledge of the concrete particulars as a basis for speculating about possible causes and alternative courses of action. Kathy and Debi have already internalized this habit of mind, as their journals reveal. Over time Carole too learns to talk and write more specifically about her practice. At this stage, however, she is struggling to define her role and set clear limits and expectations for the children.

Kathy, February 4, 1994
Carole's confidence in what to do and what to say is fragile. I sense an uncertainty and the children sense it, too. Will she insist Terry stop tapping on his desk in that dreadfully annoying way? . . . What is allowed in this classroom? What are the limits? Can the other children figure out why there are limits by what Carole says? I think this is crucial. How to state and restate your expectations and why they are your expectations without laboring the point. . . . Maybe this

would help: thinking of many examples of clear pointed things to say in different situations.

Carole, February 7, 1994
I have felt that same defiance from Terry, but also from others in my class. What is it? Am I contributing to the cause by something I am doing? I do not have many strategies to draw on when I come in contact with that kind of defiance. Kathy asked me, "What are you going to do? The kids are waiting for you to do something." That phrase has come into my head several times. Maybe I have let too much go so now each time becomes a struggle to see who will win. When Kathy and Debi are in the room, they help me focus on what behaviors are going on that need more attention, both negative and positive. They both have a way of talking about what needs to happen in the classroom to make a better learning environment. What is it that they do? I need to figure this out.

Kathy, February 8, 1994
I was very relieved to have Carole tell me that my intervention with Terry had not overstepped any bounds for her. I was so worried. Carole, I am in awe of your hard work, courage, and thoughtfulness.

Deciding where and how to set limits is a major theme in these journal entries. As Kathy pushes Carole to think about setting clear limits in the classroom, she worries about whether she is overstepping the boundaries of their friendship. Fortunately, Carole is taking a more active role in diagnosing her own learning needs. We see that her relationship with Kathy and Debi is strong enough to bear even the most direct and pointed questions.

Carole has accepted the idea that thinking about her role makes sense. She is asking her own questions, trying to define the problem by thinking about her own actions and words and what they communicate to children, and how her approach is similar to and different from Kathy and Debi's. She recalls an instance when she was clear about her role and recognizes that writing about it could help her clarify ideas about what she needs to do. She is an intentional learner.

Counting on the strength of their relationship and commitment to the work, Kathy takes a chance. She puts into writing the questions that came to mind as she watched Carole teach and gives the journal entry to Carole. She is asking Carole when she is going to take charge. This is not how teachers typically talk to each other.

We also see here a nice example of how teacher knowledge can grow out of focusing on the particulars of teaching. The first set of questions that Kathy raises has to do with the specific students and events that she observed in Carole's room. This leads to a more general insight about the need for teachers to state and restate their expectations and to be clear about why they have particular limits in the first place.

Kathy, February 10, 1994

Carole has taken charge! . . . She read aloud to us what she had told the children about how things were changing and they weren't going to ignore her anymore. She took back her authority and her job and she told them. It was great!

As Kathy's journal reveals, Carole is working incredibly hard to communicate her expectations clearly. She tells the students over and over again that her job is to help them get what they need to learn. Despite her persistence, the same six students continue to ignore or defy her and the whole class seems angrier than ever. Carole feels very discouraged. Debi and Kathy are also worried, but they keep thinking, writing, and talking about what is happening in Carole's classroom, trying to get a better handle on the problem.

Kathy, February 24, 1994

I knew there was something wrong with the way that Carole and the children were interacting and feeling about each other but I was stumped. . . . Once we started talking I realized the something important that we had missed. I remember getting the idea when Carole said something about the children not believing her when she told them she wanted to help them. . . . We tried to figure out how you could show children you care with your actions. . . . Another thing I remember about putting actions with your words had to do with looking at children, really looking deep into their eyes when they talk to you. It is sort of startling the power this has. Children can feel your attention and your caring by your concentration on them. And you can feel the connection, too.

Carole, March 3, 1994

I have learned new ways to say things to my class, but they don't seem to believe me. . . . What does that mean? The words, just saying them isn't enough. . . . We also talked about adding a dimension of play. Get down with them and be involved — trace, build with blocks, swing, throw the football — whatever it takes. I have done this and I love it. The kids love . . . I have also been paying attention to when I look right into the kids' eyes when they talk to me and not be doing something else.

As Kathy and Carole continue to talk about why things are not falling into place in Carole's classroom, they realize that not only does she need to persuade students that she is serious about their learning, but she also has to get them to believe that she cares about them. Words alone are not enough; they need to be connected to actions.

Carole already knows how to play with children in ways that let them take the lead. She also knows how to use play to show children that she really cares about them. This conversation gives her permission to do something that is not widely endorsed by the school's culture.

Carole, March 8, 1994

Today I blew it. . . . Things were messy and not quiet. So I decided to watch Debi. Things seemed calmer than in our room. They (the students) were waiting for each other. Nobody refused to help or sit down. Brad and Carl were having the hardest time. Debi kind of played with them. "Who am I going to find when I turn around to put on my happy face list?" She turned around and was smiling, really big. Debi has a very even voice, talking calmly, waiting, telling them what she needs for them to work. How can I get that to happen?

Carole knew she had had a bad morning. She deliberately went into Debi's room to see whether by watching Debi work with her own students, she could learn something that would help her. Any inhibition about intruding into someone else's classroom or asking for help had no place in her quest. In Debi's classroom, Carole saw the children she knew so well waiting, listening to Debi and to each other, sharing ideas, and being serious about their learning. Debi was enacting Carole's vision of teaching and learning right before her eyes.

Watching Debi work with her students and seeing their reactions helped Carole visualize new ways of interacting with students. Over time she developed a repertoire of nonconfrontational strategies along with the confidence to persist.

Kathy, September 7, 1994

Carole told an important story about Charles. It was a beautiful example of Carole's changing practice. . . . She told of talking directly, explaining what she wanted Charles to do. When he didn't do it, she tried another approach, focusing on children who were doing what she wanted, describing it and rewarding it. She didn't just let it go. She persisted. The class witnessed this. Carole said that she hadn't really recognized the event for what it was until we began talking.

Having developed new ways of talking about teaching, Carole came to Debi and Kathy with a success story. Kathy and Debi helped Carole appreciate her accomplishment and what it entailed. The class saw in Carole's words and actions that they could trust her to take care of them by protecting their learning time. This conversation helped us refine our collective understanding of the need for persistence as well as a repertoire of strategies to use with children who resist engaging in the work at hand.

Debi, September 25, 1994

Last week I was in Carole's room to pick up her students for the morning. They were finishing a math lesson so I sat down quietly. Carole was in the back directing the conversation and a student was up at the board sharing an idea. Alex was tossing a red toy up and down, up and down. Steven was in his seat at the front of the room banging on his desk. Nick was moaning about a toy Carole had taken away. I hadn't seen Carole's room like this in a long time. Why didn't she stop and say, "This is your first warning, Alex"? . . . I went home and wondered about my brief time in the room. I hated the feeling in there. I wondered what Carole had been feeling . . . I was debating what to do when Carole called . . . I told her that I wondered why she had let Alex toss the toy. She said it was his birthday so she didn't want to confront him.

Carole, September 26, 1994

Last week Debi asked me why I had let Steven, Alex, and Nick keep disrupting the learning. It really brought me up short. I felt those old feelings sneaking back in. . . . Her question really helped me to refocus again.

Carole's practice is open to scrutiny. She cannot hide behind an edited story of what happened. Debi (and Kathy) not only see what is going on, but they question her about it. Once Carole hears Debi's question, she knows that she has to think about it if she is going to learn from the experience to be better prepared to adopt a different course of action in the future.

Two characteristics make this a remarkable interaction. First, most teachers would be threatened by the prospect of exposing their practice to their colleagues. This is understandable since teachers generally work alone, away from the gaze of their fellow teachers. Second, teachers are not in the habit of asking a colleague to explain his or her practice. Fortunately, Kathy, Carole, and Debi have developed a sturdy relationship that can sustain both observation and tough questions. For them, this is part of the work of teaching and learning to teach in new ways.

Kathy, September 26, 1994

I am elated. Carole is making it happen in a way that she never has before. Tonight as we talked, she was smiling, animated, leaning back in her chair, explaining her decisions and stating emphatically, "I am determined." I asked her how this had happened and she looked at me like I was nuts and talked about the work we have been doing together as making the difference. Then she added that Debi's question about her room had made her realize that she was letting things go and that she didn't want to. The difference, though, is that now she has tools and strategies to use. She said she thinks it has taken her until now to realize that the boys' behavior is not her fault, that she didn't make them act the way they did. Then she stopped herself and said that probably sounds strange because "I know that it is up to me to make things happen." She also said that my experience with Latitia had helped her. That seeing the way I approached the problem, not in terms of "What is wrong with me?" but "How am I going to work with Latitia?"

Carole, October 1, 1994

I felt I worked very hard today. I didn't realize why until I talked with Kathy and Debi. Things seemed in a real uproar this morning, but what I kept trying to do was to bring order and calmness and accomplish some work at the same time. I know I am different in what I'm doing in my classroom. I am no longer angry when children come in and don't get to work. What I am doing is firmly and softly telling students what they need to be doing. If the noise level goes up, I stop everyone with 1-2-3-4-5 timer, while saying, "It needs to be quiet to write and think up your ideas. We need to be serious learners." . . . I am trying to talk slower also, making sure that people know what they should be looking and sounding like and what they should be doing.

In the beginning stages of our work, Carole felt frustrated, helpless, alone. She blamed herself for not being able to solve the problems children brought to school. She was angry with the children for not engaging in learning. She wondered how much her own confusion was contributing to the general confusion in the classroom.

Through hard work with Kathy and Debi, Carole developed a new demeanor. She now exudes a calm and quiet manner and a sense of confidence. She also has learned how to help students put aside enough of their anger to engage in serious learning. Carole has a repertoire of ways to draw students in and to manage her learner-centered curriculum. She knows how to "read" the class and how to connect with individual students. If one thing doesn't work, she tries something else, knowing that she is responsible for making it happen.

Carole, October 25, 1994

One thing that is clearer is my vision for what I want learning in my class to look like . . . having children engaged in the task of learning by digging into what it is they understand. I now see clearly that I have to choreograph the whole task by breaking it down into simple steps . . . I'm becoming more verbal with my students so they will know why we are doing something and be serious about how to learn. I am learning to give many verbal clues and to ask for what I want in ways that are not punitive but more positive. I listen to the children, asking them what they need and identifying for them what they may be feeling. Like the day Charles came in very disturbed. I went over and said, "You are very angry," and he just opened up and said his mom hit him for not bringing his coat home. I told him I'd be upset if someone hit me because I forgot where I put something because I lose things all the time. Then I told him to remain on the couch and join us when he was ready. Pretty soon he came and sat down and went to work and had a good day.

Carole has learned that having a vision of a classroom where children's ideas are listened to, valued, and central to the daily talk and learning is not enough. She also has to break the vision down into specific actions and then teach them to her students. If she wants children to listen to and think about each other's ideas during math, she has to help the students understand what this looks and sounds like in action. Simply telling them to listen to each other is not sufficient.

Carole has become an "intentional" learner—aware, articulate, and proactive in her own professional development, and better able to support children's learning. She no longer needs us to provide the focus and ask the questions. She has internalized the ways of thinking and seeing that shape our subculture of mentoring. All these changes have led to a new kind of professional relationship. We have moved from mentoring to a more collegial form of collaboration, especially in the area of curriculum. This past year Kathy worked with a very challenging class and she regularly turned to Carole for support.

THE ROLE OF THE MENTORING SUBCULTURE IN THE PDS

PDS funding enabled us to travel to the University of Pennsylvania, where we talked about our project at the "Ethnography in Education" forum, an annual meeting receptive to teacher research. On our return, we decided to make a similar presentation at Averill during a monthly PDS meeting, a regular time set aside to discuss school-wide issues and hear about individual projects. Ironically, we felt more confident describing our work to strangers in Philadelphia than we did talking about it to our own colleagues.

The audience of local teachers and university colleagues who heard the presentation was both surprised and moved. People had seen us meeting over lunch and after school, but they did not really know what we were doing. Although our project had been described briefly in the annual PDS scope of work, no one had shown much interest.

Our sense of isolation came from both inside and outside the project. Because we were engaged in an intense, time-consuming effort, we did not attend extra meetings or hang out in the teachers' lounge. Moreover, the fragility and precariousness of the work made us reluctant to talk about it. At the same time, some teachers felt uncomfortable about changes that Kathy and Carole had made, such as their decisions to follow students for 2 years or to take recess as needed rather than according to the set schedule, and they distanced themselves from us.

Three features of the work stood out to our colleagues. One person asked how important it was that we had a shared vision of good teaching. This led to an interesting exchange about the place of common values in collaborative efforts to change teaching practice. Several people noticed that the way we talked about teaching differed from more familiar patterns of teacher talk. Many recognized that the work depended on a long-term commitment. These comments about shared vision, talk, and commitment suggest ways in which the subculture we had created set us apart from the larger professional culture of the school.

Vision

The Professional Development School initiative brought new visions of teaching and learning to our school (Holmes Group, 1990). Terms like "teaching for understanding," "learning community," "inclusion," and "authentic assessment" became part of the PDS vocabulary; however, the staff did not talk much about what these terms could mean or how different people were trying to enact them in their classrooms. Everyone knew there were differences in philosophy and practice among the staff, but the staff as a whole rarely addressed these differences directly. In meetings, for instance, teachers were not in the habit of asking for or offering specific examples or evidence to illustrate or support their claims. Nor were they comfortable talking about difficulties unless they could be couched in terms of individual students and their problems.

Before they started working together, Carole actually had never seen Kathy teach, but she had observed how Kathy interacted with students in the hallway outside their room and on the playground, and she liked what she saw. She also appreciated the positions Kathy took in discussions on the management team, especially her advocacy for children. Debi had learned about Kathy's beliefs and practices when she was Kathy's student teacher. Their year-long investigation with Sharon provided a rich opportunity to construct shared meanings. Carole thought Kathy and Debi could help her create a classroom that more closely reflected her beliefs and values. In an early journal, she had written: "For decades I had an inner sense that the things I saw and did were in conflict with the way I really felt children should be treated and taught."

Having a shared vision meant that the three teachers could assume a certain level of agreement about the kind of classroom community they wanted to create and the sorts of teaching and learning activities that should go on there. Even when things did not go the way we wanted, no one in the subgroup recommended abandoning the vision. The fact that we were struggling did not mean that what we wanted to achieve was misguided.

Having a shared vision also made it more likely that everyone could find satisfaction in the work—the helpers as well as the person being helped. Even though Carole's practice did not improve quickly, all of us benefited from talking about a kind of teaching we valued and from trying to figure out what it entails and how to bring it about. Through these discussions we clarified our beliefs and constructed new understandings, something that might have been more difficult if we did not have a shared vision.

Talk

Our colleagues also noticed that the way we talk about teaching differs from the way teachers usually talk about their work. Our talk is based in the questions, doubts, and concerns that arise in the course of teaching and observing teaching. Not satisfied with vague references and generalizations, we do not hesitate to ask, "What do you mean?" or "Can you give me an example?" Nor do we experience a question like, "Why did you do that?" as an implied criticism. Rather, we value the opportunity to articulate and clarify the reasons behind our actions. We still thrive on telling about our successes and failures, but we have learned to unpack the stories, moving through the particulars to more general principles and ideas. Without that, we cannot learn from our experiences.

Neither the organization of schools nor the culture of teaching encourages this kind of conversation. Teachers are more likely to engage in storytelling and routine sharing than in sustained, critical conversations about classroom incidents or dilemmas. Teachers also tend to assume that they understand what another teacher means without checking. Nor do teachers associate these ways of talking with university researchers, who tend to favor general propositions and prescriptions that often seem remote from the realities of classrooms.

In fact, Kathy and Debi initially were surprised by the way Sharon talked and wrote about teaching compared with many of the university researchers and teacher educators they had encountered. Based on past experience, they expected faculty from the university to be more interested in telling teachers what they should know or do than in finding out what teachers actually think and why they do what they do. From the beginning, Sharon wanted to understand what Kathy and Debi thought and to engage with them in a joint inquiry about teaching and learning to teach.

Of course, the PDS initiative created more opportunities for Averill teachers to talk together, but it did not automatically promote collegial observation and critical review of practice. One teacher said she could go to anyone on the staff and "complain" about a bad day or a difficult child, but she would not expect the listener to ask for more details or offer to come and observe her teaching as a way of helping her think through what she might do differently. Venting, a common practice, does not require a serious commitment. Nor does it depend on the dispositions and skills that sustain open, critical discussions about teaching.

Commitment

In making a commitment to help Carole, Kathy and Debi were acting out of a sense of personal and professional responsibility. They could not stand by and let their friend struggle alone or fail. Nor were they comfortable watching students miss out on learning. Without knowing exactly what they were getting into, they entered into a process of observation, conversation, and writing in the belief that these activities would yield new understandings and help Carole improve her teaching. We all recognized that we were in this "for the long haul."

Because of our explicit commitment to one another and to the work, a high level of trust developed. This helped Carole cope with feelings of vulnerability and disequilibrium, the inevitable companions of serious change. It also allowed Kathy and Debi to share their own sense of uncertainty and vulnerability with Sharon as they ventured into the uncharted territory of peer mentoring. Sharon helped the teachers see how the obligations they had assumed and the subculture they had created represented a new vision of collegiality and a new form of teacher leadership.

HOW THE PDS CONTEXT AFFECTED THE MENTORING

Lord (1994) argues that "critical colleagueship" is essential if teachers are going to move from more traditional models of curriculum and instruction toward more learner-centered, inquiry-oriented approaches favored by contemporary reformers and promoted by our local PDS initiative. By "critical colleagueship," he means teachers exploring their own questions and concerns, exposing their teaching to other teachers and educators, reflecting together on new ideas and practices, and engaging in constructive criticism. More than sharing ideas and offering support, critical colleagueship depends on a willingness to analyze and justify one's practices, seek out the best knowledge available, and rely on learning through inquiry rather than by accident. In short, it casts teachers as "commentators" and "critics" of their own and each other's practices.

Kathy, Debi, and Carole developed a high level of critical colleagueship. In addition to their personal dispositions, this accomplishment depended on resources and learning opportunities made available through the Professional Development School partnership. Of particular importance were the provision of a trustworthy co-teacher and the opportunity to work with a teacher educator/researcher from the university.

Through PDS funding, teachers involved in specific projects received 2 hours a week of reallocated time. A co-teacher spent this time with their classes while they worked on various PDS projects. Kathy and Carole were fortunate to have Debi as their co-teacher, someone who knew their children and shared their vision of teaching and learning. With a less competent or compatible co-teacher, they might not have felt so comfortable leaving the classroom. The reallocated time made it possible for the three teachers to observe in each other's classrooms, to plan curriculum together, and to meet with Sharon. Especially important was the opportunity for Carole to observe her own students with a different teacher (Debi).

The PDS partnership also made it possible for Kathy, Debi, and Carole to work with a teacher educator/researcher who valued teachers' knowledge and critical discourse. Sharon helped the three teachers articulate what they were learning and appreciate its broader significance, despite the sea of frustration and discouragement that often surrounded them. We have already detailed her role in asking questions, reframing problems, and setting the work in a broader context of reform. In many ways this was a continuation of her original project with Kathy and Debi.

Since her initial involvement in the PDS, Sharon had been trying to help interested teachers at Averill study and expand their role as school-based teacher educators. She did this through the Teacher Education Circle, where she encouraged critical discussions of mentoring and learning to teach. As a leader of the new teacher certification program at Michigan State, she also drew the principal and teachers at Averill into a range of teacher education activities while continuing to collaborate with Kathy and others on studies of mentored learning to teach. Finally, Sharon connected Kathy, Debi, and Carole with other resources, such as the mathematics study group where they worked with teachers from other schools learning new approaches to the teaching of mathematics (Featherstone, Pfeiffer, & Smith, 1993).

Besides these specific resources and learning opportunities, the PDS initiative brought to the school a vision of content-rich, constructivist-oriented teaching and learning that appealed to certain teachers. Many exciting changes were taking place at Averill, including the creation of a well-stocked library/media center, a school-wide commitment to literature-based teaching, and a restructured school day that allowed time for teachers to work together on various projects and activities.

Still the school as a whole had not yet achieved a professional culture supportive of critical colleagueship. That depends on more than resources, restructuring, and new visions of teaching and learning. It is not an automatic byproduct of reform activity. Developing the skills and dispositions of critical colleagueship requires a shared understanding of how the traditions of equality, autonomy, and noninterference limit interactions among teachers. It requires well-supported opportunities for teachers to experience and practice new ways of interacting with colleagues (and with novices, administrators, and researchers) based on openness, respect, and critical thinking. It requires people involved in a PDS effort to embrace such a goal and to recognize, encourage, and celebrate progress toward it.

The peer mentoring project described in this chapter occurred because three teachers and a university researcher/teacher educator deliberately created a subculture that supported observation and critical discourse among teachers about teaching. The decision to read from our journals and talk about our experiences with fellow teachers, administrators, and university collaborators came from a desire to describe and model a new kind of colleagueship that has enriched our professional lives. Perhaps, the positive response to our presentation means that others involved in our Professional Development School are interested in moving toward more serious and sustained collaboration. Perhaps together we can "make it happen."

The research reported in this chapter was supported in part by the College of Education, Michigan State University, and by the Michigan Partnership for New Education.

REFERENCES

Cochran-Smith, & Lytle, S. (Eds.). (1993). *Inside/outside: Teacher research and knowledge.* New York: Teachers College Press.

Featherstone, H., Pfeiffer, L., & Smith, S. (1993). *Learning in good company* (Research Report 93-2). East Lansing, MI: Michigan State University, National Center for Research on Teacher Learning.

Feiman-Nemser, S., & Beasley, K. (1993). *Discovering and sharing knowledge: Inventing a new role for cooperating teachers.* Paper presented at the Workshop on Teachers' Cognition, Tel Aviv University, Tel Aviv, Israel.

Holmes Group. (1990). *Tomorrow's schools: Principles for the design of professional development schools.* East Lansing, MI: Author.

Little, J. W. (1987). Teachers as colleagues. In V. Richardson-Koehler (Ed.), *Educator's handbook: A research perspective* (pp. 491–518). New York: Longman.

Little, J. W. (1990). The mentoring phenomenon and the social organization of teaching. *Review of Research in Education,* (16), 297–351.

Lord, B. (1994). *Teachers' professional development: Critical colleagueship and the role of professional communities. The future of education perspectives on national standards in America.* New York: College Entrance Examination Board.

Chapter 3

How the Emergence of Teacher Leadership Helped Build a Professional Development School

KATHERINE BOLES AND VIVIAN TROEN

In the mid-1980s the authors of this chapter, two elementary classroom teachers each with over 15 years of experience, together made a fateful decision. We agreed to share a classroom, co-teach a fourth grade, and share the experience with others in a series of articles, as an experiment in professional development. This new arrangement was intended to allow both of us to gather insights, ideas, and methodologies leading to a strategy for the revitalization of a profession that each of us believed to be in serious need of repair. We were two teachers searching for ways to grow professionally without leaving the classroom.

It may have been the day we discovered, to our dismay, that the newest student teacher couldn't spell the word *excellent* or find Guatemala on the map. Or, it may have been when we realized that too many of the best teachers were walking away from the profession, leaving the less competent behind in classrooms. In either case, our discomfort with the state of education had reached a level where we had to either leave the profession ourselves or work to change the system.

What was it, exactly, that needed to be changed? What was wrong with the system and how could it be fixed? There was a whole lot of talking going on about school reform, but there appeared to be very little real action — at least none that was having any positive effect on teachers' lives in the classroom. It seemed to us that the whole discussion surrounding school reform was taking place far outside the classroom and that missing from the debate was a vital component: the classroom teacher.

Although we didn't realize it at the time (the term had not yet been invented), what we were searching for was a way of creating a "professional development school."

Above all, we wanted to create a model that would improve education for children while providing teachers with avenues for professional growth and renewal — a model that would encourage experienced teachers to remain in the classroom, as well as attract promising new teachers to the school community. In addition, we wanted to create an environment in which teachers could work together in collegial teams to improve teaching and learning.

That meant, we realized, redesigning the school day and reorganizing staffing patterns to provide teachers with sufficient time for reflection on educational practice as well as opportunities for meaningful dialogue and decision making at the building level. We understood that in order to improve the learning opportunities for all students, we had to improve the teaching occupation.

The most serious implication inherent in this decision was that we were determined to become teacher leaders in a profession where the two terms were seen to be diametrically opposed.

A CONTEXT FOR TEACHER LEADERSHIP

Teaching is not a profession that values or encourages leadership within its ranks. The hierarchical nature of public schools is based on the nineteenth-century industrial model, with the consequent adversarial relationship of administration as management and teachers as labor. Like factory workers in the 1800s, all teachers have equal status. Leadership opportunities are extremely limited.

Furthermore, since the mid-nineteenth century, teaching has been accepted as women's work or, as Catherine Beecher called it, "women's true profession" (Hoffman, 1981, p. 36). A woman's role was to follow, not to lead. David Tyack (1974) referred to the newly feminized schools of the nineteenth century as "pedagogical harem(s)" (p. 45) where women taught and a few men directed.

As teachers who were interested in teacher culture and the history of schoolteaching, we recognized the serious flaws of this traditional model. When the school reform reports of the late 1980s made compelling recommendations for teachers to provide leadership in restructuring the nation's schools, we were pleased. Unlike earlier reform efforts, these reports emphasized the importance of creating new roles for teachers that acknowledged the centrality of classroom teaching and extended teachers' decision-making power into school-wide leadership activities. The 1986 report of the Carnegie Forum on Education and the Economy, *A Nation Prepared: Teachers for the Twenty First Century*, went so far as to state that "the key" to the successful reform of schools "lies in creating a profession . . . of well-educated teachers prepared to assume new powers and responsibilities to redesign schools for the future" (p. 2). Recognizing that without such teachers "any reforms will be short-lived" (p. 2), the report suggested sweeping changes in education policy that would, among other things, "restructure schools to provide a professional environment for teaching," as well as "restructure the teaching force and introduce a new category of Lead Teacher" (p. 3).

A number of the reports envisioned less rigidly structured organizations where expert teachers assumed roles that were flexible and extended beyond the boundaries of the individual classroom (California Commission on the Teaching Profession, 1985; Devaney, 1987). These reports confirmed what we already knew — teachers had to be recognized as potentially powerful agents of change.

Yet, despite the apparent recognition of the importance of teacher leadership to successful education reform, teacher leadership in the 1990s is more often honored in the breach than in practice. Teacher leadership roles in curriculum, school improvement, and professional development are often limited in scope and vision, and subject to easy cancellation when budgets are cut (Johnson & Boles, 1994).

School districts often misconstrue the intent of the recommendations and proudly point to examples of teacher leadership no matter how minimal the impact on day-to-day operations. Teacher leadership often is characterized by placing one "token" teacher on a committee of 30 rather than including a representative number of teachers on all committees. That is akin to calling a banana republic a democracy if a few of its citizens are allowed to vote, with the bulk of the populace resentful of those who do vote, and the supreme power at the top of the administrative ladder watchful and suspicious lest this idea of participation spread and disrupt the status quo. Teacher leadership is not about serving on committees that rubber-stamp what the central administration has already proposed or promulgating decisions that subsequently are ignored by central administration.

POWERFUL FORCES IMPEDE TEACHER LEADERSHIP

Repeated attempts have been made to create teacher leadership positions in schools. Studies of teacher leaders describe teachers who were chosen to assist beginning teachers, fulfill roles in supervision, develop curriculum, or serve in part-time administrative positions (Lieberman, Saxl, & Miles, 1988; Wasley, 1990). These teacher leaders were screened and selected carefully. They often worked alone and frequently found teaching colleagues resistant to their leadership; they often had to leave classroom teaching in order to assume leadership roles (Smylie, 1992; Zimpher, 1988). The teachers related how difficult it was to implement their roles in an egalitarian school culture. Teachers who individually had restructured their work were warned to be quiet about the work they did so as not to stand out as special among the faculty. Teachers in administratively designated leadership roles reported that more often than not they were relegated to quasi-administrative positions and were "stuck" with scheduling and bus duty (Wasley, 1990).

Why, then, we wondered, is teacher leadership so difficult to establish? What stands in the way of creating truly meaningful teacher leadership roles? The answer, we believe, lies in the inherent characteristics of public education in America.

The Rigid Structure of Schools

Leadership by teachers is not part of the school culture. Leadership in schools traditionally has been organized with top-down mandates and little input from classroom practitioners (Tyack, 1974). The formulation and development of programs and reforms have never been considered the work of teachers: It has been the teacher's job to carry out plans developed by others at higher levels in the school hierarchy (Lortie, 1975).

"Programmatic and behavioral regularities" (Sarason, 1971, p. 62) make it seem as inappropriate for a teacher to assume leadership as it is for an assembly line worker to suggest how to improve the assembly line. (More accurately, we should say as it *was* for an assembly line worker, for automobiles today are built by teams of auto workers who increasingly are involved in restructuring their work.) As an indicator of social change, the profession of teaching seems to be less progressive than the manufacture of automobiles.

The Conservative Nature of Teachers

Teachers are not risk-takers beyond the domain of the classroom (Johnson, 1990). Concerned with teaching and most interested in life *inside* the classroom, most teachers have been reluctant to think of themselves as leaders *outside* the classroom (McLaughlin & Yee, 1988). They often view with discomfort the idea of assuming quasi-administrative or expanded teaching functions. In addition, experience has taught them that teacher leadership and risk-taking are neither valued nor rewarded in the schools in which they work.

The Egalitarianism of Teaching

The issue of the equality of all teachers inevitably arises in any discussion of teacher leadership. Teachers in Susan Moore Johnson's (1990) study of 115 "very good" teachers remarked that they and their peers often did not take advantage of available opportunities to exert formal influence because of the "norms of equity that discouraged individual teachers from stepping forth and taking the lead, and skepticism about the prospects for success" (pp. 200–201). Other researchers have noted that the "equal-status" norm is so strong that, while principals may note the existence of team leaders, teachers may deny that they exist (Cohen, 1981) or doubt their effectiveness (Arikado, 1976). In their study of the cultures of teaching, Feiman-Nemser and Floden (1986) describe a "norm of non-interference" that prevents teachers from using their regular interactions at staff meetings, in lunchrooms, and at the duplicating machine "to discuss their work or to collaborate on shared problems" (p. 509). This disinclination of teachers to discuss educational practice, follow the lead of their peers, or recognize the efforts of their peers who take leadership roles must be factored into any discussion of teacher leadership.

To introduce teacher leadership is to introduce status differences based on knowledge, skill, and initiative into a profession that has made no provision for them (Little, 1988). Seeing some teachers do something new and different, getting attention and respect, intensifies feelings of turf-protection and powerlessness in others. This brings up what is probably the most important obstacle of all to the institutionalization of teacher leadership.

The Issue of Power

Often left undiscussed in the dialogue surrounding "shared-decision making," "school-based management," and the "professionalization of teaching" is the issue of power. Decision-making power in schools is carefully allocated. Decisions about classroom policy—what to teach, how to use time, and how to assess progress—are made by teachers (Johnson, 1990). Other decisions that affect teachers' work—scheduling, class placement, assignment of specialists, and the allocation of budget and materials—are made at higher levels of the school bureaucracy. This norm, in which teachers feel powerless to affect school-wide policy, is widely accepted by both teachers and administrators. This view of power as a "zero-sum game," in which a gain in one area requires a loss in another, makes it difficult for teacher leaders to emerge in schools. Where principals fear they will be relegated to becoming operational managers as teachers assume new leadership roles, they actively oppose such changes (Koppich, 1993).

A Teacher-Initiated Professional Development School

We began with a clean slate, two tenured teachers with no power, beholden to no one, with nothing to lose. We had previously exerted some "leadership" in our system through committee work, had initiated an ESL Peer Tutoring program, and had worked on changing the delivery of professional development to the district.

Both of us had assumed leadership roles outside our school district. One of us had learned about the culture of teaching through a research project in Boston that studied the long-term effect of teaching on teachers. The other had been a political activist for years, had helped found a feminist theatre company, and had conducted workshops and seminars around issues of change in the workplace. So we had a background of activism, relatively thick skins, and didn't shrink from putting ourselves out front.

We wanted to open up teacher leadership possibilities through what we called "Alternative Roles for Teachers," both as a way for veteran teachers to grow and at the same time to encourage the academically able to pursue a teaching career. This model called for new roles such as: Teacher/Curriculum Developer; Teacher/Researcher; Teacher/Teacher Educator.

We realized that the key to restructuring the worklife of the teacher was held by the university. We saw collaboration with a college as a way to reform preservice teacher education while we simultaneously restructured our own work in our school. We believed that teacher education had to improve and that a collaboration between school and college was a vehicle for reforming education.

This was our context when we began to brainstorm about creating a program to address these issues. Our central question was: How can we develop knowledge and practices in teachers that will lead to the success of all students?

We should not minimize the amount of time and energy it took for our efforts to result in significant change. It took two years prior to the initiation of the project that was to become the Learning/Teaching Collaborative to lay the foundation for the program. And the road to successful initiation was littered with obstacles.

We wrote articles for journals and sent them everywhere we thought we could get published. We shared (often imposed) our ideas for school restructuring at conferences around the country, networking with educators and like-minded colleagues on the front lines of school reform. The number of other teachers we found there were few. Our sessions were poorly attended, but we persisted. We ran hither and yon looking for money, trying to interest a college in forming a collaborative with our public school, obtaining permission from our district, convincing our superintendent, and playing telephone tag with funders, potential supporters, anyone who could help us. As we gained attention, we gained notoriety, which slowly evolved into credibility. Increased credibility enabled us to form new coalitions. Our first supporter was our principal, Jerry Kaplan, followed by Wheelock College faculty member Karen Worth, Wheelock President Dan Cheever, Massachusetts Commissioner of Education Harold Raynolds, and American Federation of Teachers President Albert Shanker.

After many rejections and setbacks, the first collaborative team linking the Edward Devotion School in Brookline and Wheelock College in Boston was put into place and formally began operating in September 1987.

The objectives of the Learning/Teaching Collaborative were to

- Restructure the school's learning environment to provide increased learning opportunities for both children and teachers
- Improve the quality and coordination of preservice education curricula and clinical experiences
- Serve more children in the classroom by reducing the fragmentation of classroom activities caused by special education "pull-out" programs
- Provide teachers with time for developing professional avenues of interest while enhancing the value of their teaching and improving the teaching profession.

Administered by teachers, this team teaching program set out to alter the organization of instruction and create new professional roles for teachers. Even in an era of diminishing resources, the Learning/Teaching Collaborative has successfully met its goals and has grown steadily — from one team of four teachers to nine teams in five Brookline schools and one Boston public school. One reason for its increasing strength and popularity is that it meets the needs of many constituencies.

The Learning/Teaching Collaborative has successfully

- Supported a new paradigm of teacher leadership that allows the norms of equality and inclusion to remain intact
- Created an environment for colleges to support this paradigm in multiple ways

- Built an educational infrastructure that supports the learning of both new and experienced teachers.

The framework of the Collaborative consists of four major components.

Team Teaching

Teachers, functioning in teams, share curriculum and children. Five hours per month are allocated for team meetings outside the school day. In addition, principals have arranged common planning time for teachers so that teachers, their interns, and the college supervisor can meet on a regular basis.

School/University Collaboration

Graduate student interns from either Wheelock College or Simmons College work full time in the teams during the entire school year. A teacher and college faculty member teach the Wheelock interns' graduate-level curriculum seminar together; other teachers present guest lectures on their particular areas of expertise; and a number of classroom teachers teach reading and math methods courses at the two colleges. A steering committee composed of college and school faculty representatives and administrators from each of the participating institutions governs the PDS and meets four times per year. Subcommittees meet throughout the year to manage the budget, recruit interns, supervise the professional development of teachers, encourage and maintain parent involvement, and handle public relations.

Special Education Inclusion

In a number of the teams special needs children are fully mainstreamed. Special education teachers are members of the teams; they consult with teachers and give some direct service to children.

Alternative Professional Teaching Time

Each classroom teacher is provided with a minimum of one day a week (six hours) away from teaching duties to assume an alternative role: curriculum writer, researcher, or student teacher supervisor/college teacher. This "Alternative Professional Teaching (APT) Time" is facilitated by the full-time presence of teaching interns.

AN ASSESSMENT: HOW TEACHER LEADERSHIP
FARES AT THE LEARNING/TEACHING COLLABORATIVE

The Learning/Teaching Collaborative, with its emphasis on the powerful role of the teacher in the PDS, has provided teachers with a very different kind of educational experience. Teachers direct this collaborative, and it has been designed by them to meet their needs.

Research conducted since the inception of the Learning/Teaching Collaborative (Boles, 1990, 1991; Troen & Boles, 1994) has indicated that many teachers assume leadership roles through this PDS. What is particularly interesting is that the leadership roles were not designed as formal leadership opportunities for teachers. Rather, teachers assumed these new roles without seeking, or receiving, any formal designation as leaders.

Hour-long interviews with teachers who represented a range of grade levels, school sites, and areas of expertise, indicated that this PDS had enabled a new form of professional, collegial leadership to "bubble up" from among their ranks. Among our findings are the following:

- *Teaching practices have changed significantly.* Teachers have developed a new vision of teaching and learning. Teachers consistently co-teach; regularly discuss practice; conduct demonstration lessons; and together with their interns and teammates, develop more curriculum than they ever have before.
- *Professional relationships have improved.* Teachers work together in their teams and they meet together in study groups on a regular basis. In their teams they learn inquiry approaches that give them skills to make professional judgments about teaching and learning.
- *The work of the teachers in the PDS affects the work of their peers.* Teachers share what they have learned through their APT Time with other teachers in their building and in the school system.
- *The PDS nurtures teacher leadership.* Although a number of the teachers previously had assumed leadership roles in their schools and communities, all feel that leadership in the Learning/Teaching Collaborative is different.
- *Leadership activities are natural outgrowths of professional interests and work in teams.* While teachers generally gravitate toward other teachers with similar interests when they assume their leadership roles, their behavior is entrepreneurial and their activities self-determined.
- *Teachers express general satisfaction with the Collaborative.* A few teachers complain that there are too many meetings related to their

work in the Collaborative. Others feel some stress because the intern's full-time presence means they are never alone with their children. Yet they all emphasize that these are minor problems.

- *Teachers report collegial relationships with their school principals.* Principals arrange common planning time, generally support the concept of the Collaborative, and in some cases contribute to the funding.
- *Teachers acknowledge the fragility of the Collaborative.* Teachers have gained increased political awareness and realize that the Collaborative's continuation depends, in part, on factors beyond their control.

AREAS OF LEADERSHIP GROWTH AND DEVELOPMENT

Teachers' responses led to the identification of five major areas in which they experienced profound leadership growth and development. These are team teaching and collaboration, preservice teacher education, curriculum development and assessment, research, and governance.

Team Teaching and Collaboration

The team has become a forum in which teachers take risks with their teaching and expand their knowledge base. They talked about creating their own knowledge and adding to the professional knowledge base. All the teachers interviewed had changed their instructional practices as a result of the team. Many co-taught particular lessons and subject areas with other team members, special education teachers, and interns. Within the team, each of the teachers had taken the lead in an area of particular interest. All the interviewees stated that they had learned a great deal from their teammates in the areas of curriculum, classroom management, or pedagogy. All, in one way or another, stated that they could not imagine going back to teaching in isolated classrooms.

The teachers relinquished their individual control to the collective control of the group, and although they recognized what they had lost, they also were keenly aware of what they had gained.

We have definitely taken a large chunk of independence and handed it over to interdependence . . . which is great, just feeling like we are all in this thing together . . . but . . . there's a part of me that likes a maverick thing, develop your own curriculum, work in your own way.

In talking with other teachers and interns about their work, the participants could reflect on their own practice. Teachers spoke of the amount of "ongoing dialogue" they had with each other. One remarked that since joining the Collaborative, she had become a much better teacher "because of the dialogue, because of sharing ideas, because of feedback from other people, because of chances for exposure to other ways of doing things." The teachers spoke repeatedly about the ways that teaming had changed the conditions of teaching, about the new excitement they felt now — after years of teaching experience.

Within the team, it was understood that there would be no differentiation in status. Although each team had a designated "team leader" who was paid a stipend, the leadership role was rotated each year and was never defined as having elevated status. It was a job that essentially included more work: Team leaders had more clerical and organizational duties than other members.

Some of the teachers commented on the effect of teaming on their ability to change instructional strategies in the classroom.

> We sit down every week as a team and talk about children's issues. . . .
> [My teammate] inspired me to go on and work on my master's. I felt
> he knew this stuff inside out. . . . He got me to look at kids with a
> whole new lens. He inspired me as an educator.

Directly related to the teachers' work in teams was an increased sense of responsibility and accountability.

> If you are the only person in the class, you organize and run your pro-
> gram as a one-person operation. When you work on a team, you
> count on the contributions of all the members. It's a real change in the
> way I plan and how I work. I'm much more accountable to other peo-
> ple now. I used to be able to close the classroom door and do what I
> wanted.

The experience of teachers we interviewed reinforces Little's (1990) findings that teachers working in teams exert high levels of "reciprocal influence" (p. 13) on one another. Teaching had become more "public" for the teachers, and perhaps because teaching was no longer a secret, "private act" (Fullan, 1992), teachers began to venture beyond the classroom.

Preservice Teacher Education

The PDS significantly altered the role of teachers in preservice education and enabled them to assume new leadership roles — with interns and at the college level. Teachers became mentors to their students. They learned clinical supervision strategies, observed their interns regularly, gave them structured feedback, co-planned weekly, and taught lessons together. The teachers had more control over the interns' experience in the school than they had ever had with student teachers, and they influenced the structure of preservice education at the college.

Preservice teacher education provided the linchpin for the Professional Development School, increasing the teachers' authority and influence in a new realm — the college. The teachers, in collaboration with college faculty, supervised the interns and wrote their evaluations and recommendations.

> I'm much more involved with the interns. I have much higher demands than I had for student teachers and I certainly did not treat student teachers with the professional respect that I treat the interns.

All the teachers in the study mentioned the impetus the interns gave them.

> Being forced to discipline yourself, to express what it is you do and why you do it . . . informs your teaching and I would argue leads to greater success in teaching.

In addition, the interns returned from their college courses and shared their learning with team members. In one team the interns introduced the teachers to a new approach to teaching reading. As one of the teachers stated, "[The interns] were the ones who nurtured us through articles they brought us, which is an interesting model."

The teachers' work with preservice interns extended beyond the classroom to the larger arena of the affiliated colleges. Teachers served as supervisors of interns, taught math and reading courses at the colleges, and presented guest lectures.

> Expanding my role in teacher training has been a direct result of the Collaborative. . . . I do think that the Collaborative was instrumental in helping the college recognize that teachers can make a positive contribution in the training of other teachers.

Those teaching college courses reported increasing satisfaction with their roles. Although initially the teachers' new responsibilities took great energy and determined effort, the work has provided satisfaction for these veteran classroom practitioners and caused them to interact in new ways with their teaching colleagues at the school site.

Teaching college raises your level of esteem, and credibility, in my school. You're on a different level. People mention you at faculty meetings and workshops. One interesting thing from teaching college: I run around to the faculty [getting materials] to teach the course. I bug the librarian. It's touching base in different ways with my faculty — nagging them, asking them for samples.

Curriculum Development and Assessment

The teachers interviewed developed new curricula and assessment strategies at their grade levels and assumed leadership in district-wide curriculum revision. Principals arranged for teachers to have common planning time at least once a week, and paid after-school or weekend meetings for curriculum development and assessment became a regular part of each team's work. There was added impetus for curriculum development and assessment as new curriculum ideas were introduced to the teams by college supervisors and interns, who shared theories and knowledge at team meetings and in informal conversations with the mentor teachers.

One Collaborative member was selected to participate in the development of the statewide language arts curriculum framework. He regularly shared information and enabled all members to become a response group and give feedback on the framework to the state committee.

The special education teacher in another team described how her team's focus on special education inclusion in the classroom had helped the school district as it moved toward remediation within the classroom.

Where Chapter 1 [now called Title 1] regs have changed and that is now the model, I'm a model. That's why those Chapter 1 teachers from other districts come here to observe and in that way I'm a leader.

A number of teachers used their APT Time, the 6 hours per week away from classroom teaching, to develop new curricula. One teacher's long-standing interest in science education and her work on a new team science unit on oceans prompted her to take college oceanography courses and, during her APT Time, to write an extensive oceanography curriculum for her third and fourth graders. She found her own support system and recognized the relationship between the curriculum she was writing and her work in the classroom. Two of the teachers (and a number of their teammates) have been involved in math curriculum development during their APT Time through local research organizations.

Teachers within the teams coached peers outside the Collaborative in a variety of ways. One teacher, during her APT Time, supported other teachers in the school district as they learned new strategies for teaching writing. Another introduced teachers to the philosophy of the Responsive Classroom during her APT Time and invited colleagues in and out of the Collaborative to observe her as she implemented this new structure for classroom meetings.

These examples of curriculum changes directly related to the PDS illustrate the power that such a collaborative can have in developing curriculum. Teachers are developing curriculum collaboratively with the resources of the college, the assistance of the intern and their peers, and time during the day to experiment and develop the curriculum.

> We are trying to reimagine curriculum and trying to establish a role of reconfiguring the way kids learn. I would say that those are the two main roles as a member of the team.

Research

Teachers in the Collaborative have assumed leadership in classroom-based action research. Over the course of the Collaborative's history, the use of APT Time to conduct classroom-based research has become increasingly appealing to the teachers. In fact, in recent years it has become a drawing card for new teams that petition to join the Collaborative. Members have written and presented their research findings locally and to regional and national audiences.

One teacher/researcher who was interviewed noted that research has been such a "tremendously beneficial activity," that he has found himself being "much more reflective about my role in the classroom." His research on children's writing choices and their attitudes about writing led him to re-examine his own teaching and to improve his teaching of writing through "listening carefully to the voices of writers as they participated in the process of writing fiction."

As the teachers assume research roles in conjunction with a support network of other teachers, their investment in research grows. They see the effect on the children they teach.

> You can see the byproducts of your research, the halo effect, and the kids feel empowered and feel important . . . so the benefits are there.

Teachers have become interested in going beyond the role of teacher as "deliverer of knowledge." They have created knowledge by working on research in their classrooms and across schools and communities. They have come to believe that teachers have a responsibility for systematic research and inquiry directed at the improvement of their practice.

> My role as teacher/researcher is definitely in the theater of leadership in the sense that I'm committed to developing a viable voice for the teacher/researcher in the context of the larger research world. So that is what I'm presenting to teachers — here is one way to look at kids, and here's one way to look at the writing process.

Governance

Although the organizational structure of the Collaborative has changed over its 8-year history, a consistent aspect has been that all teachers must assume leadership and play an active role in the Collaborative's governance. They make decisions about everything from budget to personnel. This work has taught them administrative skills and introduced them to fund raising and to the complicated work of managing the Collaborative's budget. In addition, it has introduced them to the politics of school change and given them an awareness of the fragility of this teacher-initiated PDS.

Overseeing the entire Collaborative is the steering committee, consisting of one member from each team as well as college faculty members and representatives of college and school administration. The majority of steering committee members are teachers, and the committee has been chaired by a teacher since the PDS was initiated.

The professional development committee organizes 4 full days of training for teachers during the year. During the first 4 years of the Collaborative, teachers examined the role of the mentor teacher and the supervisor in the PDS, learned mentoring skills, and redesigned the roles of the college supervisor and the mentor teacher. This was followed by a 2-year focus on strategies for teaching curriculum development and implementation to the interns. The past 2 years have concentrated on the role of parents in the Collaborative and on teacher research.

Each of the teachers in the Collaborative previously had had years of staff development workshops, but all agreed that the Collaborative workshops were different. The workshops were designed and conducted by the teachers themselves, and were presented to school and college faculty members.

A member of the professional development committee described his committee work in this way:

> This committee has the finger on the pulse of what many people think are the priorities of what should be the agenda of professional develop-

ment, what people think should be on the agenda next . . . so in one sense we lead, but in another sense we follow.

On the interview and recruitment committee, teachers interview prospective interns and play a major role in selecting the incoming group of graduate students. Working with school and college faculty and administration, they developed a process for admitting new teams to the Collaborative. The budget committee raises money for the Collaborative, develops a budget, and monitors the allocation of money throughout the year.

Finally, a parent involvement committee has begun to develop ways in which parents can be more closely involved in the workings of the Collaborative.

IMPORTANCE OF THE PDS IN THE DEVELOPMENT OF TEACHER LEADERSHIP

The *raison d'etre* of the Professional Development School is the improvement of the preservice education of teachers and the enhancement of the teaching career — all for the improvement of learning for children. This focus has always been at the forefront of the work the teachers do.

At the same time, we have found that the partnership culture inherent in the PDS can be a vital force for the encouragement and nurturing of teacher leadership. Here is how we view the effect of the Professional Development School structure on the development of teacher leaders.

New Access to the Theoretical Knowledge Base of the College

Veteran teachers learn more about the theory and practice of teaching as they begin to teach preservice teachers. Theory is demystified quickly as intersections between research, theory, and practice are built through collaborative meetings, discussions, and informal interactions. Teachers find their own knowledge base deepening, and they recognize that their teaching becomes more reflective.

Teacher Leverage Beyond Their Schools

Once the relationship between the school and the college has been established, the teachers acquire leverage outside their classrooms and schools. The college connection enables teachers to redefine their roles and increase their responsibilities beyond the walls of their classrooms without leaving classroom teaching. The Collaborative provides teachers with increased visibility and expands their professional influence and self-confidence, enabling them to assume "boundary-spanning roles" (Troen & Boles, 1995, p. 3) that none had experienced previously.

The teachers discovered that working in the Collaborative gives them more clout than they had as individual teachers. As one teacher noted: "When teachers work more closely together and are teaming, they speak to the administration with a collaborative voice. They don't speak merely for themselves."

The PDS has established a new subculture in the schools that supports risk-taking, values leadership, and simultaneously maintains the norms of equality and inclusion among teachers.

Discretionary Use of Time

In all of the school reform reports of the 1980s there were repeated pleas for a reconceptualization of the school day so that teachers would have more time to accomplish their work (Holmes Group, 1986; Sizer, 1984). Most of the recent reform experiments, however, have been unable to institute such blocks of time.

What is striking in our interviews, more for its absence than its presence, is any discussion about the *lack of time*. While teachers in the Collaborative certainly work much harder than they ever did before, the Collaborative has managed to fulfill the promise of creating more time by providing full-time graduate student interns to work in teachers' classrooms. Not only are there two teachers in the classroom during most of the week, but the teachers have time during the school week, up to one full day per week, to pursue their own professional development through APT Time.

In large part, this occurred because the graduate student intern functions as a team member to replace the teachers in the classroom. Discontinuity is eliminated, and the teachers are confident that the children in their classes are receiving competent, consistent instruction. What is more, the intern values and benefits professionally from the time alone with the class—time that is used to hone his or her independent teaching skills. Time is a clear "power tool" (Kanter, 1984, p. 159) that gives the teachers freedom and enables them to move in leadership directions.

A NEW PARADIGM FOR TEACHER LEADERSHIP

Our study of the Learning/Teaching Collaborative has caused us to re-examine both the definition of teacher leadership and the possibilities for it in a Professional Development School.

With a collective form of leadership assumed by many individuals, the paradigm modeled by Professional Development Schools such as the Learning/Teaching Collaborative helps teachers develop expertise according to their individual interests. Participating teachers are given the option of choosing work that opens new opportunities outside the classroom or that enriches their work in the classroom. They continue to feel professionally independent, yet they are part of a working team. No teacher has higher professional status than any other, and a range of leadership roles is available to all. Thus the role of teacher leader is reconfigured to be inclusive, rather than exclusive, and is available to significantly more teachers. According to Little (1988), such leadership changes "the professional environment of the school" so that leadership becomes "less a matter of individual career trajectories than . . . a matter of rigorous professional relations among teachers" (p. 81).

Research indicates that teachers' interests lie less in moving into a few administratively designated leadership positions (Yee, 1986) and more in enlarging their professional roles and enhancing the professional aspects of their careers (Little, 1988). This new definition of leadership taps into the embedded norms of teacher equality (Lortie, 1975) and honors the norms of inclusivity, connectedness, and collaboration identified with the predominantly female teaching force (Belenkey, Clinchy, Goldberger, & Tarule, 1986).

Although this description is different from the traditional definition of teacher leadership, closer examination of the literature indicates that this new definition is legitimate. Kegan and Lahey (1984), in an article entitled "Adult Leadership and Adult Development," state that

> a person whose way of being in the world . . . amounts to the exercise of authority on behalf of facilitating the development of those around him or her, is the person who can truly be called a leader. (p. 226)

Kouzes and Posner's (1990) definition of leadership also supports this new leadership paradigm. They define leaders as individuals who challenge the process, who are role models and planners who model the way. This is exactly what teachers have done as they assume new roles through the Collaborative.

Further, teachers in this PDS provide powerful role models for their interns and colleagues; they initiate curriculum reform and govern their own individual teams and the Collaboration as a whole. The notion of collaboration and role-modeling that undergirds this PDS is very different from the more traditional culture of schools and the culture of teaching (Feiman-Nemser & Floden, 1986; Sarason, 1971). Teachers who consistently co-teach, regularly discuss practice, and visit one another's class-rooms, are risk-takers who challenge the status quo of teaching as an iso-lated act conducted in the privacy of the individual classroom (Little, 1990; Lortie, 1975).

Kanter (1977) discusses leadership in terms of power. She describes power as "the ability to get things done, to get and use whatever it is that a person needs for the goals he or she is attempting to meet" (p. 166), and she describes effective leadership as

> power outward and upward in the system: the ability to get for the group, for subordinates or followers, a favorable share of the resources, opportunities, and rewards possible through the organization. This has less to do with how leaders relate to followers than with how they relate to other parts of the organization. (p. 166)

STEPS TO INSTITUTIONALIZE TEACHER LEADERSHIP

We have learned that teacher leadership will not be successful if it is tacked onto the existing school structure; nor will it flourish in the prevail-ing teacher culture. Both structure and culture must be reconsidered and revised in order for new leadership to emerge.

What must be done, then, in order to further the goal of institutionaliz-ing teacher leadership?

Reform the Workplace

Working in isolated classrooms and competing for scarce resources, teachers often eye each other suspiciously as they lead their children down school corridors. The "egg-crate" mold of the school, with its secretive and competitive aspects, cries out to be broken. When a philosophy of collaboration and risk-taking replaces teacher isolation, teacher leadership will emerge. When teachers work in teams and teaching becomes a more public act, teachers will venture beyond the classroom. Teams can become a forum in which teachers can take risks with their teaching and expand their knowledge base.

It would be wise, we believe, not to reject the egalitarian ethic but to reconsider it. There is much to be said for teachers as equal members of their profession. Currently, teachers are not at all equal. They live in rela-tive isolation, competing for the scarce resources available to them, know-ing that some teachers have more access to those resources than others. If teaching were truly egalitarian, we would value each teacher's contribution to the education of children, and also be able to recognize teachers' individual areas of expertise and celebrate their leadership initiatives.

If teachers are to assume leadership roles that positively affect their practice, they need time for reflection and opportunity to conduct professional inquiry. Time in the work day must be restructured so that it can become a resource, not one more reason why teachers are unable to assume leadership.

Redefine the Role of Principal

Because principals are encouraged to be instructional leaders, they often feel threatened when asked to move over and make room for teachers. Principal preparation programs could be restructured so that principals are charged with the mission of developing a community of leaders within their schools (Barth, 1990). Principals must participate in teaching teachers how to be leaders, and develop strategies to facilitate teachers' assumption of leadership roles by providing them with the reason, the time, and the opportunity. Principals in schools could learn that power is not "zero-sum"; indeed that if power is shared with others, the quantity of power for each participant increases. Principals' influence over classroom teaching will be enhanced, not diminished, by involving teachers in decision making on matters of curriculum, instruction, scheduling, and budgets. Finally, the role of the principal, with its plethora of administrative tasks, should be redesigned so that principals have the time to become educational leaders in their own right.

Leithwood and Jantzi (1990) found that principals successful in promoting teacher leadership employed five broad strategies. These principals:

- Strengthened the school's culture to support teacher leadership
- Used a variety of bureaucratic mechanisms to stimulate and reinforce cultural change
- Fostered staff development
- Engaged in direct and frequent communication about cultural norms, values, and beliefs
- Shared power and responsibility with others.

Preparation programs for teachers and principals must be restructured so that all understand the importance of developing a *community* of leaders within schools. Principals who are provided with strategies to facilitate teachers' taking on leadership roles will participate in teaching teachers how to be leaders. Principals need to provide teachers with both the reason and the opportunity, including time, to lead. In turn, teachers themselves must understand that their influence over classroom teaching will be enhanced when they have decision-making power over matters of curriculum, instruction, scheduling, and budgets.

Support the Role of Teacher as Leader

The phrase "teacher leader" will remain no more than an oxymoron if the education community continues to treat it as such. Teachers themselves must advocate for the creation of leadership roles. Building on their expertise in teaching and learning and their understanding of the needs of children, teachers who acquire leadership skills and an understanding of organizational theory and behavior are in a better position to facilitate change.

Teachers will become resources for one another and hold each other accountable for the work they do. No longer should teachers stand by helplessly as teacher colleagues "sink or swim" in their first few years in the classroom. No longer can teachers turn a blind eye to the teacher who is behaving unprofessionally or to those who are just not working hard enough.

Collaborations between colleges and schools are a key way for colleges to support teacher leadership. Leadership by teachers will not become the norm unless colleges of education recognize the importance of teacher leadership and strengthen their commitment to teaching those skills to every preservice teacher.

TEACHER LEADERSHIP CAN EQUAL TEACHER ACCOUNTABILITY

It is time for us, as professionals, to bite the bullet on teacher accountability. We believe that a strong case can be made for tying teacher leadership to accountability for improved student learning. That means leaving behind those discussions surrounding teacher leadership that seem to take place in a parallel, separate universe from the teaching and learning that go on in classrooms.

Teacher leadership in the Learning/Teaching Collaborative is grounded in the vision of teaching and learning that places the teacher in a central position of responsibility. Teachers view the child's progress through school as a continuous, coherent, and cumulative sequence of learning experiences. There is an expectation of cooperation and interdependence. The culture supports participants as they engage in critical dialogue based on careful scrutiny of concrete practices and outcomes within a professional community. Teachers examine student work as a basis for standard setting. Teachers observe videotapes of participants teaching. Professional Development days provide opportunities for teachers to share their inquiry-oriented, school-based practices. It is an explicit goal to connect professional learning to new practices that improve student learning. This nonhierarchical, nonbureaucratic cultural form of accountability not only can assess the effect of teacher leadership on children's learning but can be a vehicle for professionalizing teaching.

CONCLUSION

Our study of this Professional Development School has demonstrated the need to extend the definition of teacher leadership and to examine its many alternative forms. All too often we attribute a teacher's reluctance to assume leadership to the norm of equality among teachers. This study suggests that it is possible, given the right environment, to respect the norm of equality and still develop forms of leadership and accountability among teachers.

The teachers involved in the Collaborative take their work very seriously and want to be accountable to each other, to the children, and to the community. They know that they influence the creation of policy and are privy to the details of the organization's functioning. No longer isolated in "egg-crate schools" (Lortie, 1975, p. 14), they are demonstrating their strength in ways they never would have imagined just a few years ago. The PDS has broadened their horizons beyond the school and exposed them in new and meaningful ways to the world of theory. They have seen their practice reflected back to them through the interns' eyes. As they assume new leadership roles, they have deepened their understanding of policy, curriculum, and the value of research to practice. The PDS has provided renewal and stimulation for veteran teachers; it has made teachers accountable to each other for the work they have done together; and it has caused them to become engaged, in the words of Lieberman and Miller, in "continuous inquiry into practice" (Levine, 1992, p. 106).

This new leadership paradigm, created by the partnership of two institutions — the college and the school — and marked by an increase in leadership opportunities for teachers, shows promise of significantly enhancing the development of preservice and inservice teachers and improving the education of children.

This chapter is an outgrowth of a larger study, *The Learning/Teaching Collaborative: Nine Years of Teacher-Initiated School Restructuring*, which was conducted by Katherine Boles under a postdoctoral Spencer Foundation fellowship awarded by the National Academy of Education.

REFERENCES

Arikado, M. S. (1976). Status congruence as it relates to team teacher satisfaction. *Journal of Educational Administration, 1*(14), pp. 70–78.

Barth, R. S. (1990). *Improving schools from within.* San Francisco: Jossey-Bass.

Belenkey, M. F., Clinchy, B. M., Goldberger, N. R., & Tarule, J. M. (1986). *Women's ways of knowing: The development of self, voice, and mind.* New York: Basic Books.

Boles, K. C. (1990). *School restructuring: A case study in teacher empowerment.* Cambridge, MA: National Center for Educational Leadership.

Boles, K. C. (1991). *School restructuring by teachers: A study of the teaching project at the Edward Devotion School.* Doctoral dissertation, Harvard University, Cambridge, MA.

California Commission on the Teaching Profession. (1985). *Who will teach our children?* Sacramento: California Commission on the Teaching Profession.

Carnegie Forum on Education and the Economy. (1986). *A nation prepared: Teachers for the twenty first century.* Washington, DC: Author.

Cohen, E. (1981). Sociology looks at team teaching. *Research in Sociology of Education and Socialization, 2*(2), pp. 163–193.

Devaney, K. (1987). *The lead teacher: Ways to begin.* Paper prepared for the Task Force on Teaching as a Profession. New York: Carnegie Forum on Education and the Economy.

Feiman-Nemser, S., & Floden, R. E. (1986). The cultures of teaching. In M. C. Wittrock (Ed.), *Handbook of research on teaching* (pp. 505–526). New York: Macmillan.

Fullan, M. (1992, April). *Arming yourself with knowledge of the change process.* Paper presented at the annual meeting of the American Educational Research Association, San Francisco.

Hoffman, N. (1981). *Women's true profession: Voices from the history of teaching.* Old Westbury, New York: Feminist Press.

Holmes Group. (1986). *Tomorrow's teachers: A report of the Holmes Group.* East Lansing, MI: Author.

Johnson, S. M. (1990). *Teachers at work.* New York: Basic Books.

Johnson, S. M., & Boles, K. C. (1994). School-based management for teachers: Strategies for reform. In S. A. Mohrmann & P. Wohlstetter (Eds.), *Designing high-performance schools: Strategies for school-based management* (pp. 109–138). San Francisco: Jossey-Bass.

Kanter, R. B. (1977). *Men and women of the corporation.* New York: Basic Books.

Kanter, R. B. (1984). *The change masters.* New York: Simon & Schuster.

Kegan, R., & Lahey, L. L. (1984). Adult leadership and adult development: A constructivist view. In B. Kellerman (Ed.), *Leadership: Multidisciplinary perspectives* (pp. 199–230). Englewood Cliffs, NJ: Prentice-Hall.

Koppich, J. E. (1993). Rochester: The rocky road to reform. In C. T. Kerchner & J. E. Koppich (Eds.), *A union of professionals: Labor relations and educational reform* (pp. 136–157). New York: Teachers College Press.

Kouzes, J. M., & Posner, B. Z. (1990). *The leadership challenge: How to get extraordinary things done in organizations.* San Francisco: Jossey-Bass.

Leithwood, K., & Jantzi, D. (1990, April). Transformational leadership: How principals can help reform school culture. Paper presented at the annual meeting of the American Educational Research Association, Boston.

Levine, M. (Ed.). (1992). *Professional practice schools: Linking teacher education and school reform.* New York: Teachers College Press.

Lieberman, A., & Miller, L. (1992). Teacher development in professional practice schools. In M. Levine (Ed.), *Professional practice schools: Linking teacher education and school reform* (pp. 105–123). New York: Teachers College Press.

Lieberman, A., Saxl, E. R., & Miles, M. B. (1988). Teacher leadership: Ideology and practice. In A. Lieberman (Ed.), *Building a professional culture in schools* (pp. 148–166). New York: Teachers College Press.

Little, J. W. (1988). Assessing the prospects for teacher leadership. In A. Lieberman (Ed.), *Building a professional culture in schools* (pp. 78–106). New York: Teachers College Press.

Little, J. W. (1990). The persistence of privacy: Autonomy and initiative in teachers' professional relations. *Teachers College Record, 9*(1), 5–28.

Lortie, D. (1975). *Schoolteacher: A sociological study.* Chicago: University of Chicago Press.

McLaughlin, M. W., & Yee, S. M. (1988). School as a place to have a career. In A. Lieberman (Ed.), *Building a professional culture in schools* (pp. 23–44). New York: Teachers College Press.

Sarason, S. B. (1971). *The culture of the school and the problem of change.* Boston: Allyn & Bacon.

Sizer, T. R. (1984). *Horace's compromise: The dilemma of the American high school.* Boston: Houghton Mifflin.

Smylie, M. A. (1992). Teachers' reports of their interactions with teacher leaders concerning classroom instruction. *Elementary School Journal, 93*(1), 85–98.

Troen, V., & Boles, K. (1994, April). Teacher leadership in a professional development school. Paper presented at the annual meeting of the American Educational Research Association, New Orleans.

Troen, V., & Boles, K. (1995, April). Boundary spanners in professional development schools. Paper presented at the annual meeting of the American Research Association, San Francisco.

Tyack, D. (1974). *The one best system—A history of American urban education.* Cambridge, MA: Harvard University Press.

Wasley, P. A. (1990). *Teachers who lead: The rhetoric of reform and the realities of practice.* New York: Teachers College Press.

Yee, S. M. (1986). *Teaching as a career: Promotion versus development.* Stanford: Stanford University School of Education.

Zimpher, N. L. (1988). A design for the professional development of teacher leaders. *Journal of Teacher Education, 39*(1), 53–60.

Chapter 4

Reinventing Leadership in Professional Development Schools

ROBERTA TRACHTMAN AND MARSHA LEVINE

To date, little attention has been paid to the kind of leaders needed to build Professional Development Schools, or to the nature of effective leadership for collaborative, restructuring environments. Indeed, frequently leaders are not even identified. Most literature about Professional Development Schools focuses on the changing role of teachers in school–university collaboration or on the characteristics of the new school culture. In fact, PDSs typically are thought of as teacher-centered projects. Participants and theorists have paid too little attention to the role in PDS development of those in formal organizational leadership positions: deans, school principals, superintendents, union leaders, and other school-based leaders. What have they been doing? How have they contributed to both the successes and failures in these efforts? How do traditional leaders view their roles, and how might they need to change what they do in order to provide leadership in these emerging institutions?

For this discussion, we will look across institutions at formal organizational leaders. While we acknowledge and support the valuable and significant leadership roles played by teachers in Professional Development Schools, here we explore the behaviors and activities of more traditional leaders, and examine how the development of teacher leadership influences their work.

The basic characteristics and goals of PDSs have important implications for how leaders need to function and view their responsibilities. Such environments are not "business as usual" for either schools or universities. First, by definition, PDSs are collaborative ventures. They always involve universities and schools, higher education faculty and school teachers, and sometimes district personnel and teachers' unions. Leadership in collaborative environments is different from intra-institutional leadership because boundaries are blurred, turf issues arise, and new cultural norms need to be established. Second, PDSs are learning communities designed to support professional inquiry, student achievement, and the education of new practitioners. Their creation requires that participants rethink the role of education leaders.

In addition to these basic characteristics, some other factors are important in considering PDS leadership requirements. How PDSs come into existence, who initiates them, and who is present at their planning and design combine to influence how leaders in formal positions view their roles. Similarly, the context in which the PDS is developed (i.e., the school and the district) bears strongly on how leadership is played out. With these impacts on leadership in mind, we describe below some of the ways that formal organizational leaders have functioned in the design and implementation of Professional Development Schools. Data come from two important sources—the survey of PDS sites completed by the National Council for the Accreditation of Teacher Education's (NCATE) PDS Standards Project (Trachtman, 1996) and the experiences of participants in the three Professional Development Schools included in Part III of this text.

METAPHORS AND MEANING

We have chosen metaphor as a device for illuminating the various forms that leadership may take, although, at best, metaphors provide a way of making sense of a perspective rather than of displaying the whole. Real human beings are rarely unidimensional, and so our metaphors should not be mistaken for the real people in Professional Development Schools. The real people are "mixed metaphors," combinations of the images presented below, and much more than that. They are products of their time, their place, and their history. Most significantly, across institutions and across roles, the leaders in Professional Development Schools are complicated people and are participants in complex organizations. Nevertheless, we offer these metaphors as a way of stimulating discussion on the important role of leadership in the creation of Professional Development Schools. Importantly, since we believe that all organizational participants are potential leaders, our metaphors will hold for those who already have leadership positions and traditional authority bases, as well as for those who have the skills, knowledge, and dispositions to engage in the practice of leadership, irrespective of their formal roles.

The Bureaucrat

As organizations, schools and universities continue to mirror Max Weber's bureaucracy—tasks are subdivided, written policies and rules control behavior, and authority is hierarchically defined. Not surprisingly then, many formal leaders at PDS sites continue to respond like bureaucrats, measuring requests against a backdrop of rules, allocating resources based on what is rather than what might be, and elevating the needs of the whole organization above the needs of small groups or individuals.

Some administrators in PDS sites and at the district level continue to behave in ways sanctioned and encouraged by the norms of "real schools" (Metz, 1990); the school leaders respond to the demands of their jobs in ways that previously have worked for them and their colleagues. As they carry on business as usual, their guiding mental models of school leadership remain intact, at times obscuring their vision and limiting the promise of the Professional Development School initiative. So, for example, requests for PDS "banking" time for professional development, block scheduling, or clustering students and teachers together for more than one year may be unsupported.

Some university leaders as well seem to stick to the "old rules." College administrators may continue to focus on the needs and demands made by their immediate supervisors and subordinates, those directly above and below them in the university hierarchy, who themselves are guided by traditional, bureaucratic expectations. Leaders in higher education not only find themselves caught between these two sources of traditional demands, but also find themselves having to provide direction in areas where they traditionally have played no active role. For example, unused to focusing directly on the needs of student teachers, deans may fail to revise course credit allocations or class schedules for PDS participants. In some places, new courses designed by university and school-based faculty and delivered on site are undervalued because no "credit" is attached to them. Similarly, because student teachers in PDSs are off campus and out of view, university administrators cannot easily understand their experiences. Unlike the laboratory schools located on the university campus, the PDS does not provide administrators with easy access.

Finally, because the overwhelming majority of university students and faculty continue to enact traditional roles, the very small number of faculty and teacher education students at the professional development sites may be left on their own, given no special attention by university administrators, and little recognition for the hard work of redesigning teacher education. Some faculty members even suggest that their PDS work disadvantages them over time, since few universities have changed their formal tenure and promotion structures to support field-based teaching and research.

The Parent

The school administrator as parent is both compelling and persistent in the literature. A decade ago Deal (1987) described the school as an extended family, with principals as parents who nurture and support students and teachers. It seems, however, that when principals see themselves as heads of families, they may rely more on principles of equality than of equity. In some PDS sites, principals find themselves caught among the traditional expectations of the central office, the needs of non-PDS participants, and the changing needs of the PDS faculty. Since so many PDSs begin as small schools-within-schools, principals find that their resource allocations are insufficient to meet the needs of both the larger school and the newly created one. As principals worry about the potential schisms between PDS members and their colleagues, some respond by limiting the ways that the PDS is allowed to differ from the rest of the school. When principals opt for keeping the family together, they reject the Professional Development School as a lever for whole school improvement. As one teacher explained, "The principal recognizes the importance of the PDS only to the degree that it doesn't interfere with the needs of other staff."

The Cheerleader

In writing about school improvement, Fullan (1993) and others (e.g., Louis & Miles, 1990) identified principal participation and engagement as critical ingredients. Yet, as they rush to manage crises, principals at PDS sites are sometimes unable to find the personal energy and organizational resources to support the initiative. Some school- and university-based leaders limit their support to public cheering. But, as cheerleaders, they remain on the margin, hoping for the best, doing little, and risking less.

The Ostrich

Teachers have been described as artisans, as bricoleurs (Levi-Strauss, 1974) who "work alone, learn alone, and who derive the most important professional satisfaction alone" (Huberman, 1990, p. 12). Like teachers, school-based administrators have been socialized to function on their own, working hard at what they do while expecting and receiving little support from others (Cuban, 1990). These norms, however, are not conducive to building learning communities.

Some teachers' union leaders, school superintendents, school board members, principals, and deans remain mostly out of sight during the creation and implementation of Professional Development Schools. While some feel left out, others are relieved not to be involved in a contentious, untested school improvement initiative.

The Storyteller

The hard work of participants in restructuring organizations needs to be trumpeted by leaders in their role of institutional storyteller (Gardner, 1995). As storytellers go about their task, they serve to link insiders and outsiders, joining participants with nonmembers. Weaving tales, and bringing the news, they work to demystify the change process by making it open to all. At one site, the principal used the case study written by PDS participants as a way for the whole school organization to learn about and make sense of the participants' work. As a storyteller leader, he invited nonparticipants to "come and listen" so as to become a part of the work in progress. The story, as such, became a mediating structure, joining school-based PDS educators together with nonmembers. While this principal did not write the PDS story, he used the tale to bring people together.

In another PDS, the vice principal on site sought to bridge the distance between PDS participants and the revolving succession of school building principals. According to teachers, as the only continuous administrator on site during the PDS's first 3 years, the vice principal had to tell and retell the PDS story to each new site leader; in an important way, the vice principal became the PDS's historian, the keeper of the vision and the teller of its tale.

People crave meaning in their work lives. The process of telling stories is a way of making sense out of work. The storyteller leader challenges the overwhelming silence in organizations and offers members a venue for voicing their sense of meaning in their work.

The Gardener

Gardeners approach their tasks mindful of conditions—the soil, the sunshine, the water, and the temperature. They respect the beauty of the young plant, but recognize its fragility, its needs, and its vulnerabilities. They know that seedlings face their greatest survival risks at the beginning, risks that increase or diminish with the gardener's skill and knowledge.

Leaders in developing collaborative organizations need the skills of the gardener. They need to protect the innovators from the naysayers.

Recognizing the dangers posed by inhospitable climates, gardener leaders pay special attention to the disparate needs posed by members from organizations with distinct histories, purposes, and ways of doing business. In one community, school district leaders work to support the beliefs and practices of the PDS by locating all district professional development resources at the PDS site. In this way, the PDS is seen as supported by the district, even though it is housed in only one school. In contrast, at another site, when the supportive district leaders changed jobs, resources for the PDS diminished.

The Juggler

At the circus, the juggler is always a hard act to follow. Demonstrating remarkable hand–eye coordination and extraordinary manual dexterity, the juggler engages the crowd in a game of control and coordination. We watch and wait for the juggler to drop one ball or smash one plate, knowing full well that just one slip will bring down the act. We marvel as jugglers assume more and more risk, wildly applauding their grace under pressure.

Like circus jugglers, effective educational leaders engage in continuous balancing acts. They hold the purse strings at the site, using resources judiciously while they seek to spread limited organizational wealth among participants. Careful juggler leaders learn how to support what matters most to them, even when resources are tight. For example, at one PDS site, the university president provided a permanent allocation to the school of education to support the PDS. In this way, the PDS is protected from the uncertainty that results from tying program support to budget vagaries. At another PDS, the university dean makes time to regularly participate at the school site. The dean meets with PDS school and university faculty bi-monthly to examine the moral dimensions of teaching. This same dean also directs his grant makers toward securing PDS resources.

Often poised on one foot, juggler leaders work the crowd, balancing the demands of conflicting constituencies, insiders and outsiders, supporters and detractors. They maintain their balance by holding fast to the vision, knowing that the vision is in a continual state of becoming. In Professional Development Schools, the juggling is harder, faster, and somewhat more precarious than in other settings, given the unique demands of interinstitutional collaboration. Political considerations grow exponentially when two distinct organizations participate in joint activity. Juggler leaders know how to build coalitions, compromise, and fight fair. Importantly, they are comfortable in the public arena as they take on new and different responsibilities related to shared work.

The Jazz Player

Jazz musicians explore new relationships among the basic elements of their music: the rhythm and the harmony. Some explore the relationships between their music and that of others—between jazz and rock, for example, or jazz and classical. Playing together, they must learn to listen to each other's sound, building on each other's inventions. Each takes a turn at leading the music, yet each is disciplined by the same underlying structure.

Leaders in Professional Development Schools need to be like jazz musicians (see DePree's, 1995, expanded discussion of leadership as jazz). They listen carefully to all the players within and across the collaborating institutions. They need to be able to improvise and experiment with new ideas and ways of doing things, and they need to develop strategies for working together that are appropriate to their goals. At the same time, like the jazz musician, they must keep the guiding principles of the work firmly in mind. That set of principles can be "played" in many different ways, but musician leaders must always be held accountable to them.

PDS leaders, unlike the symphony conductor who is always in control, pass the lead around and accept leadership from all participants, not only from those in traditional leadership roles. As one PDS principal said, "The principal must be strong enough to be 'weak.'" According to this principal, "the stakeholders cannot have power if the principal keeps the power." Jazz-like PDS leaders create an environment where leadership can, and does, come from many directions. Producing a harmony, rhythm, and melody that work to support Professional Development Schools requires playing together in a very different way than universities, schools, districts, and unions are used to playing. As another PDS principal concluded, "We have not formally changed roles; we have combined and enlarged them."

THE PREPARATION OF SCHOOL LEADERS

Little (1993) has argued persuasively that in order for teachers to meet the demands of school reform, they need to engage in new ways of learning. We would like to make a similar argument regarding the preparation and development of formal leaders who work in Professional Development Schools. PDS leaders need opportunities to learn across boundaries. They need to acquire new skills, new dispositions, and new knowledge to effectively meet the challenges posed in a cross-institutional organization dedicated to the ongoing and simultaneous reform of school and university practices, and the development of children and adults. While formal leaders in a PDS no longer have to do everything on their own, they have to do different things in different ways.

TRADITIONAL SCHOOL ADMINISTRATION PREPARATION

The most compelling argument for changing administrator preparation and professional development comes from the recognition that neither the traditional preparation model (see Cooper & Boyd, 1987; Hallinger & Wimpelberg, 1991) nor more recent state efforts to reform preparation are consistent with the needs of adults in learning organizations. Whether administrators find themselves leading a PDS or some other type of restructured school, they will not be able to get by with the knowledge and skills that served bureaucratic leaders well (Prestine, 1994). Since the turn of the century, the traditional administrator preparation model has been university-based and credit-constrained. According to Mulkeen and Cooper (1992), most preparation programs

- Are conglomerates of courses prescribed by an accreditation agency
- Value empiricism, predictability, and scientific certainty
- Train administrators as management functionaries
- Are grounded in the belief that school administrators manage most effectively and efficiently by relying on a system of rules, regulation, penalties, and rewards tied to a hierarchical structure of authority.

Educational Leadership Reform by the States

During the 1980s the states attempted to change schools by changing administrator preparation, licensure and certification, induction, evaluation, and professional development (see Doyle, Cooper, & Trachtman, 1991). However, like other centralized reform initiatives, state efforts to reform school leadership lacked clear incentives for implementation and significant sanctions for noncompliance (Murphy, 1990). These efforts were not successful in changing the roles and leadership patterns in the schools, for they changed neither administrators' orientation to their work nor the ways that they practiced. Instead, the states (1) attempted to expand the pool of administrators by offering alternative certification routes; (2) tried to improve practice by increased testing of first-year administrators; and (3) sought to enlarge the knowledge base of prospective administrators by requiring that they spend more time as interns.

A Framework for Reinventing Leadership

Out of the experiences of implementing Professional Development Schools, and out of the literature on change and leadership for change, we can begin to build a framework for reinventing leadership in Professional Development Schools. The changes for administrators mirror the changes for teachers and for students. Thus, reinventing teaching and learning, and reinventing leading are part of the same process, especially because they often involve the same people. To begin we will need to reimagine the leaders, their work, and their contexts. The reconstruction will have several interactive components.

Develop the Characteristics of Leaders

Leaders involved in PDSs need to be both risk-takers and learners. Their orientation toward inquiry and reflection needs to be broad and deep. What they read, whom they talk to, and whose advice and opinions they seek become very important as they negotiate unknown terrain and work with partners across institutional boundaries. Leaders also need to be nurturers. Like the gardener, they need to plant, protect, and nourish new ideas and new practices. They need to be able to juggle the political and developmental demands of PDS leadership, and they need to be able to share leadership across boundaries. Professional Development Schools need new kinds of leaders, women and men who are prepared to lead against the grain (Cochran-Smith, 1991).

Set Policy to Support New and Multiple Leaders

All Professional Development School leaders do not occupy formal leadership positions, but they all need power. Creating new opportunities for leadership, as among teacher leaders, and creating structures where they can assert influence, challenge the traditional system. We need new policies to support new practices.

Define Roles Differently

How PDS leaders define themselves and how they see themselves in relation to other individuals and institutions will be an important part of reinventing leadership. Leaders will have to have both an internal and external focus in order to expand what is in their purview and to develop structures to support new roles. As holders of formal organizational authority, principals and deans are well positioned to legitimate the work of Professional Development School faculty by creating new rewards, bringing extra resources to bear, and insisting on formal PDS governance structures, with discrete roles and responsibilities for members. In important ways the reinvention of schools will demand multiple and intersecting reinventions—for students, for teachers, and for administrators.

Create an Organizational Culture

The larger school and university contexts significantly support or impede leaders. Just as we have paid close attention to developing professional teaching cultures, we must ask the same with regard to administrators in schools, universities, school districts, and unions. Organizations that support learning, collegiality, and a problem-solving orientation are environments where administrators, teachers, and students can thrive. In urban settings, where PDSs can have significant positive impact, compelling issues of school violence, racial tensions, low student achievement, and high dropout rates, together with inadequate financing, compete for the attention of leaders. High turnover among teachers and administrators (including those at the top) further confounds the problem. However, in places where school superintendents and college presidents view the PDS as part of the solution to school reform, they have encouraged the creation of new norms by allocating more resources and rewarding good work. As one PDS teacher recently said, "You can mandate what matters if you know what matters!"

Create Leaders Through Professional Development

In her foreword to a book on innovation in educational administration, McCarthy (1993) suggested a "new ferment" (p. xvi) in the field of educational leadership. McCarthy cited a number of promising signs of change, including increasing diversity in personality, perspectives, and experiences among educational administration faculties; renewed respect for the artistic aspect of school administration and the conceptualization of school leadership as a moral and intellectual effort; renewed interest in guiding student practitioners in developing the craft-like knowledge of leadership; changed approaches to student recruitment and selection; and expanded connections between schools and universities in the preparation of school leaders.

Given what we have learned about leadership in PDSs, we would like to advocate for one more change. We believe that school-based teachers and administrators need to learn together, so that they may better understand each other and envision their work organizations as places where leadership is shared. For that to happen, the faculties in schools of education need to begin planning new courses for the preparation of school-based educators. We urge a model of shared learning in preservice programs for teachers, administrators, and other faculty and staff.

THE NEXT STEP

A PDS needs more than the principal's blessing. It is not merely an "add-on" program, but it represents a change in the school culture and demands organizational and structural changes. It implies important role changes for everyone, including the principal. The same argument can be made with respect to college deans. Professional Development Schools imply new structures, new curriculum, new organization, and alternative reward systems within the university. The PDS also means sharing responsibility with experienced school-based professionals for the education of new practitioners.

Collaborative leadership means balancing institutional needs against the needs of the PDS. In the case of Professional Development Schools, it also means reforming or restructuring the partner institutions. A PDS will not succeed if leaders treat it like a new tail on an old dog. Professional Development Schools have the potential for providing models for professional practice and for institutions that support good practice. They can be important instruments of education reform. In order to fulfill this potential, PDSs will require a different kind of leadership than traditional organizational leaders have been expected to provide. We have suggested some metaphors that may be useful in evaluating current modes of leadership, and a framework for beginning to reinvent leadership. We hope these ideas will stimulate yet another step in the process of education reform.

REFERENCES

Cochran-Smith, M. (1991). Learning to teach against the grain. *Harvard Educational Review, 61*, 279–310.

Cooper B. S., & Boyd, W. (1987). The evolution of training for school administrators. In J. Murphy & P. Hallinger (Eds.), *Approaches to administrative training in education* (pp. 3–27). Albany: State University of New York Press.

Cuban, L. (1990). Reforming again, again, and again. *Educational Researcher, 19*(1), 1–5.

Deal, T. E. (1987). Effective school principals: Counselors, engineers, pawnbrokers, poets . . . or instructional leaders. In W. Greenfield, Jr. (Ed.), *Instructional leadership* (pp. 230–245). Newton, MA: Allyn & Bacon.

DePree, M. (1995). *Leadership as jazz*. New York: Bantam/Doubleday.

Doyle, D. P., Cooper, B. S., & Trachtman, R. (1991). *Taking charge: The role of the states in the 1980s*. Indianapolis: Hudson Institute.

Fullan, M. (1993). *Change forces*. London: Falmer.

Gardner, H. (1995, September 13). A cognitive view of leadership. *Education Week*, pp. 34, 35.

Hallinger, P., & Wimpelberg, R. (1991). *New settings and changing norms for principal development* (Occasional Paper No. 6). Cambridge, MA: Harvard University, National Center for Educational Leadership.

Huberman, M. (1990, April). *The social context of instruction in schools*. Paper presented at the annual meeting of the American Educational Research Association, Boston.

Levi-Strauss, C. (1974). *The savage mind* (2nd ed.). London: Weidenfeld and Nicholson.

Little, J. W. (1993). Teachers' professional development in a climate of educational reform. *Education Evaluation and Policy Analysis, 15*(2), 129–151.

Louis, K. S., & Miles, M. B. (1990). *Improving urban high schools*. New York: Teachers College Press.

McCarthy, M. (1993). Foreword. In J. Murphy (Ed.), *Preparing tomorrow's school leaders: Alternative designs* (pp. iii–xx). University Park, PA: UCEA.

Metz, M. (1990). Real school: A universal drama mid disparate experiences. In D. E. Mitchell & M. E. Goertz (Eds.), *Education Politics for the New Century* (pp. 75–91). London: Falmer.

Mulkeen, T. A., & Cooper, B. S. (1992). Implications of preparing school administrators for knowledge work organizations: A case study. *Journal of Educational Administration, 30*(1), 17–28.

Murphy, J. (1990). The reform of school administration: Pressure and calls for change. In J. Murphy (Ed.), *The education reform movement of the 1980s* (pp. 277–304). Berkeley: McCutchan.

Prestine, N. (1994, April). *Sorting it out: A tentative analysis of essential school change efforts in Illinois*. Paper presented at the annual meeting of the American Educational Research Association, New Orleans.

Trachtman, R. (1996). *The NCATE professional development school study*. Washington, DC: NCATE.

Chapter 5

The Idea of the University in an Age of School Reform: The Shaping Force of Professional Development Schools

NONA LYONS, BETH STROBLE, AND JOHN FISCHETTI

In the late 1980s, when school reformers at last shifted their attention to teachers and suggested that they needed to be at the center of school change, effectively reaching all students, it became clear that the restructuring of education had to go hand and hand with the renewal and reform of teacher education (Carnegie Forum, 1986; Goodlad, 1990; Holmes Group, 1986; Wise, Darling-Hammond, & Berry, 1987). Good schools would need a steady supply of excellent teachers, with new habits of mind and new habits of work (Meier, 1992). At that moment, by extension, the school reform movement reached the university, especially the colleges of education and their teacher education programs. If students in schools were to be constructors of their own knowledge and understandings, teachers too would need to be in new kinds of knowledge relationships with students (Elmore, 1996). There had to be two features to school renewal: changing practices for teachers and students in new relationships around knowledge and learning, and changing practices for learning to teach. To date, however, reporters of school reform have riveted their attention on elementary and secondary schools; little discussion has focused solely on the university. This chapter takes up that subject. It tells the stories of the teacher education programs in two institutions, the University of Louisville, Kentucky, and the University of Southern Maine (USM), and explores how school reform arrived at these institutions through the creation of a Professional

Development School: that school–university partnership where the education of new teachers and their mentors takes place in a school committed simultaneously to school renewal and to the transformation of teacher education.

The chapter contrasts the PDSs at the two institutions: USM, where the PDS is the sole model for teacher education within the university's postgraduate program; and Louisville, where all teacher education at the graduate level now takes place at school sites. It then examines specific examples of change brought about by the PDS at each institution. It addresses the central concern: What difference do PDSs make to the dual vision of new practices for student learning and for teacher education. Finally, it addresses a larger issue: what a university, its colleges, and schools need to become in an age of change and school restructuring. It considers this question as certain aspects of change through PDSs begin, however slowly, to come into focus in the context of a world in dynamic, irreversible change.

After some 10 years of school reform, renewal, and restructuring, and the proliferation of Professional Development Schools across North America, several characteristic features of change emerge (Darling-Hammond, 1994; Elmore, 1996; Goodlad, 1994; Levine, 1992; Meier, 1992, 1995; Osguthorpe, Harris, Fox-Harris, & Black, 1995; Robinson & Darling-Hammond, 1994; Sarason, 1990; see also Clark, 1995; Cushman, 1992; Darling-Hammond, 1994; Grossman, 1994; Lieberman, 1995; Lieberman & Miller, 1992; Muncey & McQuillan, 1991).

- The process of renewal, restructuring, and creating partnerships for teacher education is a long-term undertaking — some would argue a 10-year process at least.
- School reform may be more possible by designing a new school culture than by changing an existing one; PDSs may be considered a new kind of culture.
- Reform depends on the strength of intense, shared commitments to students and their teachers, to learning about learning, and to the ongoing assessment of these efforts. Without a shared vision of what students could be, especially intellectually, and what teachers need to do, reform will not be sustained within either institution. Nor will the creative work of developing the necessary skills and competencies and programs take place. National dialogues can help the process, facilitate local action, and serve as catalysts to sustain the enterprise, but the hard work at the grassroots is sustained by a common vision and commitment.
- Renewal and change are highly context-dependent, perhaps even context-driven, depending on the history, practices, and regularities of the insti-

tutions (Sarason, 1982, 1990), as well as the people involved, their relationships to one another, and the continuity of these relationships. The commitment to changing environments is crucial.

- Reform and change are complex and multidimensional. This may be especially so in the new partnerships between schools and universities needed to create Professional Development Schools. As they engage in a common enterprise—to support the learning of their students and the transformation of teacher education—each institution has its own agenda, history, and way of operating. The two organizations are separate yet joined—by intertwining visions and goals, engaged in creating a new entity. No map or blueprint is readily available to chart a direction. Invention and ongoing inquiry are what partnership must be about.

- Not surprisingly, partnership relationships are not without dilemmas, tensions, and critical questions. At heart is the question of how they can be sustained.

- To date the university, unlike partner schools, shows the least overt institutional change. Yet radical change is occurring in the roles university faculty take on in Professional Development Schools. This change, once in motion, is taking its direction from what has gone before, altering colleges and universities in apparently simple, almost invisible, yet ultimately far-reaching ways.

The two cases presented here illuminate through their detail some of these issues. This chapter argues that changes within the university generated by Professional Development School activities, although slow, are incremental, with the ripple effects of a quiet revolution, however fragile. Professional Development Schools, a new, jointly defined school culture, are subtly altering the traditional tasks of the university, raising compelling questions such as: What counts as knowledge? Who constructs it? How? Who are its faculty? These changes may foreshadow the university of the future: the idea of the university not simply as an institution of learning but as an institution of learners, a learning organization, carrying out its missions primarily through partnerships, whether with schools or other institutions, engaged in a simultaneous and ongoing process of renewal demanded by the dynamics of a changing worldview.

Each case study presented here reveals the context, history, and nature of the Professional Development School partnership for teacher education. Each considers the interconnected challenges of PDSs; changing the process of teacher education and engaging in school change, especially creating effective relationships between students and their teachers and learning.

Discussion of these examples leads to consideration of the larger issue: the future of the university in an age of school reform and a new worldview.

THE TEACHER EDUCATION PROGRAM OF
THE UNIVERSITY OF SOUTHERN MAINE

If you drive 10 miles along Route 25, heading west from Portland, Maine, leaving behind the turnpike and suburban malls, passing through gently rolling farmland, you reach the outskirts of the village of Gorham. On your right, set well back from the road, you pass an elementary school. A simple white and green sign announces: The Naragansett School: A Center of Inquiry. The school, a modest, one-story brick building extending out to jungle gyms and playing fields, looks as it did when it was built in the 1960s. But its simplicity belies the bold changes represented within the school and its school system, the Gorham Public Schools.

Changes within the school are as little visible as those revealed by a second set of buildings you come to if you continue a short distance west on Route 25. There you see on the hill to your left the classic white clapboard and brick buildings of a New England college. A bright blue sign announces: The University of Southern Maine. Nothing there would make you think that the two school systems—the Gorham Public Schools and the University of Southern Maine—were in any way connected. But they are in their most recent history and the connection has been profound—especially for the education of teachers. When the education faculty of USM voted in 1989 to eliminate its undergraduate major in education and to create a new, postbaccalaureate program for prospective teachers, it did so in unusual local and national contexts that have imprinted the program in lasting ways. Now these changes are affecting the College of Education and Human Development, and even the university as a whole, subtly transforming the nature of its work and faculty.

The Context of Change

In 1987, in the community of Gorham, Maine, site of the University of Southern Maine's College of Education and Human Development, a group of people also had been discussing school reform and restructuring, but from their own perspective. Encouraged by the College of Education's dean and a faculty member, a colleague of John Goodlad's who suggested forming a school–university partnership, six local school superintendents joined the university faculty to form the Southern Maine Partnership (SMP) as a way to improve their own schools and students. Informal conversations, often held at night, sometimes over dinner, focused on issues that the superintendents wanted to pursue: early childhood education, tracking in high schools, and so on. Conversations begun in small groups broadened to include principals and teachers, and shifted to a growing strand of interest: What was known about student learning? How could teachers voice what they knew about learning? Needed to know? How could they follow their own hunches? Design their own knowledge about teaching and learning? Could a school become a center of inquiry, not simply a dispenser of knowledge? A center of its own inquiry?

The conversations became small investigations, conferences, and then joined larger audiences. The Southern Maine Partnership gained stability with several grants for teacher research. Local schools joined larger, national projects. Howard Gardner's Harvard project on multiple intelligences found a new site in the Gorham Public Schools. A new statewide committee, representing business, educational institutions, agencies, and citizens, re-examined expectations for Maine students and created the Maine Common Core of Learning, a set of standards for all Maine students. New standards and practices demanded new kinds of assessments — and a new line of investigation was under way for Southern Maine Partnership schools.

At USM's College of Education and Human Development (CEHD), the momentum of ideas from the outside met with that from within. Administrators and faculty, looking critically through the lenses of reform, reconsidered an undergraduate major in education and opted to eliminate the existing program — to the dismay of some. To the credit of all, CEHD faculty turned to the development of a new program with two criteria in mind: a postbaccalaureate program rooted in liberal arts learning and a sustained experience of teaching in a Professional Development School setting. Faculty reviewed the models then being proposed by Goodlad (1990) and Darling-Hammond (1994) and those of earlier advocates of Professional Development Schools (Stallings & Kowalski, 1990), as well as the best practices already in place in their own existing program. These reviews supported the idea of a year-long teaching internship in schools and the necessity for a close link to schools in delivering the program. The fact that area schools were members of the Southern Maine Partnership, committed to and engaged in school renewal and restructuring, made them attractive sites for a new clinical teacher education program.

In this context, after 5 years of collaboration between local schools and USM's education faculty, the new program, the Extended Teacher Education Program (ETEP) emerged. The first school system chosen to elaborate the design and pilot the program was the Wells–Ogunguit Public

Schools, a Southern Maine Partnership member that by consensus agreed to participate.

The New Program

The Extended Teacher Education Program has three key components: (1) an undergraduate minor with practicum courses that allow USM students to explore the possibilities of a career in teaching, to test their interest, and to deepen it; (2) an intensive, year-long internship of practice for graduates of liberal arts programs committed to learning to teach, which leads to certification; and (3) a 2-year, follow-up program in which beginning teachers meet in the summer and on Saturdays. These 3 years of study — certification and 2 years beyond — lead to a Master of Science in Education. Teacher education begins in the undergraduate years, continues across an intensive internship, and concludes after the first 2 years of practice. Several features characterize the ETEP.

An Intensive Internship. The center of the ETEP is an intensive internship taking place over the course of a year. Beginning each summer, some 80 new teacher interns in cohorts of 12 to 15 students join with university and school faculty at each site. Students, following the school calendar, come at the opening of school and stay until May, during which time they work primarily in schools, taking their university courses at their school sites as well as at the university. Teacher interns become part of the school faculty, participating in all aspects of school life.

Mentoring by Site Coordinators and Cooperating Teachers. ETEP students at a site are mentored by cooperating teachers and two site coordinators, a university faculty and a school faculty member, who jointly share in the responsibility for their learning. Sometimes school faculty and cooperating teachers serve with university faculty as co-instructors.

Partnership Relationships. The internship year of the ETEP takes place in five partner school sites, ranging from Portland — a federal relocation site for immigrants from Southeast Asia — to the coastal communities of Yarmouth and Wells-Ogunguit-Kennebunk, to inland Gorham and rural Fryeburg. These schools, members of the Southern Maine Partnership, are committed to school reform, however unique to their settings and efforts. As members of a PDS, they also join in teacher education.

Partnership between school and university is part of every phase of the ETEP beginning with an admissions interview, which is mandatory for acceptance at a site, and continuing through the program year.

Performance Assessment and Collaborative Judgment. At an end-of-year presentation of a portfolio, teacher interns present a body of evidence — lesson plans, student work, videotapes of classroom teaching — to their school and university faculty, who decide whether a candidate is indeed ready to teach, that is, to take full responsibility for working with children. Faculty acting as a community of interpreters consider the intern evidence and determine whether the student should receive initial teacher certification (Moss, 1996).

The success of the ETEP is demonstrated by the support it receives from local schools and superintendents who recruit and hire graduates of the ETEP, by the high, nearly 90% job placement rate — for full and part-time teaching positions — for graduates of the program, and by the ongoing commitment to the program by the university and school faculty. The program also continues its own development. Recently, under the sponsorship of the National Association of State Boards of Education, the Maine State Board of Education, and the State Department of Education, the ETEP school and university faculty have been collaborating with Bates College and the University of Maine at Farmington to develop a set of standards for beginning teachers and to explore the use of portfolios and other performance assessments.

Change at the University: Visible and Invisible Signs

If asked how the Extended Teacher Education Program and the partnership with local schools has changed the University of Southern Maine, some would say there has been no change. From the outside and to some on the inside, the university and its College of Education and Human Development appear the same. But to others, change has been significant, although not always easily observable. Paradoxically, few, if any, new structures mark these changes, but university partnership faculty report fundamental changes — even transformational ones — in their life and work. This double-sidedness of change may be the most significant aspect of it: its reality and its near invisibility. While the work of the university faculty seems to flow seamlessly from past efforts, real change is going on at the university: in the nature of faculty work, in who does it and how, and, especially, in the new kind of knowledge being constructed by faculty and interns about teaching about teaching. At the moment, then, it seems that the burden of change at the university is being carried through its faculty and the changing work that engages them. But who are the faculty and what is the nature of their work? Of their new knowledge?

Redefining Faculty Membership. University faculty in the ETEP share their responsibilities with school site faculty. New titles were created to go with these roles: University and school partners are called site coordinators. In the spring of 1996, university faculty voted to give school site coordinators adjunct faculty status with voting privileges. The rationale was that both share in the delivery of the teacher education program, so both need to be fully responsible for it. This change—the sharing of traditional roles and decision-making power—although not visible in ways that a new office, program, or department might be, is a significant one.

One other aspect of the partnership of site coordinators is the increasingly collaborative nature of their interactions, whether in teaching, carrying out research, or crossing institutional boundaries. Site coordinators are collaborative teams. They support and nurture each other's learning as they do that of their students, supporting the work, too, of restructuring in both their institutions.

The Transformation of Faculty Work. Traditionally defined, university work centers on courses, course credits, and faculty load. It usually is confined to the university site. Work within most Professional Development Schools not only has meant moving out of the university to schools, but has shifted time frames, the schedule, and the nature of work. The focus of most PDSs, such as the ETEP, is the intensive year-long internship of learning to teach. Of necessity, university faculty follow a school calendar. Teaching is not limited to a 2- or 3-hour course that meets once or twice a week. Nor is supervision of students limited to several observations a semester. These activities are more likely to extend to everyday interactions. Seminars and courses delivered on site are usually open to all school faculty. For university faculty, being on site means greater interaction with school faculty and administrators, and more responsibilities for facilitating school–university relationships. Some examples of the changing nature of faculty work are:

- *Facilitating Ongoing Inquiry Between Theory and Practice.* Working in a clinical setting, particularly in these schools with their restructuring agendas and projects, both faculty and teacher interns are more likely to ask: How does learning take place? In this class? With these students? How can student learning be facilitated by this teacher intern? What evidence is appropriate to judge this learning? Why? How might this lesson or portfolio be done more effectively to reach these students? This focus on student learning and teaching of necessity brings together theory and practice and is likely to be a part of daily experiences and conversations (see Goodlad, 1984; Hunkins, Wiseman, & Williams, 1995; Schlechty & Whitford, 1988; Shulman, 1994). Both student and teacher can point to the same puzzling situation in a classroom, seek some way to understand what has been going on, re-examine situations in the light of theory, and, then, try new teaching solutions.

- *Participating in a New Learning Organization.* Re-examination of theory in the light of practice is not always initiated by university faculty. Rather, in some situations, schools are nudging the university. For example, a teacher intern working with junior high school students who are assessing their exhibitions and portfolios on the basis of Gardner's model of multiple intelligences is working in a context where a re-examination of class practices is a central organizing feature of the school. Teacher interns and university faculty are of necessity engaged in firsthand experiences of a new learning organization. The focus of the school has shifted from an organization transmitting knowledge to one engaged in constructing it collaboratively, joining teachers, students, and those learning to teach. The school, too, is addressing more formally issues once relegated solely to the university, that is, the education of new teachers. Often the university as an organization has not itself taken on such a commitment to ongoing inquiry, investigations, or change in its own teaching and learning practices, while its faculty in a PDS may have. They may be helping to create it. While clearly not every PDS site is fully in this mode, there are those that are.

- *Exploring New Habits of Mind and Work in Everyday Inquiry.* The nature of the inquiry embedded in school restructuring, which looks constantly at learning and teaching, asking about its effectiveness and about reaching all students, is shaping new habits of inquiry and reflection, ones that can be a model for teacher interns.

- *Constructing New Knowledge.* Perhaps the most significant change in the work of PDSs is the new knowledge that faculty are constructing. Teacher educators are deepening their understanding of the dynamics of learning to teach, of the kind of mentorship that this entails, of questions to be posed, and of experiences to be facilitated. In exploring the use of a standards-based model of teacher education and initiating a process of constructing and presenting portfolios by the teacher interns, ETEP faculty report significant new insights about these performance assessments, student teacher learnings, and their own changing understandings of the possibilities of performance assessments. For example, portfolio presentations in several ETEP sites originally were done as celebratory end-of-year events. Interns presented their portfolios in public forums and people clapped. Now several sites have shifted to an interpretive assessment mode, offering students feedback on their presentation, much as in a doctoral defense (Moss, 1996). At the conclusion of the questioning of the presentation, the intern may leave the room and the faculty caucus to determine whether the student should receive initial teacher certification.

Not all ETEP sites follow this procedure, but all use portfolio presentations as evidence for certification. For faculty and interns, teacher development and assessment are becoming aligned.

- *Making Knowledge Public.* A significant result of the ETEP PDS model with its portfolio process has been to make public discussions of teaching practices. What before remained behind closed doors when teacher interns took over a class, or even in conferences between an intern and a supervisor, has become part of a larger, public dialogue. Now, especially through portfolio presentations, discussions about effective teaching practices or ways of engaging students in their own learning are likely to involve a whole cohort of interns and their mentors. Reflections on teaching, on how to change one's practices, are no longer private ruminations; they have become community deliberations. Just as some reformers have argued for making public what counts as good student work, for example, what makes an A, a B, or a C grade (Wolf, 1994), so that students know what that means, what makes effective teaching practice also has become open to scrutiny.

Joining the Twin Agendas of School Reform: The Fragility of Knowledge

It is this kind of deepening knowledge about teaching, and about learning to teach, that is slowly accruing to faculty and interns. It is this kind of knowledge and experience that are at the heart of university change. But it is not easily observable. At the moment, it is carried in the faculty, through their experiences and their own learning and that of their students. It is elaborated in faculty discussions. It may be found eventually in recommendations to the state about a new model for teacher certification. It is a fragile kind of knowledge, easily lost if someone leaves a site, goes on sabbatical, or decides not to continue as a PDS coordinator. It is not yet well documented; clearly it is not fully shared throughout the university system. Yet it needs to be. One agenda for the future of PDSs emerges with enormous potential, that is, documenting this knowledge of teaching for understanding and learning to teach.

THE DEPARTMENT OF SECONDARY EDUCATION AT THE UNIVERSITY OF LOUISVILLE

The Department of Secondary Education at the University of Louisville entered into a school–university partnership with Fairdale High School and Iroquois High School in Jefferson County, Louisville, Kentucky, to aid simultaneous restructuring of high schools and teacher education. In 1996 the department moved sections of courses that had met on-site at Iroquois High School to the Manual and Ballard sites. With professional year courses prior to student teaching moved to partner school sites, the new program prepares candidates for student teaching by immersing them in the culture of diverse, urban high schools that are undergoing major renewal and restructuring, through links to Kentucky school reform and national school improvement initiatives. This move clearly has changed the experience of students, but it has had effects on the School of Education and the larger university as well, sometimes with challenging results. This section describes the history of the development of a Professional Development School for the new Secondary Education program.

University Teacher Education Program Changes

In October 1987 the School of Education faculty voted to join the Holmes Group. The next fall, with funding through 1992, the Department of Secondary Education launched an experimental accelerated teacher preparation program to prepare career change students for teaching. The program provided paid internships alongside a professional year sequence of courses. Because many of the internship placements were housed at Fairdale High School, a high school with which faculty had collaborated in several team and department projects, relationships with teachers and administrators in the school grew gradually through mutual interest and support.

Fairdale High School is located in a mostly white, working-class community in Jefferson County. Some 30% of the students — mostly African American — are bused in from Louisville, some 15 miles away. Jefferson County Public Schools are the result of a 1975 merger and desegregation of the Louisville Independent Districts and the Jefferson County Schools. A new superintendent was hired in 1981, and a commitment to school restructuring was undertaken. With significant local and national foundation support, several important staff development and school renewal programs were launched, gaining nationwide attention. In these efforts, the University of Louisville faculty joined school faculty, especially through the activities of the Jefferson County Schools' Gheens Professional Development Academy. In 1987, a major comprehensive effort focused on creating Professional Development Schools was launched and all local schools were invited to participate. It was these earlier experiences that led to the experimental work of the Secondary Teacher Education Program (Whitford, 1994).

The Secondary Teacher Education Program

During 1992 and 1993, members of the secondary education department, faculty at Fairdale, and others met to redesign the regular Secondary Teacher Education Program. Approved in 1993 as an M.A.T. professional year degree, the new program for all University of Louisville secondary students incorporates many of the aspects of the pilot experimental program, including the sequence of professional courses in a single year, the employment of a cohort, and on-site courses. For two semesters (spring or summer) and through their fall pre-student teaching, the 110 students in the program work at Fairdale High School, duPont Manual High School, or Ballard High School, the three PDS sites. The addition of the Manual and Ballard sites as course locations began in 1996. Some students stay at the PDSs for student teaching; most go on to other high schools in the area as part of the evolving notion of the professional development community.

While changes in individual courses and in the structure of the program have resulted from local initiatives and naturally evolving relationships, the Secondary Teacher Education Program also has functioned within a national policy context. Collaborative efforts between university and local high school faculty have been supported by funding from both public and private sources. Policy frameworks defined by the Holmes Group, National Center for Restructuring Education, Schools, and Teaching (NCREST), Coalition of Essential Schools, Foxfire, and the philosophy and mandates of Kentucky Education Reform have had shaping influences (Mussington & Whitford, 1993).

The preservice teachers enrolled in the Secondary Teacher Education Program are often mature students, with an average age of 30, making career changes. The program is able to draw upon the diverse backgrounds and work experiences that these candidates bring to teaching. Many continue to support families by working part- or full-time during their coursework prior to student teaching. Because few of them have recent direct experience with public schools, their knowledge of national reform efforts and Kentucky's unique state education policy context is limited. The hands-on opportunities to work in an urban PDS immersed in rethinking their processes of teaching and learning allow them to develop expertise in the change process and in school restructuring issues.

While completing a three-semester sequence of professional courses, taught largely at one of the three PDS sites, students also enroll in content courses to complete a teaching major in their certification area. The first course in the professional sequence, Exploring Teaching, is a prerequisite to admission to the professional year. In this 6-hour block, students assist in classrooms as part of their teaching visits, provide community service as a required program component, and study topics typical of introductory foundations and educational psychology courses. In the second semester, students enroll in Pre-Student Teaching, a 6-hour block team taught by university instructors with assistance from on-site educators. This class meets twice weekly for 16 weeks at Fairdale or duPont Manual High School. Class sessions consist of authentic, performance tasks tied to pre-service teachers' experiences in high school classrooms and an additional 3 hours of weekly teaching visit experiences in content-oriented classrooms. Because these experiences are common among members of the class, they focus the content of class sessions.

The course becomes a laboratory for the high school classroom experiences. Further, the teaching visit assignments for the course emphasize teaching and direct, systematic experiences with adolescents, rather than observation. The preservice teachers act on their knowledge of content, their emerging roles as teachers, and their growing relationships with learners by organizing at least four teaching events in high school classrooms. They support each high school's reform efforts by fully involving themselves in the life of the school. For example, candidates meet in team planning sessions, assist teachers and students with assessing school reform components, participate in School-Based Decision-Making Council meetings, and facilitate interdisciplinary cooperative learning group projects. Students then complete their professional year, going to a variety of local area high schools for their semester-long student teaching experience accompanied by a student teaching seminar.

The current program has the goal of "developing reflective educators who view learning as a constructive and lifelong experience" (*Basic Program for Secondary Education*, 1993). By organizing the curriculum to help students construct meaning from their experiences, by providing opportunities for them to interact and apply their understanding in real-world contexts, and by using cooperative learning groups, portfolios, and increasingly more complex projects (Dittmer, Fischetti, & Kyle, 1993; Ross, Bondy, & Kyle, 1993; Sizer, 1992), the program models an expanding knowledge base for teaching and challenges the old notions of passive learning and "teaching as telling" (Kyle, Dittmer, Fischetti, & Portes, 1992).

Portfolio Development and Assessment

A significant feature of the Secondary Teacher Education Program is the use of performance assessments, including portfolios. The assessments are designed to equip students for the state-mandated assessments they will be expected to use in their own classrooms, to bring authenticity to measures of their performance, and to provide instructors and students with better information with which to guide instruction.

Teacher educators (who have long assembled their own portfolios for purposes of promotion and tenure) have found professional portfolios a useful tool for authentically documenting school/university/community partnership experiences as well as a tool for classroom assessment (Hamm & Adams, 1991; Mosenthal, 1994). Used alongside of or in lieu of traditional assessments, portfolios serve as a catalyst for change in the curriculum of teacher education programs. Because successful portfolios should include evidence of teacher education candidates' success with young people, portfolios can exert important program influences. Beginning teachers must have the opportunity to be immersed in schools and school change and to reflect upon those experiences. Students must have significant experiences and then make meaning of those experiences in the same way that they design classrooms where their students construct knowledge out of the curriculum experiences designed for them. These experiences should translate to real and relevant bodies of work that will assist graduates in demonstrating to potential employers their ability to do the job. Local school districts are requiring prospective teachers to submit portfolios for interview and selection purposes. In addition, state-level certification offices are incorporating portfolio assessments for licensure and continuing assessment of entering and experienced teachers and administrators.

Portfolios first became a part of the teacher education program as assessment components of individual courses. As members of the department team taught courses and shared their portfolio experiences, the portfolio process became much more student-owned. The portfolio shifted from a collection of class materials to selected samples of work to represent what had been learned. While faculty use Kentucky Teacher Standards and program themes as the organizers for the portfolio entries, decisions about selection criteria and final assessments rest with students. They use the portfolio as a visible record of their reflections across a semester and as evidence of their personal and professional growth. Asking students to create assessment criteria in the first week of a course gives them a focus for their work, which, in turn, allows them to reflect explicitly and continuously about the value of that work as evidence of their learning (Stroble, 1995).

Later, the portfolio is a way to bring coherence to the program and to connect with external audiences. Using a common framework for the portfolios allows students the opportunity to make links among the school, the university, and the community.

Simultaneous with program efforts to use the portfolio to link theory and practice in authentic ways and to bring coherence to the multiple requirements for program completion (state certification, school district employment, and first-year internship) was the State Professional Standards Board's adoption of nine New Teacher Standards. The standards are used as the guidelines for the portfolios that students first assemble for admission to the program and that continue to evolve throughout the program: leadership, designing instruction, establishing a positive learning climate, communicating assessment results to students and parents, collaborating with colleagues and the community, developing as a professional, mastering subject content, managing instruction, and reflecting on and evaluating one's teaching. They allow students to continue to develop evidence that they can use at program completion and through Kentucky's first-year internship program. Now faculty are much more likely to ask whether they have provided the experiences students will need if they are to meet these standards. As faculty members face the challenges of making judgments about student performance and program strengths, they have evidence that matters not only to teacher educators but to those who make licensure and employment decisions as well.

Changing the Work Life of Teacher Educators

Moving to school sites and focusing on a performance-based curriculum have significantly changed the experiences of teacher education students. In addition, the PDS approach has been a catalyst for changing the roles of teacher educators in the program in each of the categories of teaching, learning, research, and service.

By teaming the prerequisite Exploring Teaching course, faculty in Secondary Education work together with colleagues in Educational Psychology and Special Education. The course, offered at a PDS site, takes advantage of the school resources to provide a meaningful context for course readings and reflection and a more coherent approach to the important basics of teacher education. The goal of producing student portfolios for admission provides a focus for developing the curriculum for the 6-hour course. Minus the portfolio, the tendency would be for each instructor to create separate syllabi and a variety of inconsistent assessments. The portfolio requirement challenges faculty to work together and with school colleagues.

In the next phase of the M.A.T. program, Pre-Student Teaching, professors from Secondary Education team teach and work with teachers and administrators at the PDS sites to infuse the curriculum with projects related to school change. Portfolios from Exploring Teaching are reviewed and improved upon as a result of the additional classroom and reform-oriented experiences of this course. The team approach gives teacher educators the chance to function in a team environment. Because of the emphasis on the portfolio as a device for program admission, continuation, graduation, and the first-year internship, Pre-Student Teaching instructors must be in close communication with Exploring faculty, content methods instructors, and those who work with student teachers and interns. In the past, this aspect of the program was evaluated as the weakest by graduates because course requirements did not emphasize the accumulation of authentic evidence as a goal. For professors, however, the familiarity with each other's teaching has proven beneficial in providing specific evidence of success with students as they move forward in the promotion and tenure process. Traditionally, it was difficult to prove superior performance in teaching because few actually had the chance to be part of each other's classes.

Collecting, Evaluating, and Acting on the Evidence for Change

As portfolios have become not only a catalyst for change but also a tool and an instrument for transition in the Secondary Teacher Education Program, the challenge has become to face now what teacher educators have always identified as issues to be resolved later. Portfolios provide access to more information about student performance and the nature of students' involvement with students and adults in school sites. Portfolios demonstrate how students draw meaning from their experiences and they supply evidence demanding attention and action.

Supporting Best Practice. In the past, faculty knew anecdotally about the weaknesses of the program. The portfolios provide authentic evidence of the value of students' experiences at the PDS site. In portfolios, the pressure that the students place on classroom teachers, administrators, and staff becomes clear. Many portfolios show excellent evidence of teacher interns working successfully with restructuring leaders devoted to all students' ability to learn. Other portfolios show evidence of outdated practices and teacher-centered paradigms. This evidence helps in making decisions about placements, but challenges program commitment to students and to colleagues at the PDS site. As a result, faculty work with building administrators more closely to make matches between students and school faculty, meet with interested faculty to reach agreement on expectations for students' work and leadership in their classrooms, and use an assessment form to communicate those shared expectations among the school faculty and students. Program faculty foster honest, professional conversation among the students about the contradictions they may face. On occasion, they move a student to a new placement.

What is not yet clear is how the challenges posed by the school-wide restructuring projects in which the students engage may alter the program.

When teacher education students step on toes with their sometimes brash and inexperienced leadership, should the program pull back on such projects or trust that leadership from PDS faculty and staff will provide a moderating influence and appropriate model? Further, the portfolio process enhances the need to more fully honor the diverse members of the professional development community who contribute to the success of students.

Students' portfolios routinely identify the following aspects of the program as important in teacher preparation: locating the classes in a "real" environment, developing a spiraling curriculum linked to strong content standards and student success, and building habits of collegiality and reflection through cohorts (Stroble, Fischetti, Collins, & Keill, 1994).

Counseling Students. A few portfolios also reveal students who are minimally committed to teaching or who do not believe that all students can succeed. They may not have engaged themselves completely enough in the work of the PDS site to see the links between their teacher education courses and the agendas of the school. Or they simply may have gone through the motions in the program, paying lip service to a constructivist approach. When portfolio evidence makes these problems apparent, a response must be formulated. Again, it is necessary to confront the consequences of gathering evidence in an authentic environment. A working committee in the School of Education is preparing a plan for continuous assessment based on a portfolio framework that will serve as a guide for self-assessment and revamped statewide accreditation.

Developing Shared Program Assumptions. As the rules and relationships change for those working in PDS sites, staff roles also must change (Metcalf-Turner & Fischetti, 1995). Teacher educators must struggle to include university colleagues in decisions about the direction of the program without diffusing its focus. Just as not everyone in the PDS site shares assumptions about students and their success, not everyone in the school or department shares assumptions about teacher education students and their success. Agreement has not been reached about which experiences students should have across sections of the subject-area methods classes or even about how the portfolios should function as a curriculum and assessment tool. The different experiences that students have across course sections and at PDS sites become obvious in their portfolios, however, and such evidence challenges program staff to take leadership on behalf of students, while respecting the academic freedom of their colleagues. When portfolios depend on making meaning of one's experiences, differences in experiences result not only in very different portfolios but in very different opportunities to learn.

One of the challenges facing those in partnership to prepare, certify, employ, develop, and nurture teachers is bringing coherence to these multiple purposes that PDS work implies. Further, this era of restructuring in teacher education will indeed move teacher education programs past the traditional time-based, transcript orientation to allow a performance-oriented curriculum to emerge. It will be necessary to overcome the history of teaching as telling and provide experiences that connect teacher education students' learning about teaching to the lives of their students. The clearest measure of success to this point has been the success of program graduates in the job search process. Marilyn Hohmann, former principal at Fairdale High School, said this about program students:

> After several years of this program, we now have at least four or five new teachers prepared for real classroom experiences at rigorous levels and trained to put a rational, systematic emphasis on the way kids learn. They have had practice in working with diverse student populations in student-centered classrooms. (Cushman, 1993, p. 3)

CONCLUSION

While the idea of a Professional Development School for teacher education has had a long history in the United States, models emerging today differ significantly from previous ones. John Dewey's Laboratory School at the University of Chicago (1896) and James Conant's (1963) "clinical" school reverberate in today's PDSs, in the recent recommendations of the Holmes Group, and in Goodlad's (1990, 1994) conception of "partner schools"—those created through partnerships among schools, colleges of education, and colleges of arts and sciences. All are concerned with teacher education. Yet today's models—PDSs and partner schools—are different in two primary ways: in the central questions that concern them and in the profoundly different context of change that characterizes today's world.

The compelling concerns of today's partners in education are focused on how to teach well and how to teach to reach all students in the real, complex, messy settings where teachers and students live and work. The changing characteristics of today's world reflect a letting go of predictability—what some call a Newtonian worldview. That view is being replaced by the uncertainty of a world of little predictability. Individuals must go beyond routine, exercise personal judgment, understand the technical and human systems of which they are increasingly a part, and participate in them in thinking and inventive ways (Resnick & Resnick, 1992; Senge, 1990; Zuboff, 1988; see also Bateson, 1972).

Conditions of work are likely to continue to be subject to radical changes, especially technological ones, requiring a new kind of human adaptability. The computer networker and the forklift operator may have more in common than ever before. The networker can communicate with others around the world. The forklift operator, with a switch of the computer, can act on some distant object, remove a needed product in a warehouse 3,000 miles away, and send it on its way. The web of technological connection is powerful, linking all kinds of jobs, and demanding new kinds of abilities and human responsiveness.

In this new world a narrowly defined idea of hierarchy is replaced by fluid relationships. Competencies focus on the ability of individuals and groups to adapt to situations and environments, and to new ways of doing things, and to shift dramatically if necessary. The university of today, too, of necessity must look to the future, increasingly connecting to local institutions and to regional needs. It seeks, like the University of Southern Maine, to "pursue national standards while working on a local level." It must work in close collaboration with the community, be "deeply concerned about teaching, be of service, and provide programs responsive to regional needs and student development in an increasingly competitive and fast changing world" (Pattenaude, 1995).

What is remarkable is that the features of PDSs that are emerging from the first years of their growth map onto this dynamic new worldview. PDSs are focused on relationships, on fluidity and invention, and on the force of change occurring in schools and the power of visions to enact new possibilities for teaching and learning. They cannot be separated from their contexts. But it is precisely these new dimensions that can create tensions. Considering the characteristic tensions found in today's PDSs, it is necessary to think about what a college of education or its university could become in an age of such dynamic change.

Sustaining a PDS: Invention, Flexibility, and Relationships

While the stories of the development of USM's Extended Teacher Education Program or Louisville's PDS are bright ones, seen as exemplars by others seeking to create Professional Development Schools of their own, these teacher education programs are clearly not without their dilemmas, tensions, and critical questions.

When teacher interns move out of the university to live and work in their partner schools, subtle institutional adaptations occur. Schools expand to receive teacher interns, inviting them to work with their students, asking them to participate in the larger activities of the school year, such as faculty meetings, conferences with parents, staff development activities, school reform projects. School personnel are usually grateful for the increased resources the student interns provide and they value the new opportunities for teachers to take on professionally enhancing roles in collaboration with the university—acting as course leaders, site coordinators, mentors, and so on. Flexibility characterizes the school as it adapts like an organism to a new life. Similarly, university faculty also adapt. University and school faculty collaborate in research, course development, and delivery.

Yet while school and university adapt to new exigencies, neither has the experience of a PDS. This new entity exists neither in the school nor in the university but in the relationship between the two in a new fragile culture. These adaptations can place stress on the institutions and their members. For example, each of the five USM internship sites celebrates its autonomy and the richness of its school-based context for learning to teach, but university administrators—as well as site faculty—worry about the consistency and control of the program across sites. Since university faculty members spend most of their time on site, they are not easily available for informal faculty meetings. Program development and consistency are hard-won achievements.

Partnership Roles: Overlapping Arenas of Action

As both school and university faculty have discovered, their roles and relationships are the critical center of a PDS. As such, faculty must take on unusual, shared roles, ones that never were a part of their job description. The roles of school and university site coordinators overlap, spanning boundaries of each other's jobs, often creating new demands with little guidance for how to respond. School faculty members find themselves speaking for the program; university faculty members find themselves deeply involved in the life of schools. The realities of these overlapping roles, with more direct demands on faculty time and with subtle, new commitments, shift traditional understandings of job descriptions. Faculty responsibilities may not be fully understood by other faculty or administrators of either schools or universities.

The Need for a Shared Vision

The stories of the two PDSs presented here, and especially their experiences with portfolio assessments, point to the power of a shared set of assumptions to facilitate program evaluation and ongoing development. What is equally clear is that lack of a shared commitment, for whatever reason, can radically affect what can be achieved. Shared visions and commitments are critical.

Time and Resources

In a time of economic stringency, when state institutions like USM are at or near level budgeting, with small hope for increased university funding, there are real issues about how to support continued growth and development of intensive programs such as a Professional Development School. In the USM's ETEP model, the university pays a stipend (a portion of a teacher's salary) for teachers who serve as site coordinators and supervisors of teacher interns. These positions are not "frills" of the program; they are the heart of it. Without stretching schools beyond their limits, they make possible real contributions by schools to teacher education, such as providing for a substitute teacher when a mentor teacher must be available elsewhere. Similarly, issues of stretching university faculty members in terms of the time they need to spend in schools is an ongoing issue.

Envisioning a Future

While these issues can challenge institutions and their faculties, it is important to consider this work in the framework of a time of unprecedented change both in the way schools deliver an education and in life in general.

Recently, Lee and Smith (1994) at the University of Michigan have found a direct relationship between schools demonstrating commitment to restructuring and student achievement. Similarly, at a time of national concern about the adequacy of teacher education, it seems useful to ask what difference a PDS experience makes to success in learning to teach, to actual teaching practices, and to student learning. While there are anecdotal data, there is a clear need to begin systematic work, following graduates of these programs and considering real-life consequences to students and their new teachers.

Several considerations emerge from the examination of the two PDS models now under development at the University of Southern Maine and the University of Louisville.

First, the best way to encourage the work of PDSs may be to continue to support faculty invention, to foster the connections members are making with school systems, and to give the resources that would make it possible to deepen this interconnection of school and university systems. Such a path would allow for the real issues — whether of finance, governance, or structure — to emerge in their particularity.

Further, creating structures need not be the first order of business or of concern; new structures may not be necessary. Some organizational theorists argue that, given the world of change, action should go first, then planning and structures (Wheatley, 1994).

Lastly, the PDSs of today may portend the future. Colleges of education and their universities also need to be characterized by an ability to adapt and to forge linkages with other systems and other institutions. The primary goal is fostering human adaptiveness — that is, learning.

The vision today for schools and universities in partnership relationships is focused on children and adolescents and their possibilities, on what they could be and become, and on their teachers and how to foster the skills, understandings, knowledge, and competencies necessary for them to act and live and create order in a complex, changing world. It is a powerful, if still fragile, field for action.

REFERENCES

Basic Program for Secondary Education. (1993). Unpublished manuscript, University of Louisville, Department of Secondary Education, Louisville, KY.

Bateson, G. (1972). *Steps to an ecology of mind.* New York: Ballantine.

Carnegie Forum on Education and the Economy. (1986). *A nation prepared: Teachers for the twenty first century.* Washington, DC: Author.

Clark, R. W. (1995). Evaluating partner schools. In R. T. Osguthorpe, R. C. Harris, M. Fox-Harris, & S. Black (Eds.), *Partner schools: Centers for educational renewal* (pp. 229–262). San Francisco: Jossey-Bass.

Conant, J. B. (1963). *The education of American teachers.* New York: McGraw-Hill.

Cushman, K. (1992, November). What works, what doesn't: Lessons from essential school reform. *Horace, 9*(2), 1–4.

Cushman, K. (1993, September). Teacher education in essential schools: The university–school partnership. *Horace, 10*(1), 1–7.

Darling-Hammond, L. (Ed.). (1994). *Professional development schools: Schools for developing a profession.* New York: Teachers College Press.

Dewey, J. (1896). The university school. *University Record, 5,* 417–442.

Dittmer, A., Fischetti, J., & Kyle, D. W. (1993). Constructivist teaching and student empowerment: Educational equity through school reform. *Equity & Excellence in Education, 26*(1), 40–45.

Elmore, R. F. (1996). Getting to scale with good educational practice. *Harvard Educational Review, 66*(1), 1–26.

Goodlad, J. (1984). *A place called school: Prospects for the future.* New York: McGraw-Hill.

Goodlad, J. (1990). *Teachers for our nation's schools.* San Francisco: Jossey-Bass.

Goodlad, J. (1994). *Educational renewal: Better teachers, better schools.* San Francisco: Jossey-Bass.

Grossman, P. L. (1994). In pursuit of a dual agenda: Creating a middle level professional development school. In L. Darling-Hammond (Ed.), *Professional development schools: Schools for developing a profession* (pp. 50–73). New York: Teachers College Press.

Hamm, M., & Adams, D. (1991, May). Portfolios: It's not just for artists anymore. *The Science Teacher,* pp. 18–21.

Holmes Group. (1986). *Tomorrow's teachers: A report of the Holmes Group*. East Lansing, MI: Author.

Hunkins, F. P., Wiseman, D. L., & Williams, R. C. (1995). Supporting collaborative inquiry. In R. T. Osguthorpe, R. C. Harris, M. Fox-Harris, & S. Black (Eds.), *Partner schools: Centers for educational renewal* (pp. 99–123). San Francisco: Jossey-Bass.

Kyle, D., Dittmer, A., Fischetti, J., & Portes, P. (1992). *Aligning the Kentucky internship program with the Kentucky education reform act*. Frankfort: Kentucky Department of Education.

Lee, V., & Smith, J. B. (1994, Fall). *High school restructuring and student achievement: Issues in restructuring schools* (Issue Report No. 7). Madison: University of Wisconsin, Center on Organization and Restructuring of Schools.

Levine, M. (Ed.). (1992). *Professional practice schools: Linking teacher education and school reform*. New York: Teachers College Press.

Lieberman, A. (1995). *The work of restructuring schools*. New York: Teachers College Press.

Lieberman, A., & Miller, L. (1992). Teacher development in professional practice schools. In M. Levine (Ed.), *Professional practice schools: Linking teacher education and school reform* (pp. 105–123). New York: Teachers College Press.

Meier, D. (1992, Summer). Reinventing teaching. *Teachers College Record, 93*(4), 594–609.

Meier, D. (1995). How our schools could be. *Phi Delta Kappan, 76*(5), 369–373.

Metcalf-Turner, P., & Fischetti, J. (1995, February). *The ABCs of PDSs (professional development schools): Problems, practices, and possibilities*. Paper presented at the annual conference of the Association of American Colleges of Teacher Education, Washington, DC.

Mosenthal, J. (1994, April). *Statewide assessment: Alternative approaches and alternative needs*. Paper presented at the annual meeting of the American Educational Research Association, New Orleans.

Moss, P. A. (1996). Enlarging the dialogue in educational measurement: Voices from interpretive research traditions. *Educational Researcher, 25*(1), 20–28.

Muncey, D. E., & McQuillan, P. J. (1991). Preliminary findings from a five year study of the Coalition of Essential Schools. *Phi Delta Kappan, 74*(6), 486–489.

Mussington, C., & Whitford, B. L. (1993). *Professional development schools: Where we've been, where we are, and next steps*. Unpublished manuscript.

Osguthorpe, R. T., Harris, R. C., Fox-Harris, M., & Black, S. (Eds). (1995). *Partner schools: Centers for educational renewal*. San Francisco: Jossey-Bass.

Pattenaude, R. L. (1995). Crafting the comprehensive university – USM in the 21st century. *University of Southern Maine report of gifts, 1994–1995*. Portland: University of Southern Maine.

Resnick, L. D., & Resnick, D. P. (1992). Assessing the thinking curriculum: New tools for educational reform. In B. Gifford & M. C. O'Connor (Eds.), *Changing assessments: Alternative views of aptitude, achievement and instruction*. Boston: Kluwer Academic Publishers.

Robinson, S., & Darling-Hammond, L. (1994). Change for collaboration and collaboration for change: Transforming teaching through school–university partnerships. In L. Darling-Hammond (Ed.), *Professional development schools: Schools for developing a profession* (pp. 203–219). New York: Teachers College Press.

Ross, D., Bondy, E., & Kyle, D. W. (1993). *Reflective teaching for student empowerment: Elementary curriculum and methods.* New York: Macmillan.

Sarason, S. B. (1982). *The culture of the school and the problem of change* (2nd ed.). Boston: Allyn & Bacon.

Sarason, S. B. (1990). *The predictable failure of educational reform.* San Francisco: Jossey-Bass.

Schlechty, P. C., & Whitford, B. L. (1988). Shared problems and shared vision: Organic collaboration. In K. A. Sirotnik & J. I. Goodlad (Eds.), *School–university partnerships in action* (pp. 191–204). New York: Teachers College Press.

Senge, P. M. (1990). *The fifth discipline: The art and practice of the learning organization.* New York: Doubleday Currency.

Shulman, L. (1994, January). Portfolios in historical perspective. Presentation at the Portfolios in Teaching and Teacher Education conference, Cambridge, MA.

Sizer, T. (1992). *Horace's school: Redesigning the American high school.* New York: Houghton Mifflin.

Stallings, J. A., & Kowalski, T. (1990). Research on professional development schools. In W. R. Houston (Ed.), *Handbook of research on teacher education* (pp. 251–266). New York: Macmillan.

Stroble, E. (1995). Portfolio pedagogy: Assembled evidence and unintended consequences. *Teaching Education, 7*(2), 97–102.

Stroble, E., Fischetti, J., Collins, G., & Keill, K. (1994, April). *Making teacher education real: Assessing preservice teachers' growth in a school-based program.* Paper presented at the annual meeting of the American Educational Research Association, New Orleans.

Wheatley, M. J. (1994). *Leadership and the new science: Learning about organization from an orderly universe.* San Francisco: Berrett-Koehler.

Whitford, B. L. (1994). Permission, persistence, and resistance: Linking high school restructuring with teacher education reform. In L. Darling-Hammond (Ed.), *Professional development schools: Schools for developing a profession* (pp. 74–97). New York: Teachers College Press.

Wise, A. E., Darling-Hammond, L., & Berry, B. (1987). *Effective teacher selection: From recruitment to retention.* Santa Monica, CA: RAND Corporation.

Wolf, D. (1994, January). *Creating a portfolio culture.* Presentation at the Portfolios in Teaching and Teacher Education Conference, Cambridge, MA.

Zuboff, S. (1988). *In the age of the smart machine: The future of work and power.* New York: Basic Books.

Part II

Building Professional Development Schools in the Context of Education Reform

Chapter 6

The Organization and Governance of Professional Development Schools

LEE TEITEL

The governance structures of Professional Development Schools sometimes have been affectionately called "systematic adhocracies" (Miller & Silvernail, 1994), a phrase that captures one of the issues and tensions in the organizing and running of PDSs. Many PDSs attribute their innovative spirit to their spontaneous, bottom-up roots. Yet without systematic connections between and within the institutions that developed them, PDSs may find themselves unable to promote institutional renewal or otherwise be woven into the fabric of their institutions.

For PDS participants, figuring out how best to organize and govern their school is a challenge for several reasons. PDSs are interorganizational collaborations, and the models for successfully linking two or more institutions are less well developed than those for intrainstitutional governance. Even in the best of circumstances, interorganizational relationships are often prone to breakdowns in communication, disagreements over resource allocations, differences in expectations, and so on. PDS partnerships add several overlays to the usual challenges of collaboration, since they represent two institutions committed to mutual renewal that are trying to expand professional development opportunities at both institutions, engage in research and development, and improve the education of schoolchildren and prospective teachers.

In addition, PDSs challenge the status quo and bring into question entire sets of assumptions about who is responsible for teacher education. In the traditional model, universities take primary responsibility for preparing new teachers, yet relegate student teaching — arguably the most important component of the teacher preparation experience — to cooperating teachers, who are often haphazardly or only tangentially connected to the college or university. Most important decisions about teacher preparation are made unilaterally, with a powerful disconnection between where the decisions are made and where they are implemented. To be effective, PDSs not only have to change two institutions (each of which is probably strongly resistant to change in its own right), but they have to change the nature of the ways those institutions work with each other: how they make decisions together and how they grow together to take a shared responsibility for teacher education.

The question that frames this chapter, then, is whether there are some approaches to governance that best support PDSs in making these changes in a lasting way.

The chapter is organized into three sections. The first examines the governance tasks faced by PDS partnerships, exploring why performing them can be so challenging. The second section is a brief survey of the governance models and approaches currently being used. The chapter concludes with some recommendations that do not identify one best model for PDS governance, but rather suggest a framework that may help PDS partnerships approach their evolving governance challenges more effectively. The framework indicates that governance is not static, but a mechanism whose definition must be reviewed periodically and revised to keep meeting the needs of the PDS and its partner organizations. Finally, and perhaps most important, I identify the core commitments — around a shared vision of teaching and student-centered learning, of simultaneous and mutual renewal, and of equity — that are, indeed, unchanging and that provide the guiding light for all PDS decisions.

GOVERNANCE IN PROFESSIONAL DEVELOPMENT SCHOOLS

The most extensive and well-developed body of literature about interorganizational relations (IOR), issues, and how best to address them grew out of the demands of the federal government in the 1970s for coordination among public sector agencies delivering related services (Schermerhorn, 1979; Whetten, 1981). This literature provides a useful base for discussions about governance in Professional Development Schools by identifying tensions that would tend to affect any collaboration.

Tensions Between Informal, Personal Connections and Formal, Structural Ones

Partnerships are made by people who look outside the boundaries of their own organization and see that the benefits of collaboration with others outweigh the costs. Partnerships, especially in the beginning, are often based on strong personal connections between one or a few individuals from each organization. Thus, if relationship activities are not structured into job descriptions, partnerships are highly susceptible to staff turnover (Whetten, 1981).

In Professional Development Schools, tensions are heightened because schools must work with universities and sometimes other external groups, as well as develop new linkages within their districts; universities must link with schools and sometimes outside agencies, and with other subunits within them, such as faculties of arts and sciences or of nursing or social work. Fostering the necessary personal interactions may be difficult, and providing a structural context for the relationship may be even more challenging. The low status that teacher education has in the university, and that professional development activities have in schools, can make these connections harder to establish (Darling-Hammond, 1994).

Tensions Between the Status Quo and Change. Partnership efforts exist on a continuum, ranging from low levels of cooperation ("mutual adjustment") to higher levels of collaboration (Rogers & Whetten, 1982). In PDSs, examples of mutual adjustment might be a university placing a cluster of student teachers in a single school without changing the approach to supervision or to any other aspects of the student teachers' experience, or a university agreeing to allow an interested faculty member to teach an existing course on site at the school. These are minor mutual adjustments that do not challenge the status quo in either institution. In partnerships closer to the collaborative end of the spectrum, the school and the university would meet to jointly plan common activities, with the understanding and expectation that the activities would be different from "business as usual" because they were being done jointly. More fully developed PDSs are further along the continuum toward collaboration and recognize that governance has to promote a real change agenda whose goal is the renewal of both organizations.

Tensions Between Marginalization and Centrality. It is much easier to set up partnerships on the fringes of organizations, but harder for marginalized partnerships to bring about change at either institution. Darling-Hammond (1994) sums this up as follows:

> The usual dilemma of school reform is magnified here. Because new ideas and projects threaten the "behavioral and programmatic regularities" of schools (Sarason, 1982), they frequently need to be created at the margins of the institution so they can be ignored long enough to take root. The dilemma, of course, is that if [new] initiatives continue to live at the periphery of the

organization, they fail at their overall mission. In the case of the PDS, the difficulties are doubled, since it is the core of two previously separate institutions which must be infiltrated, connected and simultaneously transformed. (p. 22)

Tensions Between Dissimilar Organizations. The IOR literature highlights how much harder it is to form collaborations between dissimilar organizations that differ in philosophy, culture, goals, and organizational structure. Yet schools and universities are very different.

> The missions of the two groups of institutions that seem to be logically linked, are, in fact, different. Each group of institutions has different reference groups, different governance and control mechanisms, different financing, and radically different reward structures. Tasks involved in renewal are vulnerable to the imperatives of separate missions. (Herman, Dowhower, Killian, & Badiali, 1994, p. 64)

Schools and school districts usually have more hierarchical decision-making structures than do universities, increasing the chances of conflict. Educators from schools and from universities are likely to have differing views on what constitutes knowledge, on theory and practice, on what kind of research or documentation constitutes evidence. Institutional differences in focus, tempo, reward, and power are so pronounced that Brookhart and Loadman (1989) describe school–university collaboration as "multi-cultural education."

The Ladder of PDS Decision Making

Besides considering the tensions inherent in interorganizational relations, it is also useful to look specifically at what decisions get made, by whom, and how. The concept of a "ladder of decision making" illuminates very specifically the concept of shared decision making in the PDS context.

Some PDS decisions are self-contained, with only a limited impact on the rest of the workings of the school or university. Matching student teachers with cooperating mentors and selecting the content of field-based courses are examples. But as PDSs move beyond these mutual adjustment-type choices, and begin to explore broader aspects of the PDS change agenda, decisions will have greater impacts. As they develop, PDSs may begin to explore the whole scope and sequence of the teacher education curriculum, or push for a greater role in the budgeting processes in their districts. It helps to view the types of decisions made by PDSs as being on a hierarchy, or ladder, where decisions on each successive rung mean wider impact and higher stakes.

The following (adapted from a suggestion by Lynne Miller) is a ladder of decision making from the perspective of a university involved with teacher education:

Higher Stakes/Higher Impact

- Certification of, and accountability for, new teachers
- Continuation of teacher candidates (establishing what counts as successful completion of courses, or practica)
- Admission of teacher candidates
- Overall teacher education curriculum
- Budgeting
- Curriculum or instruction decisions about a course taught at college
- Curriculum or instruction decision about a field-based methods course
- Field placement decisions

Lower Stakes/Lower Impact

This ladder of decision making is an illustration of a useful concept, not an exhaustive list of the choices facing PDSs. Within each of its broad categories, there would be whole subsets of decisions, each with its own hierarchy. For instance, field placement decisions might include a number of subissues (from higher to lower stakes): placement with specific teachers (and who decides), length of placements (one semester or a school year), blend of placements (mixes of urban, suburban, etc.), expectations of student teacher work during the placement, and so forth. The ladder of decision making is useful even though at different institutions (or between individuals or groups at the same institution) there may be disagreements about the relative position of items. For instance, some would argue that budgeting was more of a high-stakes decision than overall curriculum, or that length of placements had greater impact than deciding on the mix of urban and suburban placements.

Identifying something as a lower-stakes/lower-impact decision does not imply that it is unimportant or deny the powerful symbolic role that making any joint decision may have in some partnerships. Decisions on low-stakes matters are usually an ideal place for partnerships to start to develop their collaboration. By focusing attention on the substance of governance, the ladder of decision making provides a useful window on the state of the PDS partnership and governance. The ladder shown above focuses on the university view of one of the key elements of a PDS: the preparation of new teachers. Comparable ladders could be built for other PDS functions, such as the professional development of experienced educators at school and college, improvement of education for K–12 students, or exploration of a research agenda. The ladder can be refined to look at different levels of collaboration around decision making: Some decisions will be unilateral; others will be jointly decided as equal partners; for still others, one partner may take lead responsibility while consulting with the other.

The comparable ladder for school district decision making might include high-stakes issues like resource allocations, staffing, curricula, and so forth, as well as relatively lower-stakes decisions about which teacher gets a student teacher. The hierarchical ladder makes discussions of parity more concrete, illustrating, for instance, whether the PDS partnership is making high-stakes decisions in areas that were formerly the university's domain, but is limited to low-stakes school district decisions.

Overall, PDSs need to be attentive to the challenges of simultaneous and mutual organizational change, and to provide opportunities for partners to play new roles in each other's processes, without getting stuck at low-stakes decision making, which can stymie any real mutual change.

MODELS OF PDS GOVERNANCE

There are three basic PDS governance mechanisms: liaisons, school or site steering committees, and multisite coordinating councils. They are not mutually exclusive and, indeed, some PDS partnerships have all three. In this section, I describe each mechanism, and discuss the types of decisions commonly made using that approach and the advantages and disadvantages of each in furthering the partnership. The section concludes with a look at some emerging approaches to PDSs that seek to more radically alter the status quo.

Liaisons

Liaisons and the person-to-person contact they engender are very important ways of connecting schools and colleges involved in PDS partnerships. From the university side, the liaison is typically a faculty member with a quarter- or half-time commitment, who usually spends the equivalent of a day a week at a site, sometimes augmenting the facilitating role by conducting research in the PDS, or participating in a study group or some other sort of staff development activity. In some cases, university classes are taught at the school site, or the liaison is a supervisor of student teachers, so faculty members go there more often. A school liaison, if one is assigned, is typically a classroom teacher (occasionally an administrator) who coordinates the placement of student teachers and interns, arranges on-site seminars, and often facilitates faculty professional development. School liaisons usually do this work on top of their regular teaching load, although in some PDSs they have part-time releases.

Most PDSs have formally designated university liaisons; some have school liaisons and some both. The range of decisions made by liaisons, as well as their scope and authority, vary from site to site. Usually, when liaisons operate without steering committees or broader coordinating councils, their scope is limited to low-stakes decisions about day-to-day operations of the PDS. They may choose how to use the time they personally devote to the PDS, may plan workshops, and may have discretion over a small budget. For decisions that involve greater resources or other people, liaisons generally need to consult with deans, principals, or other decision-making bodies.

Typically, the strong personal connection that develops between the school and college liaisons serves as the linchpin of the partnership and the connecting point of each organization. Liaisons have the tasks of involving others in their own institution and of interpreting for them the culture of the other institution. In PDSs where there is a university-based and a school-based liaison, sometimes the powerful personal link between the liaisons becomes the de facto governance structure, even if there is also a steering committee. When there is only one liaison (usually from the university side), this de facto decision making can still take place, but only from one side.

The primary advantage of a liaison structure comes from the personal connections that help transcend the organizational boundaries. The university liaison, for instance, often becomes the personification of the university, making a distant institution concrete and palpable. When they work with each other well, the liaisons often can make decisions quickly and easily. Frequently they also have a fair amount of autonomy, unless their decisions or plans start to lead to changes that affect more people in their institutions.

The liaison approach also has a number of drawbacks. The people with the time and energy for the day-to-day work as liaisons in PDSs often do not have much positional power within their own organizations; in some cases, no real structural legitimacy has been given to the role. Since the PDS initiative can come to be seen as the liaison's individual "project," the liaison's lack of structural legitimacy may mean that decisions that affect others may be difficult to implement.

Turnover is always a potential problem with liaisons. The model that Berry and Catoe (1994) described at the University of South Carolina is typical of many PDSs: College of education faculty members "act as individual partners with their respective schools, and if a faculty member were to cease working with the school, then progress would probably come to a grinding halt" (p. 178).

The sheer amount of time and effort that partnership and PDS development take represents a third disadvantage. Liaisons often are stretched with the new and seemingly endless demands of PDS formation, while still needing to meet the rest of their obligations to their own institutions and positions. Further, disproportionate numbers of liaisons are untenured in many universities, but it remains unclear how much PDS work really counts for tenure.

School or Site-Based Steering Committees

Many PDS partnerships start with some form of liaison structure and evolve into the use of a steering committee. Others establish steering committees from the outset, as ways of broadening input and involvement, gaining legitimacy, and helping to ease transitions when a liaison leaves. At the simplest level of a partnership between one school and one college or university, steering committees typically comprise the school and university liaisons, several school-based faculty members, one or more university faculty members, and the principal or another building administrator. More developed PDSs may have an increased university presence on the committee, such as graduate students and faculty members from arts and sciences or the health professions. Other members may be parents and representatives of external organizations involved in the partnership. Usually a steering committee will meet at the school regularly to deal with all the details of the collaboration. Because these building-based steering committees typically have only one or two representatives from the university, many of the advantages and disadvantages described above in the university-based liaison model also apply.

Steering committees typically deal with the day-to-day decisions of running the PDS as well as some of the longer-range issues. Committees usually are involved with student teacher placement and the planning of professional development activities. In addition, in more developed PDSs that are embracing a simultaneous renewal agenda, committees have responsibility for the broader school or university improvement agenda, focusing, for instance, on curriculum and instruction at both institutions or pursuing a joint action-research agenda.

Steering committees can be useful mechanisms to involve others, within the school or university, or in the community, among parents or other stakeholders. The Michigan Partnership, for instance, recommends that its constituent PDSs invite community and business members to sit on the steering committees that make decisions about the school (Grant, 1994). In Cambridge, Massachusetts, parent liaisons (a paid part-time position in each school) sit on the steering committee that each school has with its college partner (Bromfield, 1994). At the University of Louisville, steering committees help connect PDSs to the Wellness Project, which tries to move toward "full-service schools," by bringing in other representatives from the medical, nursing, and dental schools and other units of the university as well as community agencies (Whitford, 1994). In some states, including Wyoming and Hawaii, representatives of the state departments of education play active roles on PDS steering committees (Dolly & Port, 1994; Porter & Collins, 1994).

In addition to providing greater involvement of others, steering committees offer increased legitimacy for the decisions that are made, sometimes because their members have positional power as principals and deans. Legitimacy also can result from the committee's formation by some consensus process or a higher authority. The involvement of more people also means a broader division of labor and a smoother transition in case of departure.

Since they are dedicated to the development of the PDS, steering committees can maintain a strong task focus. But this also can be a disadvantage, since in some settings committees duplicate existing governance structures, such as school improvement councils. Separate committees take up time, and schools that are restructuring can be overwhelmed by a sense of too many groups, too many projects, too many committees. Furthermore, the work of separate PDS steering committees may be less connected to the mainstream of the school or college than if the work was embedded into the existing governance structures. Some partnerships begin with a separate PDS steering committee and then integrate it into regular governance, or they set up semiautonomous PDS steering committees as subcommittees of the school improvement council.

Another disadvantage of a steering committee in the eyes of some is that it adds a layer of bureaucracy that can stifle the spontaneity and bottom-up nature of PDS collaboration, which often benefits from the ad hoc contributions of participants as it develops.

Multisite Coordinating Councils

Liaisons and steering committees are most appropriate for PDSs that are isolated partnerships between one school and one college (and possibly a community agency). Multisite coordinating councils are best suited to the many PDSs that are part of multisite collaboratives. These projects may involve a large district and several colleges, or multidistrict, multicollege collaboratives, but more frequently they are centered around a university, like Indiana University with its 10 school sites, or the University of South Carolina with its 11.

In Cambridge, Massachusetts, where three area colleges have PDS links with one, two, and three Cambridge elementary schools, respectively, the six partnerships come together under a citywide coordinating council. The council comprises teachers from each school, some of the principals, city school officials, and representatives of the Cambridge Partnership, a business/education group that has supported the effort. Decisions that concern citywide policy or the work of all the colleges, or that might affect current or future grants, are made at the district-wide level. Each PDS school site also has a planning team of teachers, the principal, and one or more college faculty members that meets more frequently to consider school issues.

The Brookline/Boston Learning and Teaching Collaborative is an example of a partnership that is not solely college-based or district-based. It began as a partnership between a four-person team in one Brookline school and Wheelock College and expanded over the last nine years to include another college and eight more teams in five more schools in Brookline and Boston (Troen, Boles, & Larkin, 1995). The Learning and Teaching Collaborative has no school-level governance, since in many schools only one team is involved. A coordinating group meets quarterly and includes deans, assistant superintendents, teachers, and university supervisors and faculty, and sets policy for all sites. It has five subcommittees that meet to do work in between and to resolve issues or questions as they arise: budget, recruitment, professional development, parents, and public relations (Troen, Boles, & Larkin, 1995).

The district-based and multisite, multicollege collaboratives are the exceptions; more of the networks are centered around universities, as schools and colleges of education have established multiple PDS sites to ensure sufficient placement opportunities for their preservice teachers. They often combine liaisons and local-level steering committees with a broader coordinating council to shape collaborative-wide policy and recommend some parameters for school-site decision making. How these are organized and how much decision-making authority each has can vary considerably.

The Puget Sound Professional Development Center was planned by a group including a principal and a teacher from each middle school, six University of Washington College of Education faculty members, a union representative, one student from the existing teacher education and educational administration program, and a representative of the state's office of public instruction. The representative PSPDC-side "Steering Committee" focuses on larger policy issues; implementation is left to the site committees, which, for instance, can decide how to compensate supervisor and cooperating teachers, from the allotted funds (Grossman, 1994, p. 62).

At the University of South Carolina with 11 sites, PDS site councils make local level decisions about issues like placement of student teachers. A PDS planning council with at least a teacher or principal from each site, along with university liaisons, meets monthly to plan common activities like a summer professional development conference, but have little influence on high-stakes decisions that concern the university. For instance, decisions about whether to add more PDS sites (which has resource implications for the members) are made at the university without input from this group (Berry & Catoe, 1994).

In contrast, at the University of Southern Maine, decisions about most everything are made by a group in which all the teacher coordinators participate as equal members. This group makes broad policy for the Extended Teacher Education Program and includes its teacher coordinators in such high stakes decisions as promotion and tenure and the search for a new dean (Walters, 1995). The involvement in high stakes decisions led the former director of teacher education at USM to note that, "For all practical purposes, the teacher education program is planned and implemented by the site steering committee" while "governance and day to day management of teacher education has become localized in [each school district]" (Miller & Silvernail, 1994, p. 43).

Other university-based networks have backed away from the formal use of a coordinating committee. Winthrop University, for example, set up one at the beginning of its efforts to coordinate its six PDS relationships, but the committee has not been active. Instead, decision making takes place by what one faculty member calls "trickle-up" governance. Retreats are used, some of which pull together the planning teams for all the PDS sites; the associate dean meets monthly with the principals and (separately) with the university liaisons. Although they are planning to add more of a "solid governance structure," the PDS planners at Winthrop argue that the primary focus is to ensure that people understand, believe in, and have a voice in the process (Gottesman, Graham, Caldwell, Winecoff, Ferrante, & Nogy, 1994).

The existence of a coordinating council does not in itself mean that it will be used for high-stakes decisions. In fact, the existence of multiple levels of governance puts into high relief the issues of centralization and decentralization that suggest the need for an analytic framework like the ladder of decision making to help pinpoint what decisions are made at which level and by whom.

Emerging Approaches to PDS Governance

The liaisons, steering committees, and network coordinating councils described so far leave existing school and university structures intact, and offer ways to best link them. More radical approaches may be necessary to meet the challenges of forming a PDS and to fulfill its agenda of expanding professional development opportunities at both institutions, engaging in research and development, and improving the education of children, adolescents, and prospective teachers. In fact, pursuit of these goals may have far-reaching impacts on the way schools and colleges are organized. A few approaches to PDS governance suggest that substantial redesign of existing organizational structures is necessary for real collaboration and simultaneous renewal to take place. To some extent this has taken place on the school side, where it is common for schools to move from a hierarchical principal-driven structure to more of a shared decision-making approach. Many PDS networks require evidence of a shared governance system as a prerequisite for the participation of a school (Gottesman et al., 1994; see also Woloszyk & Davis, 1993).

Goodlad's (1990) proposal for a "center of pedagogy" represents a radical restructuring at the university level that specifically focuses on the simultaneous renewal agenda. Goodlad sees the lack of "a clearly identifiable group of academic and clinical faculty members for whom education is the top priority" as the "most serious deficiency in all programs" (p. 276). The creation of centers of pedagogy calls for major structural reorganization, with profound implications for governance, personnel, and resource issues. Several of the universities participating in the National Network for Educational Renewal have begun the process of making those structural changes. Metropolitan State College of Denver, for instance, has reorganized its Department of Teacher Education, identified faculty with appointments in the School of Letters, Arts, and Sciences whose primary responsibility is teacher education, and pulled them together into a newly created Professional Education Unit. Representatives of these faculty members and their department chairs, along with students from the teacher education program and partnership school faculty, constitute a Professional Education Council. This "broadened membership in decision-making for teacher education" set the stage, according to O'Shea, Taylor, and Foster (1994), for a "new institution-wide commitment to change in the preparation of teachers" (p. 34). They go on to note that the college can now work more effectively with its 13 partner schools, many of which "had been waiting on the sidelines for the College to clear up its governance problems."

This sort of major restructuring is not simple to implement and can have unexpected impacts. Roper and Davidman (1994) describe how creating the University Center for Teacher Education at Cal Poly in San Luis Obispo, California, involved obstacles over information flow, academic governance, union contracts, and personnel policy. Because so many university policies assume a departmental or college structure, the Center, which cuts across those lines, found itself out of the information loop, disenfranchised, and uncertain about how promotion and tenure issues should be resolved for faculty coming from other disciplines but working in teacher education. Roper and Davidman note the progress they made in resolving these issues, not without observing the irony that at times their attempt to organize teacher education into a center to give it more centrality and importance in the university instead had the effect of making it more peripheral. Other accounts of the development of centers of pedagogy by institutions in the National Network for Educational Renewal are reported in a special edition of the *Record in Educational Leadership* in Spring/ Summer 1994, and highlight the promise, as well as the pitfalls, of these early steps toward restructuring attempts at the college or university side.

CONCLUSIONS AND RECOMMENDATIONS

PDSs are dynamic, growing entities with tremendous potential to renew schools and teacher education simultaneously. The governance structures of PDSs have powerful, and often conflicting, demands on them. Participants in PDSs have developed a number of creative governance approaches to address. Although it is too soon to try to correlate governance approaches with specific types of PDS outcomes, or to attempt to draw conclusions about which approaches work best in which situations, there are useful lessons to be learned.

These lessons are important not only for the development of PDSs in individual schools and colleges, but as part of a move toward the professionalization of teaching. If a key part of being in a profession is playing a role in establishing entry criteria, standards, and policy, then teachers need to play dramatically increased governance roles. Governance necessarily begins at home: Teachers taking an active part in shaping their own PDSs are gaining vital expertise in a collaborative leadership approach that can and should contribute to a broader governance structure for the profession. Shared governance over the preparation and qualifications of those who will become teachers is an important move in the direction of professional accountability. This is a major change, with high stakes and significant implications for the profession.

In contrast to the way that historically a few teachers were screened and selected to serve quasi-administrative roles or to focus on administratively sanctioned special projects (in curriculum development, for instance), leadership in PDSs is more broadly inclusive and presumed for many teachers. At work is nothing less than a redefinition of what a professional teacher is: one who performs a substantial role outside of the classroom in addition to teaching. Indeed, two teacher leaders active in founding the Learning/Teaching Collaborative PDS in Brookline/Boston have proposed that the National Policy Board for Professional Teaching Standards include a sixth "proposition," defining standards for what teachers should know and be able to do: "Teachers are leaders who reform their work, facilitate the development of others, and have influence in domains outside the classroom" (Troen & Boles, 1994, p. 14).

Darling-Hammond, Cobb, and Bullmaster (1995) suggest that what may be the most important part of the process whereby PDSs move along a continuum from "rigid, top-down structures to more collegial, teacher-participatory approaches" is for teachers to gain

> access to images of what is possible and an openness to seize opportunities for participation, inquiry and engagement in the continual rethinking of teaching and learning. As teachers grab hold of these emerging, unexpected opportunities, the possibilities for leadership may grow, and with them the possibilities for a profession of teaching committed to ongoing inquiry and invention in support of student success. (p. 34)

Although the specific form of such a governance structure for the teaching profession falls outside the scope of this chapter, it would have a good deal in common with the considerations for local governance recommended here. Below I suggest a framework for helping PDS participants evolve structures to help partnerships reach their goals.

My conclusions are shaped by the belief that to realize their potential to improve schools, the preparation of teachers, and the professionalization of teaching, PDSs need to move in from the margins of their school and university creators and become central to both. This means involving more and more people from both institutions and overcoming the cultural chasm between them. The many goals of PDSs will be served best only if school and university people take seriously the notion of simultaneous and mutual renewal and share decision making at all levels of the organization. Finally, I believe that for PDSs to be effective in promoting the simultaneous renewal of schools and teacher education, they must be institutionalized and woven into the fabric of schools and universities.

These beliefs lead me to return to the fundamental questions that frame this chapter: Are there some approaches to governance that best support PDSs in making change in a lasting way? Or, more explicitly, do PDSs need formal, stable, and powerful governance structures to become institutionalized? I began writing this chapter implicitly answering "yes" to this question, although I now see other possibilities. Even the word *institutionalization* implies a structural model that I see now as relied on too heavily. PDSs need to be woven into the fabric of the school and university not as rigid, inflexible structures but as dynamic and vibrant parts of the mission and operation of each institution.

So, rather than thinking of PDS governance in terms of a particular structure, it is useful to consider it as a starting point and a direction. Structures that work well in one setting will not necessarily transfer well to another, and, more important, structures that work well at one stage of a PDS partnership will not necessarily continue to be effective as the PDS evolves. For instance, the governance model that might have worked well for a small marginalized start-up PDS may be inadequate to the tasks of managing a larger, more central partnership. PDSs need to be fluid in their structures, but consistent in the visions and goals and directions in which they seek to move. Specifically:

- PDSs need multiple, personal connections and need to constantly engage the widest participation possible. Whatever the starting point, PDS advocates need to move toward greater and greater involvement of their colleagues from all partnership organizations, drawing them into contact with one another, and building those contacts into relationships. The boundary between two organizations should not be the narrow intersection of the liaisons and a handful of others, but the longest possible border, with multiple large and small connections. This engagement of many people is not only important in changing the culture of the collaborating institutions, but critical to developing a web of connections and relationships to help sustain the PDS and support the kind of flexible institutionalization that is needed.
- PDSs need legitimacy within their own organizations, especially for making higher-stakes decisions, so PDS advocates need to steadily seek recognition and legitimatization at the appropriate levels of power within each institution, and to move their school in the direction of embedding or at least integrating their work into existing structures. Doing so will not always be possible in the beginning, but it should be a goal of governance. One step can be setting up a PDS subcommittee of the school- or

district-based planning team, or of the appropriate body of the college or department of education. The direction should be toward obtaining sanction and high-level involvement, and toward being active and present on the agenda of each institution's governance bodies.

- PDSs embody core commitments around a shared vision of teaching and student-centered learning, of simultaneous and mutual renewal, and of equity. Thus, PDS actions and processes must constantly reconnect to those core commitments. The vision needs to be shared, with new participants socialized into the nature of the commitments, and not simply trained to engage in PDS activities.

- PDSs can easily get "stuck" at low-stakes decision-making levels, so advocates should use the ladder of decision making as a tool to help assess the decision-making process and to understand how best to move the partners in the direction of genuine simultaneous and mutual renewal. PDSs need some force that will keep them revisiting their progress toward the directions they set. This may be the task of a visionary leader, or of a person who is the designated "nudge." It may come through involvement in a network or through interaction with "critical friends" who periodically visit and promote the kind of dialogue that keeps movement and change on the agenda.

A final story illustrates what effective PDS governance might look like in real life and demonstrates how a direction and movement toward a PDS can transcend specific structural approaches. Wheelock College in Boston began its involvement with Professional Development School partnerships 8 years ago in a collaboration that involved one (part-time) Wheelock faculty member and a four-person team of teachers in Brookline. That relationship has grown to become the Learning/Teaching Collaborative (described above and in Chapter 3 of this volume), which is governed by a steering committee that includes central office personnel from two districts, deans and other faculty from two colleges, and representatives of nine teams in six schools.

In addition, Wheelock has more than a dozen other PDSs, which have very different kinds of governance structures. Some have developed as part of the Cambridge Partnership relationships (also described earlier), which are governed by school-based steering committees as well as a district-based coordinating group. Several more PDSs are part of the Teachers of Students with Special Needs program, which is run by a management team of representatives of the faculty, admissions office, field placement office, and financial aid office (Troen, Boles, & Larkin, 1995). A few more PDSs are "independent," usually having grown out of informal linkages between school and college faculty. Although the degree of formalization and the structure and governance of these PDSs vary enormously, what connects them is a growing commitment to a collaborative ideal of working closely with schools to improve the lives of children and families and of involving the voice of practice in the teaching of the college. School-based teachers have been very vocal in ensuring that the partnerships are mutual; they have pushed for roles in decision making and to have the partnerships make increasingly higher-stakes decisions collaboratively.

All these apparently disparate PDS partnerships are starting to have a powerful integrated and interactive impact. Wheelock's graduate dean, Mario Borunda, has become a passionate advocate for PDSs and has recently begun to set up meetings that pull together all the different Wheelock-related PDS initiatives. He sums up the types of interconnections he envisions:

> Although the structures are very different, I see all these PDSs moving toward a similar form — not at the detail level, but up one, at the concept level. We are working at the college on this conceptual overview, bringing together all these different PDSs — not to try to standardize their structures, but to pull together and help fill in the pieces of our direction together.

Because of the proliferation of PDSs, more than half of the Wheelock faculty are involved with one or more partnerships; dozens of school-based educators are playing increasingly important roles in planning, teaching, and serving on committees at Wheelock. A powerful and growing sense of shared commitments, combined with the multiple personal connections that have been established, increases the likelihood that the PDSs will be able to make real changes in the participating institutions and that they can survive turnover or departure of key individuals.

The story of Wheelock and its partner schools helps put issues of structure and governance into perspective. It illustrates how PDSs can move toward a flexible form of institutionalization, not on a solely structural path, but through common vision, strong commitments, multiple personal connections, increasing support of people in positions of power, and a willingness to consider and move toward higher stakes joint decision making. It highlights the potential that can be found in the definition that Miller and Silvernail (1994) provide for "systematic adhocism."

> Systematic ad hocism is characterized by having a map, rather than an itinerary, being long-range, being adaptive, and being values-based. This approach to planning has . . . enabled experimentation and risk-taking and encouraged authentic partnership. Most importantly, it has encouraged constant assess-

ment and invention—which may be essential ingredients in the transformation of teacher education. (p. 48)

I wish to thank a number of colleagues who provided background information or who otherwise shaped my thinking on these issues of governance: Barnett Berry, Mario Borunda, Liz Larkin, Marsha Levine, Sandra Spooner, and Vivian Troen. A special thanks to Lynne Miller and a dozen other participants at a workshop session on Models of PDS Governance as part of the New England Conference on Professional Development School/College Partnerships (May 5–6, 1995). Their feedback and suggestions on an early version of this chapter were very important influences on my thinking about these issues.

REFERENCES

Berry B., & Catoe, S. (1994). Creating professional development schools: Policy and practice in South Carolina's PDS initiatives. In L. Darling-Hammond (Ed.), *Professional development schools: Schools for developing a profession* (pp. 176–202). New York: Teachers College Press.

Bromfield, M. (1994, April). Presentation at the Starting and Sustaining a Professional Development School mini-course at the annual meeting of the American Educational Research Association, New Orleans.

Brookhart, S., & Loadman, W. (1989, April). *School university collaboration: Why it's multicultural education*. Paper presented at the annual meeting of the American Educational Research Association, San Francisco.

Darling-Hammond, L. (Ed.). (1994). *Professional development schools: Schools for developing a profession*. New York: Teachers College Press.

Darling-Hammond L., Cobb, V., & Bullmaster, M. (1995). Rethinking teacher leadership through professional development schools. *The Elementary School Journal, 96*(1), 87–106.

Dolly, J., & Port, A. (1994, Spring/Summer). Restructuring teacher education at the University of Hawaii. *Record in Educational Leadership, 14*(2), 37–40.

Goodlad, J. (1990). *Teachers for our nation's schools*. San Francisco: Jossey-Bass.

Gottesman, B., Graham, P., Caldwell, B., Winecoff, S., Ferrante, R. A., & Nogy, C. (1994, Spring/Summer). The big picture: The South Carolina collaborative to renew teacher education. *Record in Educational Leadership, 14*(2), 67–76.

Grant, J. (1994, April). Presentation at the Starting and Sustaining a Professional Development School mini-course at the annual meeting of the American Educational Research Association, New Orleans.

Grossman, P. (1994). In pursuit of a dual agenda: Creating a middle level professional development school. In L. Darling-Hammond (Ed.), *Professional development schools: Schools for developing a profession* (pp. 50–73). New York: Teachers College Press.

Herman, S. J., Dowhower, S. L., Killian, D. L., & Badiali, B. J. (1994, Spring/Summer). Liaisons: A journey in nurturing university–school partnerships. *Record in Educational Leadership, 14*(2), 63–66.

Miller, L., & Silvernail, D. (1994). Wells Junior High School: Evolution of a professional development school. In L. Darling-Hammond (Ed.), *Professional development schools: Schools for developing a profession* (pp. 28–49). New York: Teachers College Press.

O'Shea, M., Taylor, M., & Foster, J. (1994, Spring/Summer). Barriers and breakthroughs to educational renewal at Metropolitan State College. *Record in Educational Leadership, 14*(2), 32–36.

Porter, W., & Collins, J. (1994, Spring/Summer). The Wyoming partnership: Centers for teaching and learning. *Record in Educational Leadership, 14*(2), 90–93.

Record in Educational Leadership. (1994, Spring/Summer). National Network for Educational Renewal. Dayton, OH: Wright State University.

Rogers, D., & Whetten, D. (1982). *Interorganizational coordination: Theory, research and implementation.* Ames: Iowa State University.

Roper, S., & Davidman, L. (1994, Spring/Summer). The University Center for Teacher Education: An organizational catalyst for change. *Record in Educational Leadership, 14*(2), 23–26.

Schermerhorn, J. (1979, Spring). Interorganizational development. *Journal of Management, 5*(1), 21–38.

Troen, V., & Boles, K. (1994). *The case for including teacher leadership as a criterion for national board certification: Introducing proposition six.* Discussion paper prepared for the Education Policy and Reform Working Group of the National Policy Board for Professional Teaching Standards.

Troen, V., Boles, K., & Larkin, E. (1995, April). Boundary spanners in professional development schools. Paper presented at the annual meeting of the American Educational Research Association, San Francisco.

Walters, S. (1995, April). *Walking the fault line: Boundary spanning in professional development schools.* Paper presented at the annual meeting of the American Educational Research Association, San Francisco.

Whetten, D. (1981). Interorganizational relations: A review of the field. *Journal of Higher Education, 52*(1), 1–28.

Whitford, B. L. (1994, April). Presentation at the Starting and Sustaining a Professional Development School mini-course at the annual meeting of the American Educational Research Association, New Orleans.

Woloszyk, C. A., & Davis, S. (1993, February). *Implementing institutional change through the professional development school concept.* Paper presented at the annual meeting of the American Association of Colleges for Teacher Education, San Diego.

Chapter 7

Professional Development Schools: Their Costs and Financing

RICHARD W. CLARK AND MARGARET L. PLECKI

During recent years of school reform, the four core components of Professional Development Schools — school renewal, restructured preservice education, professional development, and research and inquiry (Clark, 1995) — have been reviewed extensively. To date, there has been little written about Professional Development School financing, however. Here, in an effort to fill the gap, we briefly review the state of education reform and funding over the decade following publication of *A Nation at Risk* (National Commission on Excellence in Education, 1983), and then examine the costs associated with the development and operation of different types of PDSs and the many variables that affect these costs. Further, we identify costs borne by the school districts and universities that manage the PDSs, and the sometimes considerable savings and other benefits that accrue, again based on the many context, program, and economic variables that make each school unique. Finally, we discuss the overall — but sometimes largely intangible — value of PDSs, in terms of both generating a well-prepared, highly qualified, and committed pool of teachers and providing a richer education experience for a diverse student population.

SCHOOL REFORM AND EDUCATION FUNDING

Before discussing PDS funding specifically, it is useful to put it into context by providing some perspective on the overall state of reform and funding of education. Education in the United States is directed by a complex web of policy makers and funded through an equally complex set of national, state, local, and private funders. When decisions need to be made about which particular approaches to reform to attempt, and how to fund them, different parties advocate different solutions (Clark, 1988). Therefore, it is impossible to present a list of discrete strategies, or to describe precisely how the various reform efforts have been funded. What is clear, however, is that K–12 and higher education reforms seem, in three ways, to parallel reforms in education financing.

Since 1983, reform efforts in both area have been made to: (1) add more, (2) address issues of equity, and (3) either centralize or decentralize decision making.

Add More

Less than 3 years after the release of the landmark national report, *A Nation at Risk* (National Commission on Excellence in Education, 1983), and in the midst of an avalanche of reports that followed close on its heels, Odden (1986) noted that all the states expanded their school improvement programs, nearly all increased high school graduation requirements, most stiffened college admission requirements, many deepened the content of course offerings, and many enacted a variety of policies to strengthen the teaching profession. On top of this first wave of reform, subsequent initiatives added new emphases on staff development, teaching methods, teacher empowerment, and calls for higher levels of student performance to catch up with students in other nations. Special services also were added to address problems of violence in schools, respond to a growing crisis of drug abuse, and react to health problems such as AIDS. Younger children were included, causing the common reference to schools as K–12 to change to P–12, in recognition of the growing prevalence of preschools.

Meanwhile, in teacher education, additions also were made. Various members of the Holmes Group (1990) began experimenting with 5-year and graduate-level initial certification programs. Commonly, students were expected to complete majors in a subject-matter field rather than in education. States such as Washington passed legislation requiring master's degrees for initial certification. States such as Minnesota began to add a residence year after initial certification to requirements for teacher preparation. Institutions in those states, while claiming that their preparation programs were undergraduate programs, developed requirements so extensive that students frequently could not complete the required work in 4 years (Goodlad, 1990).

However, by the end of the decade after the publication of *A Nation at Risk*, the adding-more solution had lost favor among most reform advocates. There was dissatisfaction with the results of adding more requirements for K–12 students. Perhaps, people had begun to recognize that doing more of the same wrong thing was unproductive. Darling-Hammond and McLaughlin (1995) made this case well for both public school and university-based teacher development. As the second and third waves of reform moved forward, educators focused more on school renewal and staff development as necessary means of improving students' performance. As they did so, they began to recognize that these reform efforts needed to be closely linked.

For many of the same reasons that adding more lost favor in grades K–12, it began to be rejected as a solution to reforming teacher education. In Washington state, before the new requirement for a master's degree was fully implemented, new legislation was passed repealing it. Underlying much of the rejection of the adding-more solution at both K–12 and higher education levels were the high costs of trying to make reforms in this manner (Lewis, 1990; Verstegan, 1990). The possibility of more efficient school renewal and improved education for educators became one of the primary drivers of interest in PDSs.

Adding more also has a long history as a strategy of reform for education financing. During the 1980s, there were substantial increases in K–12 funding beyond that needed to meet inflation or educate additional pupils. Odden (1994) reported that "real dollars per pupil for the schools rose by 48 percent" (p. 1) for that period, and that the increase for the 10-year period ending in 1993–94 still was 47%. During this same timespan, private and corporate foundations began to invest in public school and teacher education reform efforts. Foundations such as Annenberg, the Pew Charitable Trusts, the DeWitt–Wallace Reader's Digest Fund, Annie E. Casey, Mac-Arthur, Carnegie, Exxon, and Rockefeller all have invested in a variety of K–12 and higher education reform efforts, making added funds available. In some instances these funders also began to influence reform policy in ways beyond simply giving money (McKersie, 1993).

At the time of this writing, however, it appears that the adding-more solution is unlikely to persist for either grades K–12 or higher education. Odden (1994) noted that state shares of school budgets had begun to decline as of 1992 and that there was a brewing revolt against raising local taxes. In fact, several states placed severe controls on the right of local communities to generate tax revenue. What new revenues were created at the state level seemed to be used to close gaps between income and expenditures, to build prisons, to offset federal reductions in areas such as health care, or to reduce the state tax burden on individuals. The elections of 1994 promised continuing reductions in spending at both the state and federal level (Pipho, 1995). These promises were kept by Congress and many state legislatures. The results of the national election of 1996 suggest continuing support for proponents of budget cutting. As publicly funded higher education was running into the same taxpayer resistance that faced K–12 schools, private schools were finding that their clients were rejecting continuing increases in tuition and fees.

In short, it appears that any approach to reform of K–12 or teacher education that is to be attempted in the near future should not count on adding more as a solution to either program reform needs or funding. Instead, it should seek ways of reallocating existing resources so that they bring better returns.

Equity

In the name of equity, courts and legislatures have mandated substantial reforms of school district structures and occasionally of specific practices within school districts and schools. Equity concerns have been fundamental in court and legislated decisions concerning the need for special attention for students whose primary language is not English, for students with special learning needs, and for students who are discriminated against because of race, religion, or gender. Such actions have affected both K–12 and higher education. Higher education has been particularly stung by the need to expand enrollment among underrepresented ethnic groups.

Equity issues have long dominated reform efforts in education financing. Most recently the courts have become major players regarding this issue. Between 1971 and 1991, 27 state school finance systems were challenged, and in 13 of those states courts found the inequities to be great enough to overturn then extant funding laws (Firestone, Goertz, Nagle, & Smelkinson, 1994). The most extensive of such suits led to the total overhaul of state educational systems, such as Kentucky's (Adams, 1994).

Equity issues have not been solved. Real differences persist, particularly in support of schools in rural and urban low socioeconomic areas. However, in keeping with the generally conservative political trend of the early 1990s, legislatures and courts have been narrowing the gap, not by advancing the causes of underrepresented parties but by lowering the expectations concerning equity that earlier laws and rulings had established. Thus, as funding efforts fall short of their intended goal of equal financial support for all public schools (Adams, 1994; Firestone et al., 1994; Picus, 1994), the likelihood that there will be increasing programmatic or financial support to obtain such equity has diminished.

Centralization or Decentralization

In a reform mode that is curiously typical of education in the United States, both centralizing and decentralizing reforms were advanced in the 1980s and 1990s.

Early in the reform effort, state initiatives often included mandated reductions in class size along with specified changes in educational requirements. Led by governors and the president, state and national goals were adopted and professional groups worked to develop "world-class" standards in various disciplines. Increasingly, as the reform effort moved forward, dissatisfaction with the bureaucracies at the state and local level led to bypassing these agencies in favor of site-based management and market-driven privatizing initiatives such as vouchers and charter schools.

While such changes were occurring in K–12 schools, renewed emphasis on national accreditation, expanded systems of state program approval, and newly empowered professional standards boards were centralizing influences affecting teacher education. Accompanying the development of a National Standards Board offering advanced certification were refined means of assessing teacher competency for initial entry into the profession and, seemingly contradictory, state legislation limiting the amount of professional training that could be required of prospective teachers.

While these centralizing influences were occurring, decentralizing trends could be noted as schools and universities created partnerships that developed Professional Development Schools. States also appeared to be giving up some of their control as they authorized alternative routes to entry into the profession. Some of these efforts, such as Teach for America, seemed to parallel the privatization trend in K–12 education. The continued active presence of entrepreneurial colleges offering shortcut teacher preparation programs demonstrated that the market can affect cost, but it also can have a negative effect on quality in some situations.

The simultaneous advance of centralized and decentralized programmatic efforts was accompanied by similar changes in funding. Federal and state categorical funding was sometimes targeted at certain student populations, as in the case of federal Chapter 1 funding for disadvantaged students. Sometimes state funds were aimed at specific programs such as mathematics, science, AIDS education, and technology, or for reductions in primary class size. Higher education experienced similar funding as, for example, in Texas where state-provided funding for Professional Development Schools focused heavily on the use of technology in such settings.

While such categorical funding persisted, and even expanded, legislation was being passed to promote site-based management of funds. Appropriations bypassed districts and went straight to schools and classrooms, and, in some cases, such as vouchers and charters, directly to parents. Conservatives urged that the marketplace should drive schooling. Block grants (decentralist in theory and centralist in practice) took existing categorical funds and distributed parts of them to schools to decide how they should be spent. This change in funding affecting higher education is most evident in federal funding, which empowered local schools to determine professional development needs and required higher education institutions that wished access to these funds to plan with the local schools that were receiving them.

While foundation funding was available for development of reforms in teacher education, in some instances colleges seeking public funds through initiatives such as the federal Goals 2000 found that they had to develop partnerships with local schools and obtain approval from professionally led councils.

TEACHER EDUCATION FUNDING

As these reform elements moved forward, the education of educators continued in its historically underfunded condition (Goodlad, 1990, 1994; Peseau, 1982). Peseau and Orr (1980) noted that educating a teacher education candidate cost less than half the average cost of educating a college student and about two-thirds of what it cost to educate a public school student. Berliner (1984) noted that it cost 13% less to educate a teacher at his institution than it cost to educate a liberal arts student. Peseau, Backman, and Fry (1987) concluded that the failure to recognize teacher preparation programs as clinical rather than classroom programs was a significant contributor to this historical underfunding.

Here we are considering the specific issue of financing Professional Development Schools, the clinical part of teacher education as well as a vehicle for school renewal, professional development, and research and inquiry. As we do so, it is important to keep in mind that in view of the general trend against increasing public expenditures and the historical tendency to underfund teacher education, a simple solution of increasing funding is unlikely. For example, even though efforts to increase equity respond to real societal needs, they are not likely to generate assistance in obtaining short-term financial support. We are also likely to continue to experience the ambiguous and sometimes conflicting centralist and decentralist expectations of policy makers. We may find cause for both hope and despair in Ralph Tyler's (1985) observations.

> We learned that the education of teachers could be greatly improved without large additional expenditures, if the staff of local teacher education institutions and school systems worked together to identify serious problems on which to focus their efforts and for which to develop solutions, i.e., programs that used local resources and that could be practicably implemented. What we learned more than 40 years ago seems to me to be worth careful consideration in improving the education of teachers today. (p. 684)

The hope resulting from the efficacy of school–university collaboration efforts in the first half of the twentieth century was diminished but not
eradicated by the fact that such programmatic and financial collaborations
are still not widespread.

PROFESSIONAL DEVELOPMENT SCHOOL FUNDING

There are varied approaches to Professional Development Schools,
leading to different costs for different schools. One of the reasons for the
persistent difficulties in obtaining funds for PDSs may be that there is
insufficient information about the costs of such schools and an inability to
accurately compare costs across PDSs because of different classification
and accounting methods. Further, financial analysis of Professional Development Schools requires a sequence of activities beginning with clarity
about what functions are to be pursued and proceeding to determination of
the sources for the needed funds. Such listing of activities implies that the
process is a linear one, while in practice it consists of advancing forward
several steps and then, based on new information, returning and revising
earlier conclusions. For example, it may turn out that insufficient funds to
satisfy earlier plans for the program can be obtained, requiring a revision
of the original proposal. Such reassessments make preparation of a firm
budget extremely difficult, and PDS developers may opt to direct their
energies at program rather than budget development, possibly to the detriment of fund-raising efforts.

To facilitate budget preparation, Theobald (1990) speculated about
costs required for PDSs and offered some model student and staffing arrangements that could be used in estimating costs. He then identified a
sample Professional Development School funding formula that takes into
account school district and university contributions to expenses associated
with preservice preparation programs. The formula does not address the
costs for other purposes, although he acknowledges their existence, such as
continuing education (professional development) for school system staff or
research/inquiry work. In a later writing Theobald (1991a) addressed in
more detail the specific problems created when colleges of education are
asked for funds to support the developmental costs of PDSs. Discussing
the economic implications of Professional Development Schools, Theobald
gave considerable attention to costs introduced by governance structures,
issues of faculty (school and college) load, and enrollment in terms of credit
hours. While his formulation of considerations with regard to this issue is
complex, it may not have taken into account all significant variables. The
following sections expand on Theobald's work and identify variables that

must be considered when determining costs prior to obtaining financing for a Professional Development School. Such additional analysis is necessary for state, district, and higher education institution policy makers to make sound decisions regarding financing the development and operation of Professional Development Schools.

PDS resources can usually be assigned to one of the following budget categories: one-time expenditures, marginal costs, opportunity costs, indirect costs, joint funding and in-kind contributions, or intangible resources.

One-Time Expenditures

A common PDS funding technique is to identify one-time-only expenses and then seek financial contributions for them. These contributions, called start-up funds or seed money, are provided to PDSs at the beginning of their development for such expenditures as telecommunications equipment, computers, or initial training of professional participants.

There are at least two ways to account for one-time needs and their funding. One way is to create a special budget category that contains all initial expenses. This method has the advantage of providing useful information to policy makers and funders who are interested in beginning or expanding PDSs. Since not all PDSs have access to start-up contributions, they ultimately may cover one-time costs through other means, such as in-kind contributions.

A second way to account for one-time expenses is to amortize their total value over their projected lifetime in order to arrive at an annual amount. For example, if a $10,000 contribution is needed for computer equipment for a PDS, and the equipment will be useful for 5 years, then it could be reflected as an expenditure of $2,000 per year for 5 years. While such an estimation may be relatively simple for goods (such as equipment), it is more problematic for services (such as professional training activities) whose years of value to the PDS are not so clear-cut.

Moreover, as indicated later, there is a tendency to overestimate the extent to which an expenditure is a one-time developmental cost. For example, initial training, although certainly a start-up expense, is also a recurring cost, as staff members turn over and program emphases shift.

Marginal Costs

Economic cost analysis begins with the determination of marginal costs, which represent the minimal level of resources necessary to provide services (Cohn & Geske, 1990). They are the expenses that would cease if the services were discontinued. For example, the marginal costs of operating a PDS would not include many of the facility costs because the school would continue serving K–12 students even if the PDS-related functions were eliminated. Obviously, some institutions provide services at a level greater than that supported by marginal costs, but in order to appropriately compare the costs of a variety of PDS models with a variety of traditional models of teacher education, it is important to determine the marginal costs involved in each type of program.

Opportunity Costs

Opportunity costs represent the trade-offs made when a particular approach to providing services is selected and others are rejected. For example, decisions regarding use of professional development time, school curriculum, responsibilities of the school principal, technological resources, faculty research and advising activities, and opportunities for school-university collaboration and school renewal often depend on the type of teacher education model used (e.g., PDS-based or traditional, 4-year or 5-year). If a PDS aims to provide a different type of teacher preparation, while at the same time providing benefits to all educators and students located in the school, then the value of these expanded services must be factored into the costs of the PDS before comparing them with the costs of similar services provided by a school that does not experience these PDS-related benefits.

Indirect Costs

In determining the costs of any major effort such as a PDS, indirect costs must be taken into account. These costs, such as for administrative support, payroll, accounting, and purchasing, are complicated by the presence of multiple agencies with different governance structures and sets of laws and regulations determining their operating procedures. The bureaucracies of both school districts and colleges generate their own costs that must be considered in determining the costs of developing and operating PDSs.

Joint Funding and In-Kind Contributions

PDSs typically have components that either are jointly funded by the university and the PDS or are provided as in-kind contributions. For example, the costs of university faculty time for preservice activities are usually shared by the university and the school. Determination of each partner's share of the expenses often is based on an average cost per faculty member and an estimation of the average time spent in providing service. While such a formula is reasonable when forging partnership agreements regarding cost sharing, the budgeted amounts will not mirror exactly the real costs once specific faculty members begin spending real time doing PDS work. Similarly, the value of in-kind contributions of time and other resources that often are part of PDS relationships, and the value of volunteer services, are likely to be best guesses rather than accurate assessments.

Intangible Resources

Nonfiscal resources contribute considerable value to a PDS, although they may never appear on the official balance sheet. They include such benefits as professional expertise and experience, nonmonetary incentives, individual commitment and motivation, articulation of curricular efforts, and collegiality and communication among professionals. Such resources are more difficult to identify and much harder to quantify so that they can be compared from model to model.

PDS PROGRAM AND COST VARIABLES

Professional Development School programs comprise many variables in several general categories that influence their costs.

Developmental Stage

The first consideration is whether the PDS is being developed or is operational; many of the other variables apply differentially depending on how mature it is. Early developmental or start-up efforts for a PDS require more time of college and school faculty. They require extensive communication with community members served by the school and often with the power structure of the college. Several years of conversations between college of education faculty and school-based faculty, with attendant costs, may be necessary to create a well-integrated field-academy effort.

Trial operations during the early stages usually serve fewer preservice students than do more mature operations, thus making the per-student costs higher. School and university faculty are hesitant to change habitual approaches to providing clinical experiences, so for a length of time there may be duplication as old and new programs operate simultaneously. In addition, many developmental costs not initially anticipated are incurred as problems arise and new plans need to be made.

Frequently, schools and colleges seek state or foundation support for this early stage. One such developmental effort, supported by the Ford Foundation, is discussed in some depth in *Voices of Change: A Report of the Clinical Schools Project* (Anderson, 1993). Levine (1992) edited another volume, *Professional Practice Schools: Linking Teacher Education and School Reform*, which includes case reports on the early developmental stages of such schools.

Developmental costs are relatively easy to estimate, partly because they are almost always added on to existing expenditures and include paying for discrete items. Examples of these costs are a one-time outlay for technology and professional development and school renewal activities. Still, there are no reliable reports of the extent of these costs across large numbers of PDSs, and it is reasonable to assume that they vary considerably depending on other conditions surrounding the PDS.

Location

The general setting in which a Professional Development School operates influences costs. Factors such as staff and student travel costs between the university campus and the PDS vary considerably. The extent of such variation may be most obvious in rural states such as Wyoming, where the university relocates significant numbers of preservice candidates to schools 300–400 miles from the main campus, affecting student living arrangements, staff travel and housing, and provision of support services to students.

Costs also vary when students in urban settings are primarily commuters and find themselves relocated to PDSs some distance from the college campus, and when students used to living on or near the campus have to seek transportation and/or housing near the PDS.

Ensuring safety for faculty and students, and obtaining instructional materials and access to experts to complement faculty, also may require differential expenditures depending on the setting of a PDS.

Cost of living also tends to vary from area to area, and these differences affect PDS costs in several ways. Salary and benefit costs are frequently (although not always) higher in urban and suburban than in rural or semirural areas. Per-student costs for P–12 education vary considerably among different states, partly because of variance in property wealth and different regional political priorities, affecting the costs of operating a PDS in different settings. For example, in 1991–92 the per-student costs for the 50 states ranged from a low of $2,827 in Utah to a high of $8,793 in New Jersey ("Estimates of Public School Statistics," 1992). Salary costs are the largest element of this differential; thus, a PDS in New Jersey will be much more costly than one in Utah.

The regulatory environment in which each PDS exists also affects costs. Specific requirements exist in some states for ratios of supervisors to student teachers, and faculty–student ratios are sometimes spelled out in regulations. Various elements of state program approval processes also may dictate some costs.

The location-related costs just discussed apply to each PDS in a multiple-site program. In addition, it may be necessary to consider more than the number of preservice students a setting will serve, the number of students to be placed at an individual PDS for various components, and the number of staff development students each PDS will serve. As the numbers at a particular location grow, the administrative support mechanism also may have to grow. At first, such growth may permit greater efficiency—it may take about the same amount of administrative effort to support one PDS as to support four or five. No readily available data answer the question of when the number of PDSs with which a particular college is working becomes so large that economies of scale do not pertain and bureaucratic inefficiency begins.

Type of University

Among state-funded institutions of higher education, the major research universities are the most costly, because of the added costs associated with graduate programs and research work. Theobald (1991a) described the difficult reallocation decisions facing such institutions that seek to provide additional funding to PDSs. Research institutions also tend to educate small numbers of teachers. Institutions such as regional universities, which prepare the largest numbers of teachers, have some advantages of economics of scale in their operations. Peseau and Tudor (1988) began work on identifying peer program comparisons that could be used to help deans negotiate their fair share of university resources. More investigation is needed into the relative cost of private and public institutions, not just from the standpoint of student tuition but in terms of per-student expenditures, and also into general per-student costs of teacher education by institution type. Studies to date make it clear that there are cost differences inherent in the nature of these different institutional types that also will affect the eventual cost of PDSs.

Grade Level

Generally speaking, increasing specialization at the secondary level has generated higher costs for high schools than for elementary schools. Costs for laboratory science and vocational programs have been the greatest contributor to this differential. In recent years, however, mandates by local and state officials to reduce class size in the primary grades have led to higher elementary education costs and a narrowing of the gap between the costs of the two school levels.

For PDSs the main effect of grade level on preservice components appears to be in the general size of schools at different levels. Because more preservice students can be assigned to larger schools, the tendency of high schools to be larger than elementary schools can lead to reduced costs for supervision of preservice candidates. For example, one person providing general supervision for 20 preservice elementary students may have to work with two to four schools, losing time traveling between them, while the same number of high school preservice candidates may all work in a single high school. Offsetting that apparent savings, however, is the tendency for secondary schools to require external subject-matter specialist supervisors, while elementary schools require generalists. Thus, for the aforementioned 20 candidates, conventional practices may lead to the assignment of six or seven different supervisors because of the subject-matter specialization of the candidates.

Numbers of Students/Clients

The number of students who can be accommodated at each PDS site for each component (administration, teaching, other) of the program is an important cost variable. Generally, new PDSs appear to underestimate the number of students who can be assigned to a site, sometimes limiting early preservice candidates to only three or four. Once there is agreement on mission and sharing of governance among PDS faculty, and the mutual benefits of engagement in the work are clear, many more candidates can be assigned to a school. For example, after several years of collaboration at Bulkeley High School in Hartford, Connecticut, its PDS serves as many as 87 graduate and undergraduate students from the University of Connecticut and also provides professional development opportunities for Hartford teachers.

Differences in numbers of people served by PDSs are a financial consideration, but the decisions concerning how many are served turn on more than economic considerations. For example, the climate of trust between school and university faculty and the integration of preservice and professional development programs have significant impacts.

Training and Supervision

Whether teachers, administrators, other educators, or some combination of these groups are served by the PDS affects the cost of a school.

While it costs more to serve more students, combining different clinical programs at a single site may generate some savings. Establishing and maintaining relationships with a school have associated costs for a college and a school district in terms of time to plan and coordinate efforts. Thus, if productive relationships have been established between a college and a school and school district, using the school to train administrators as well as teachers, for example, can generate savings.

Program decisions about on-site training and supervision also affect PDS costs, since costs vary depending on the specific kinds of instructional activities carried out. For example, if a PDS serves as a clinical setting for an administrative training program, interns assigned to work in the PDS may replace professional staff who would have been assigned to the school at higher costs. Depending on program design, two such interns could replace an assistant principal at a high school, simultaneously increasing adult–student ratios and reducing costs.

The type of training provided affects costs as much as the number of trainees does. For example, many trainees may be assigned to a school but spend only 2 days a week there, be only minimally supervised, and attend very few workshops. Some preservice students simply may sit in on classes where interns are trained, at no extra cost. Conversely, some training programs consist of extensive supervision and many workshops, which translate into significant program costs. The 87 students attending the Hartford PDS in a single semester range from juniors doing early practica in education to graduate students doing doctoral research in social work.

Care needs to be taken to consider the added services that may result from added program components and related costs. Extensive inclusion of social service interns in PDSs in several locations has proved to be an economical way for schools to extend more support to students. For example, at one PDS committed to integrating learning about professions serving young children, candidates in counseling, social work, nursing, and other professions interact with people at the school and in the local community.

Other Program Components

As indicated above, considerably more school and college staff time has to be devoted to support a student engaged in a practicum than one who is a member of a large class that uses the PDS to observe instruction. Research projects may entail more than just staffing costs; they may call for computer support, extended communications with parents, and preparation of reports. However, the kind of activity selected also may help create a funding source or result in savings in other areas. Preservice students working as tutors can be scheduled to replace staff paid for such activity; practitioners engaged in inquiry projects may obviate the need to hire outsiders to evaluate programs; interns may replace teachers in some situations or provide low-cost improvements in pupil–teacher ratios. While there are costs associated with each activity, the extent to which they are added costs or marginal costs depends very much on the creativity of the people designing the program. The question for the PDS becomes: What expenditures could disappear without altering the accomplishment of the identified goals?

What might be a cost for one PDS may not be for another, even though they both include the same program component, depending on the extent of the school–university partnership. For example, a partnership that administers one PDS also engages in more general professional development activity, and PDS-related professional development costs are assigned to the budget of the partnership instead of the school.

Course Time and Location

If the college considers a practicum a 13-credit hour course, it will cost more than if it is considered a 6-credit hour course. However, it is not as clear whether students spending more time at a clinical setting rather than on campus will cost a preservice program more. It generally should follow that the cost of providing staff development to school employees at a PDS site will be less than conducting such training on a college campus. However, in a specific situation even that condition could vary, since this variable, like so many others, will depend on conditions peculiar to a particular setting.

There is another sense in which time is a costly variable. Both school and university faculty must have sufficient time for collaboration and for the reflective practice of their art. University-based faculty members tend to find that the time consumed in this effort is even more demanding than their usual campus-based work (Anderson, 1993). For school people whose normal work schedule includes very little time for either reflection or collaboration, additional time free of direct interaction with students is essential (Anderson, 1993; Darling-Hammond, 1994a; Levine, 1992). Although some of this additional time could be acquired through restructuring the instructional delivery system and the existing overall responsibilities of educators, the allocation of time for reflection and collaboration can represent significant costs.

Teacher Education Level

Costs also may vary depending on whether teacher preparation is a postbaccalaureate program, an undergraduate program, or a 5-year program. Several different kinds of postgraduate programs are emerging. In a number of colleges — particularly large research universities, but a scattering of other institutions of all types — teacher education and other professional training for educators have been made postdegree programs. Regardless of whether a master's is associated with the program, such approaches claim that they have certain advantages. They are also more expensive, since graduate faculty are apt to have higher salaries than those who teach only undergraduates.

Alternative certification programs that place degree-holding students in schools as interns with little prior training generally cost less than other types of teacher preparation efforts. Costs are reduced because limited instruction in professional courses is provided students, because preservice candidates often replace regularly certified teachers at a reduced wage, and because supervision of the work of the candidates is performed largely by adjunct faculty and low-paid or unpaid school faculty. If critiques such as those of Darling-Hammond (1994b) apply generally to such programs, it would be difficult to justify them on a cost–benefit basis, even if they are less expensive in the short run. Further, such programs currently affect a very small proportion of all teacher candidates and have been in operation for a relatively short period of time.

At least one state, Minnesota, is experimenting with placing degree-holding, initially certificated novices in PDSs as part of an induction process (not unlike the placement of interns and residents in teaching hospitals). It is not clear at this point what the role of colleges will be in working with such PDSs, nor is it clear how this induction year will be coordinated with other staff development efforts within the school district. It would appear that this approach will add significant cost, if for no other reason than its countermanding of the common practice of assigning beginning teachers the heaviest loads in a school rather than easing them into the profession.

Attention needs to be given to the question of whether well-designed clinical experiences, even if they have a higher initial cost, could produce better student learning, thus increasing the return on the investment. It is also possible that they could generate teachers more apt to gain and retain employment. Substantial costs of educating teachers are associated with the fact that many who are trained never teach and many who do teach leave after a few years, requiring expenditures in colleges and school districts for the training of replacements.

On the surface, the least costly approach to the initial training of teachers is to require students to experience all types of teacher education training, including clinical preparation, prior to earning a bachelor's degree. If a PDS is not willing to place significant responsibility in the hands of undergraduates, however, the opportunity to reduce costs at the school level will be hindered. If undergraduate-only preparation leads to teachers who lack adequate academic and/or professional backgrounds, the cost–benefit returns of a bachelor's degree program might be lost.

Examples of questions that might help with cost–benefit and opportunity cost analyses of teacher education in general, and of teacher education as delivered using PDSs, include

- Do teachers demonstrate increased desire to stay in the profession?
- Are teachers more committed to being advocates for children?
- Is professional behavior increased? (Is there reduced turnover rate, increased attendance, increased likelihood of attending graduate education, expanded involvement in decision making?)
- Do students learn more?
- Do students attend, and like, their school?
- Do parents respond positively to the school?
- What are indicators of student participation and persistence in higher education?

With respect to PDSs specifically, questions should cover

- Are students from PDSs more apt to become teachers?
- Are school renewal activities more prevalent at PDS sites?
- Do PDS faculty report higher satisfaction with professional development activities?

Faculty Loads

There are wide ranges in faculty loads depending on the type of university. While the National Council of Teacher Accreditation (NCATE) and other accreditation agencies seek to ensure reasonable loads, variances between research and regional universities still result in significantly different costs for using tenure-track faculty in the two different settings. In states with strong collective bargaining laws and histories, union contracts tend to specify loads for school faculty, which will determine the cost of engaging them in the work of the PDS. Of course, the load issue is another way of stating the need for time for planning, collaboration, and reflection.

Compensation for Students and Staff

Pay differentials for nontenure-track student teacher supervisors have been cost-cutting devices used in teacher training for some time. Whether these roles are continued, the extent to which tenure-track college faculty (especially senior faculty) are included, and the compensation provided to schoolteachers who serve in various ways in the PDS are all cost factors.

While it is obvious that the pay rates for employees are a major cost determinant, it also should be noted that in some instances there are compensation questions for students of the PDS. Some colleges use tuition waivers as a form of compensation, and such loss of revenue to the college must be factored in as a cost, although it may be offset by the unpaid PDS work done by the student teachers.

Some institutions provide compensation for student teachers who are postgraduate interns in somewhat the same way they provide graduate assistantships, and these are clearly PDS expenses, to be offset by the value of the interns' work.

When staff development and research activities are added to preservice work in a PDS, school faculty may be compensated for these activities beyond their salary, and these extra amounts are clearly PDS costs.

Other Variables

It is possible that facility costs will increase as a result of housing a PDS in a school building. While many such costs are not marginal, there may be remodeling expenses or the expenses of portable classrooms or additions to provide an office and dedicated classroom space for the PDS activities. Conversely, there may be facility savings at a college as a result of increased use of school facilities.

There are also a variety of communication, meeting, and publicity costs associated with a PDS, particularly in its early stages.

PDS FINANCING

External Sources of Support

Generally speaking, as with costs, there is little information in the literature about financing operating Professional Development Schools. Darling-Hammond (1994a) observed that "despite substantial moral support, the PDS movement has been launched with remarkably little funding" (p. 23). She suggested that generally there has been little external support from foundations or governmental agencies for initiating such schools, and added that historic underfunding of teacher education within higher education institutions suggests that it will be difficult to secure needed support from universities. She did identify Michigan and Minnesota as two states where some external PDS funding had been made available on a limited basis.

As of 1995, West Virginia University had received nearly $3 million from the Claude Worthington Benedum Foundation to support its developmental efforts. Robinson and Darling-Hammond (1994) indicated that 5-year funding of $1.7 million for a Kansas State project by the National Science Foundation made that project the best funded of a group of developmental projects they examined. Ishler (1994) confirmed in his report of survey findings that there are difficulties in obtaining funds for Professional Development Schools. This survey, on behalf of the Land Grant University Deans of Education, led him to conclude that

> the overwhelming majority of states have not established a funding structure nor provided legislated funds earmarked specifically for PDSs. By far the majority of respondents indicated that reallocated university and reallocated school/district funds along with moneys from private foundations were used to fund partnerships. The vast majority emphasized that funding of PDSs was indeed a problem. (Ishler, 1994, p. 10)

Ishler did report that Texas had funded substantial support for developmental costs associated with PDSs and that legislation supporting partnerships for professional development had been passed in Missouri. His survey also revealed that various private foundations — for example, Ford, Lily (Indiana), Winthrop Rockefeller (Arkansas), and Alabama Power Foundation — have helped local settings with start-up funding. The University of Southern Maine has received assistance from the UNUM Charitable Trust and the Noyce Foundation for its efforts.

Several states (e.g., Colorado, Hawaii) used Goals 2000 funds from the federal government to help with planning and development of PDSs.

Internal Allocations

As we noted at the outset, however, adding more is not a likely means of funding PDSs. The most likely means of paying for PDSs will be through reallocation of existing funds. This is accomplished most effectively when old programs are sunsetted and new programs instituted (Goodlad, 1990), although substantial external funds for start-up efforts usually are needed.

A cost-saving approach for existing PDSs is to use the same outlay to train fewer teachers. There may be political pressures, and loss of financial support, however, in response to such cutbacks.

Increasing tuition for teacher education students is one way to increase revenues, although it is unlikely to cover the per-student cost difference between teacher education and other programs even when the benefits of the students' participation in the PDS are factored in. Also, the higher tuition may be a factor in keeping enrollment lower than is needed to offset current costs.

Another means of using existing resources is to shift those available within the college of education from other programs to teacher education and/or those available within a school district from one purpose to another. Whereas sunsetting teacher education programs moves money from one approach to teacher education to another, shifting expenditures from graduate studies in such areas as educational psychology or school administration to teacher education represents a change in priorities of the college. Not only have colleges been reluctant to do this, but some have refused to even consider the question. Still, policy makers in state legislatures and elsewhere indicate that they see professional training — not research — as the main mission of their universities and as the reason they fund institutions of higher education in their state. Such views by policy makers will keep pressure on colleges of education to find funds from within to pay for new costs. To make their case to the policy makers, Professional Development School advocates will need to be able to speak with clarity about both the costs and benefits of their programs. They will need to demonstrate that their results are better than those from other approaches to preservice training, continuing education, inquiry, and school renewal that require similar expenditures. Comparable arguments will have to be used by school districts to convince policy makers to shift funds to PDSs from other approaches to professional development and school renewal.

Examples are emerging of programs that are not alternative certification programs but that deliberately reallocate school district funds to provide sufficient resources to support teacher training. Teachers for Chicago is a "break-even program [in which] three interns fill three full-time teaching vacancies in sites hosting the program; the fourth intern covers the class that the mentor is assigned. . . . The interns are paid the salary of provisional teachers, which is generally less than half the salary budgeted for each vacancy. Tuition costs for interns and partial overhead costs are recovered through this salary differential" (Gallegos, 1995, p. 784). Similar replacement strategies have been used for years at Brigham Young University in its Leadership Development Program.

New Strategies

Educators have long been interested in lessons that might be learned from other professions' approaches to training their members. Levine (1995) suggested that there may be much to learn from approaches such as those taken by medicine in updating the education of new doctors. Indeed, examination of the approaches to clinical experiences taken by other professions may help define how PDSs can be financed.

Preparation patterns for different professions vary. In medicine, campus-based undergraduate schooling typically requires 4 years and is followed by 4 years of postgraduate degree study, sometimes referred to as "undergraduate" preparation by medical educators. This phase of the training is paid for by tuition, public funds, and endowments. It is followed by another 3 to 4 years of graduate or clinical training involving internships and residencies in teaching hospitals. Young doctors are compensated during this phase of their training, with the costs paid from a combination of income from patient fees (often covered by third-party providers), Medicare/Medicaid, grants, and public support. Because the pay for interns and residents is generally quite low, the case also can be made that the future doctors contribute to the financing of this stage of their professional training by deferring earnings.

Deferring earnings and having recipients of the services pay for professional training tend to be approaches that dominate in other professions. After an accountant has completed a campus-based undergraduate program, he or she works at a low wage rate until qualifying examinations have been completed. After engineers have completed their campus-based undergraduate work (which may have been supplemented by internships during the summers), they are employed with reduced responsibility at reduced wages. Only after they have worked under the mentorship of a licensed professional in their specialty for a set length of time can they take the examinations that qualify them as licensed professional engineers. Meanwhile the most significant part of this phase of their training has been paid by the clients of the firms for which they work. Architects follow a similar pattern.

Teachers do begin work at reduced wages—and in comparison with other professions, never reach the top earning brackets frequently associated with being a professional. However, beginning teachers usually assume full loads and have only minimal guidance from mentors. While school districts have expanded professional development activities, they usually do not assume significant responsibility for the professional training of educators that is comparable to the support provided from the field for doctors, accountants, engineers, and architects.

It is also essential to recognize that the sheer number of teachers in the nation far exceeds the number of doctors, engineers, and accountants. This fact has tremendous cost implications. Along with less quantifiable variables such as historic gender biases affecting compensation, the number of professional educators influences the content, scope, length, and compensation strategies related to training teachers as compared with other professionals.

When he addressed the issue of financing PDSs, Theobald (1990, 1991a, 1991b) echoed Tyler's (1985) comments about lessons learned in the first half of the century. Both recognized the need for added engagement by school systems in such training. Theobald (1991b) observed that

Professional development schools will necessarily wed public school districts, schools and colleges of education, teacher organizations, and state governments into an economic union which involves a significant reallocation of resources within and among the four sets of institutions. (p. 89)

This returns us to our earlier review of the state of reform and finances for education in the nation. The partnership advocated here joins difficult issues of obtaining higher education funding with current troubles facing school systems as they seek support for their operations in an era that is generally resistant to even maintaining the current level of public expenditures. Odden (1994) has suggested that

The future challenge for education will be to link improvements in school finance to local tax reform and, simultaneously, to produce high levels of achievement for all students, with school budgets that grow more slowly or even decline in some states over the rest of the 1990s. (p. 4)

He indicated that this will best be accomplished if a series of policy initiatives designed to improve student learning are linked as part of systemic reform and proposed that one such policy should lead to "substantially expanded professional staff development along with dramatically revised preservice teacher training" (Odden, 1994, p. 5).

Odden (1994) also recognized the limitations of one-shot workshops that typify too many traditional staff development efforts, but proposed other traditional approaches such as intensive summer workshops, rather than the fundamental revision of training and school renewal exemplified by Professional Development Schools.

There are, then, a variety of possible sources of financing for Professional Development Schools. Ultimately they will require collaboration between the school districts and colleges engaged in systemic renewal efforts. For this collaboration to be successful, however, funds will have to be obtained during a time of limited public willingness to support education and during a time when the Professional Development School, while popular with advocates of teacher education reform, still has not been accepted as a strategy that will produce better preservice education, staff development, and school renewal than can be obtained through more traditional approaches.

CONCLUSION

To pay for the multiple costs of developing and operating Professional Development Schools, administrators often turn to foundations and state grants to help with start-up costs. They also need to rely on reallocating funds through sunsetting old programs and shifting more money to teacher education. Ultimately, for PDSs to fulfill their fourfold purpose of school renewal, preservice education, inquiry, and professional development, school districts will have to invest significantly along with universities in paying for them. To secure support from policy makers for this investment, to convince higher education faculty to reallocate funds to institutions furthering school renewal, and to persuade school people to appropriate money to institutions with major responsibility for preservice education, some questions will need to be answered. Among them are the following:

- Are more benefits in terms of better-prepared teachers, better-educated children, and/or more knowledge about schooling obtained when PDSs are used than can be obtained without them?
- How do the costs of performing the services expected of Professional Development Schools vary when services are performed in a PDS as opposed to a more traditional teacher education program?
- What are the governance structures that can successfully blend the interests of the partners whose collaboration is needed in order to develop and operate PDSs?
- How does the proposed use of PDSs to improve induction processes for new teachers affect financing questions?

While answers to these questions about the costs and benefits of teacher education through Professional Development Schools are not yet fully known, several groups are currently at work developing them. The success of these groups in defining the costs of teacher preservice and continuing education as part of systemic school renewal efforts will provide guidance for financing Professional Development Schools and provide policy makers with the information they need to fully evaluate their worth.

REFERENCES

Adams, J. E., Jr. (1994, Winter). Spending school reform dollars in Kentucky: Familiar patterns and new programs, but is this reform? *Educational Evaluation and Policy Analysis, 16*(4), 375–390.

Anderson, C. R. (Ed.). (1993). *Voices of change: A report of the clinical schools project.* Washington, DC: American Association of Colleges for Teacher Education.

Berliner, D. C. (1984, October). Making the right changes in preservice teacher education. *Phi Delta Kappan, 66*(2), 94–96.

Clark, R. W. (1988). Who decides? The basic policy issue. In L. N. Tanner (Ed.), *Critical issues in curriculum: 87th yearbook of the National Society for the Study of Education* (pp. 175–204). Chicago: University of Chicago Press.

Clark, R. W. (1995). *Partner schools.* Seattle: University of Washington, College of Education, Center for Educational Renewal.

Cohn, E., & Geske, T. (1990). *The economics of education* (3rd ed.). Oxford, UK: Pergamon Press.

Darling-Hammond, L. (Ed.). (1994a). *Professional development schools: Schools for developing a profession.* New York: Teachers College Press.

Darling-Hammond, L. (1994b, September). Who will speak for the children? How "Teach for America" hurts urban schools and students. *Phi Delta Kappan, 76*(1), 21–34.

Darling-Hammond, L., & McLaughlin, M. W. (1995, April). Policies that support professional development in an era of reform. *Phi Delta Kappan, 76*(8), 597–604.

Estimates of public school statistics, prekindergarten through grade 12, 1991–92. (1992, March 12). *Education Daily,* p. 6.

Firestone, W. A., Goertz, M., Nagle, B., & Smelkinson, M. F. (1994, Winter). Where did the $800 million go? The first year of New Jersey's Quality Education Act. *Educational Evaluation and Policy Analysis, 16*(4), 359–374.

Gallegos, B. (1995, June). Teachers for Chicago. *Phi Delta Kappan, 76*(10), 782–785.

Goodlad, J. I. (1990). *Teachers for our nation's schools.* San Francisco: Jossey-Bass.

Goodlad, J. I. (1994). *Educational renewal: Better teachers, better schools.* San Francisco: Jossey-Bass.

Holmes Group. (1990). *Tomorrow's schools: Principles for the design of professional development schools.* East Lansing, MI: Author.

Ishler, R. (1994, October 16). *Professional development schools: What are they? How are they funded? How should they be evaluated?* Draft Report of the Task Force on Professional Development School, Association of Colleges and Schools of Education in State Universities and Land Grant Colleges and Affiliated Private Universities.

Levine, M. (Ed.). (1992). *Professional practice schools: Linking teacher education and school reform.* New York: Teachers College Press.

Levine, M. (1995, February 1). 21st century professional education: How education could learn from medicine, business, and engineering. Commentary. *Education Week*, pp. 33–36.

Lewis, D. R. (1990, Spring). Estimating the economic worth of a 5th-year licensure program for teachers: Educational fiscal policy in the Reagan Administration. *Educational Evaluation and Policy Analysis, 12*(1), 25–39.

McKersie, W. S. (1993, Summer). Philanthropy's paradox: Chicago school reform. *Educational Evaluation and Policy Analysis, 15*(2), 109–128.

National Commission on Excellence in Education. (1983, April). *A nation at risk*. Washington, DC: U.S. Government Printing Office.

Odden, A. (1986, January). Sources of funding for education reform. *Phi Delta Kappan, 67*(5), 335–340.

Odden, A. (1994, May). *Including school finance in systemic reform strategies: A commentary* (CPRE Finance Briefs). New Brunswick: State University of New Jersey, CPRE Rutgers.

Peseau, B. A. (1982, July–August). Developing an adequate resource base for teacher education. *Journal of Teacher Education, 32*(4), 13–15.

Peseau, B. A., Backman, C., & Fry, B. (1987, Spring). A cost model for clinical teacher education. *Action in Teacher Education, 9*(1), 21–34.

Peseau, B. A., & Orr, P. (1980, October). The outrageous underfunding of teacher education. *Phi Delta Kappan, 62*(2), 100–102.

Peseau, B. A., & Tudor, R. L. (1988, September). Exploring and testing cluster analysis. *Research in Higher Education, 29*(1), 6–78.

Picus, L. O. (1994, Winter). The local impact of school finance reform in four Texas school districts. *Educational Evaluation and Policy Analysis, 16*(4), 391–404.

Pipho, C. (1995, April). Stateline: Getting a return on the education dollar. *Phi Delta Kappan, 76*(10), 582–583.

Robinson, S., & Darling-Hammond, L. (1994). Change for collaboration and collaboration for change: Transforming teaching through school university partnership. In L. Darling-Hammond (Ed.), *Professional development schools: Schools for developing a profession* (pp. 203–219). New York: Teachers College Press.

Theobald, N. D. (1990, February). *The financing and governance of professional development of partner schools* (Occasional Paper No. 10). Seattle: University of Washington, College of Education, Center for Educational Renewal.

Theobald, N. D. (1991a, Spring). Staffing, financing, and governing professional development schools. *Educational Evaluation and Policy Analysis, 13*(1), 87–101.

Theobald, N. D. (1991b, July). Allocating resources to renew teacher education (Occasional Paper No. 14). Seattle: University of Washington, College of Education, Center for Educational Renewal.

Tyler, R. W. (1985, June). What we have learned from past studies of teacher education. *Phi Delta Kappan, 66*(10), 682–684.

Verstegan, D. A. (1990, Winter). Educational fiscal policy in the Reagan Administration. *Educational Evaluation and Policy Analysis, 12*(4), 355–373.

Chapter 8

Worthy of the Name: Standards for Professional Development Schools

GARY SYKES

Setting standards for Professional Development Schools raises complex and difficult issues, which this chapter explores. Efforts already are under way to establish such standards. Universities across the country are creating formal agreements of various kinds with cooperating schools and districts in which standards, explicit or implied, are emerging. Also, the National Council for the Accreditation of Teacher Education (NCATE) has launched a national project to set PDS standards in the context of professional accreditation of schools of education. Activity, then, likely will outstrip the information and observations presented here, but what may be reviewed usefully are some general considerations about standard setting for PDSs, together with some tensions and issues likely to emerge through the choices that standard setters make.

The decision to set standards for PDSs signals their importance in developing a true profession of education as part of the larger effort to improve American education. The PDS, its advocates hope, will become a crucial institution supporting the preparation of educators, the conduct of applied inquiry, and the improvement of schooling. Before the question of standards is discussed, a brief account of the central aspirations for the PDS will set the stage.

PDSs AND THE PROFESSIONALIZATION OF TEACHING

At the heart of the PDS idea is the goal to improve substantially the preparation and continuing education of educators. A truism is that no one learns to teach in a university: One studies education at a university and learns to teach in a school. This point may seem obvious but the institutional arrangements to prepare teachers have never reflected it. The prevailing model tacks 15 to 20 weeks of practice teaching onto a slender collection of university courses, with these two strands only loosely connected to one another. Now, by creating long-term, deep relations between schools and universities, as exemplified by PDS programs, the historic breach may be healed and a much stronger form of professional education may emerge.

PDSs also implement a strategy within the broad reform movement known as professionalization. It seeks to create through policy and other means a teaching force imbued with the knowledge, skills, and dispositions conducive to good teaching and learning, and supported by structures and resources. Standards of many kinds play a prominent role today in this effort. They include curriculum content standards often developed by subject-matter associations; licensure and certification standards created by states and the National Board for Professional Teaching Standards (NBPTS), respectively; student learning standards defined by a variety of assessments; and school standards represented in accreditation. PDSs take their place within this mix but make a unique contribution. Each PDS functions, in theory at least, as an inclusive site where multiple professional standards may be combined in service to the development of new professionals and new knowledge. These professionals become a vital link in the chain of education reform whose other links specify what is to be learned and assessed, what constitutes good teaching, and what resources are necessary for full opportunity. While in principle all schools ought to be exemplary sites for professional learning, this ideal is not a reality within the current system; thus professional reformers seek targets of opportunity where they can concentrate effort. To this end, PDSs must be regular schools facing the full range of conditions in our society that foster special capacities to develop new professionals and new knowledge. Within a broad theory of reform, the PDS represents an answer to two critical questions: How will educators learn to teach to the new standards? How will the new standards be implemented in the range of real schools?

Furthermore, the PDS embodies the conviction that reform standards of all kinds are neither self-evident nor self-implementing. As other standard setters are discovering, a sizable learning process lies ahead in working out the day-to-day implications of new standards for teaching and learning in a wide array of school/community contexts. For example, the vanguard mathematics standards of the National Council for the Teaching of Mathematics (NCTM) certainly have supplied an important focus but they have not settled what teaching to those standards looks like. Early evidence of standards for teaching and learning indicates that they operate more as an invitation to discovery and invention than as a template directing practice (for example, see Ball, 1996). Educators working in concert within particular schools are needed to realize the vision of "systemic reform," and PDSs, along with other schools, may participate in this effort.

In terms of this larger vision of reform, the PDS represents another professional principle, articulated most clearly by Goodlad (1990, 1994), that is, that the renewal of schools and of professional education must occur in tandem. To overcome the long-standing dichotomies between theory and practice, laboratory and clinic, reformed versus received doctrine, knowledge as proposition and knowledge in use, interventions must embrace university-based professional education and school-based educational practice simultaneously. The fundamental unit of reform must include both spheres, for each contributes essential perspectives and resources.

Finally, PDSs participate in the reconstruction of educational inquiry, for many see a disconnection between the research that occupies faculty time on university campuses and the efforts to base educational improvements on new knowledge. The conduct of inquiry in education owes more to academic traditions in the social sciences than to direct concerns about educational practice. "The oft-noted hiatus between educational theory and educational practice," wrote Schlechty (1990), "exists in part because theory tends to be generated in a culture where it does not apply (the university), and efforts to apply theory are made in a culture where few theoreticians practice (the schools)" (pp. 44–45). He went on to distinguish a fundamental difference in the normative order appropriate for disciplining ideas — the liberal arts institution — and that for disciplining practice — the professional school. He summarized this clash in orientation by asking, "Should practice be based on theory or should theory be based on practice?" (p. 50). The liberal arts academy he identified with the first choice, the professional school with the second.

Schools of education long have suffered divided loyalties between these orientations. PDSs clearly come down on the side of the professional school, serving as crucial sites for creating theory out of study and experimentation with practice. They are vital institutions where new knowledge may be generated through, and employed to improve, practice.

These aspirations for PDSs — to dramatically improve teacher education, to jointly produce professionals and professional practice, to represent an integrating and implementing site for professional standards, to stimulate the mutual renewal of schools and of university-based professional education, and to ground educational inquiry more directly in practice — serve as the broad context for PDS standards.

WHAT IS A PROFESSIONAL DEVELOPMENT SCHOOL?

Professional Development Schools are usually regular K–12 schools that have entered into partnerships with universities to assist in the preparation of future educators and to serve as sites for research and development. These twin functions are deceptively simple, for their authentic pursuit establishes several ambitious requirements. One is that educational practice, evidenced in organization, management, curriculum, teaching, and community relations, be exemplary. This requirement to represent state-of-the-art practice exists because professional education must transmit best practice that is best learned from exemplary practitioners — at the school and the university.

A second requirement is that both the university and the school must alter certain of their features in order to support the partnership and its mission. For example, time and other scarce resources must support the additional responsibilities of professional education and collaborative research. Rewards and incentives must encourage these pursuits. New roles and role relationships must be created, and new governance arrangements must support joint decision making and conflict resolution.

Third, the partners must develop new capacities to manage the relationship and to carry out the shared responsibilities. Both school and university personnel must learn how to work together. Administrators must learn how to manage a more complex organization that involves new sources of authority. University and school faculty must learn how to conduct collaborative inquiry and how to supervise and evaluate the work of interns, inservice teachers, and other school personnel.

The two functions — professional education and inquiry — supported by these three requirements — pursuing exemplary practice, facilitating changes in each partner institution, and creating new capacity via learning — establish the broad parameters for standards.

ARE PDS STANDARDS NEEDED?

Whether there should be standards for PDSs is an important question to raise at the outset, and both sides have arguments.

Opponents argue that Professional Development Schools are fragile, delicate collaborations built on trust that must be nurtured carefully over time, face-to-face, through many mutually satisfying interchanges among the faculty and students of universities and schools. Particularly in the early stages, there is a potential for distrust, suspicion, miscommunication, and conflict. The educators on the spot must work through these problems patiently and help move all participants toward more trusting, productive relations. Standards prematurely invoked and enforced are likely to disrupt and distract the process of community building. Opponents also argue that the PDS by its nature is an open-ended innovation to be invented by the participants.

Guidelines, principles, descriptions, and statements of purpose all are useful aids to direct and stimulate invention, but it would be an error to regard the PDS as a detailed and tightly specified entity that must conform to certain external standards. The PDS is a concept that may take a variety of forms; its realization requires active experimentation and adaptation to local circumstances. Again, the premature development of standards by parties external to and removed from the local scene works against the promise of the PDS. Look to history, urge the opponents of standards; witness the many complex innovations attempted and found wanting long before they had received a fair trial. Perhaps in the future, when sufficient experience with PDSs has accumulated, standards may be useful. For the foreseeable future, however, they can only detract from the work, confining and repressing creative expression and necessary adaptation.

Proponents of standards offer a counterposing set of arguments and a different reading of reform history. The PDS is in theory an ambitious, even radical, reform that demands difficult, disruptive change by both partner organizations. The great danger is in losing the transformative potential of the idea to downsizing pressures and tendencies, whose most egregious act is the relabeling as PDSs of schools that do little more than accept student teachers. Champions of the PDS movement worry about the authenticity of the efforts under way, the fidelity to difficult ideals. Without a strong set of external standards, the PDS is unlikely to emerge as the pivotal institution its advocates intend. Standards provide one means for identifying the necessary elements that all PDSs worthy of the name must share. The history of educational innovation from this perspective is a chronicle of nonevents — superficial, cosmetic changes touted as bold, dramatic departures.

Another argument for standards is that they can direct and assist in the creation of these schools by defining their components and operations. Standards have the potential to educate those who embrace them, by pointing to the necessary goals to achieve. Advocates argue that the activity of standard setting can be a useful process for clarifying the PDS, moving from general principles and descriptions to more precise, concrete guidelines to direct the work.

These opposing views operate within different but overlapping spheres of action, each projecting a vision of reform. One sphere is local, where PDS educators are intensively engaged in the work. Associated with local effort is the vision of a reform network that informally connects the participants to one another for purposes of social support and the sharing of craft knowledge. Standards may flow through support networks, but in the form of advice, persuasion, and norm formation. Within this vision, like-minded reformers make lateral, informal connections with one another for purposes of mutual assistance. Reform networks tend to be nonhierarchical, voluntary, and non- or quasi-governmental.

A second sphere is state and national, where reformers engaged in the effort to professionalize teaching seek to link large-scale associations both to local action and to government. Advocates in this sphere work to forge public–professional compacts that exchange resources for the legitimacy conferred by law. The vision of professionalization connects associations representing the profession to government agencies with the authority to promulgate standards for institutional accreditation and individual licensure. Here, standards are authoritative and binding safeguards issued by the state but developed by the profession. Professional reformers rely on hierarchical, mandatory, formal, and governmental relationships to structure the process of standard setting. These latter terms may be summed up in a familiar and unsettling term: bureaucracy. Critics of standards worry that when government takes over standard setting, all the dysfunctional features of regulatory policy emerge. Advocates, however, hope to avoid this evil by creating a process managed primarily by the profession.

Finally, if Professional Development Schools are to grow in number, credibility, visibility, and centrality, they must move from temporary, project status to core significance in the plans of education schools and cooperating school districts. Long-term support from national and state levels, together with district and university levels, will be needed. External standards will serve as a warranty in persuading outside agencies to provide the support. The culture of accountability in education is so strong that no reform with systemic intentions can long delay developing publicly credible ways and means for being held to account. Standard setting, then, is part of a long-term political strategy to support the fledgling PDS movement.

Both sides in this debate have good arguments. Is it possible, then, to gain the benefits of standards while avoiding the liabilities? The design of standards must meet this test.

DEVELOPMENTAL STANDARDS AND THE PROCESS OF CHANGE

In the case of the PDS, standards serve as agents of change. This is a central argument of this chapter, and it bears repeating: PDS standards serve as agents of change. The PDS is a new idea that must be realized together by two old institutions that each must change in certain respects. As Sarason (1982) has observed, changing institutions is far more difficult than creating new ones. The PDS has no exact counterpart, although analogies with laboratory schools, teaching hospitals, and agricultural extension agencies frequently are invoked. Likewise, schools and universities have historic relationships of various sorts that provide both starting points for and impediments to the formation of PDSs. But as the critics of standards rightfully argue, launching a PDS inevitably plunges participants into complex, contentious changes in both the school's and the university's functioning. Standards must account for this process of change. A well-functioning PDS does not spring up overnight. It evolves gradually through phases of exploration, early initiation, continuing implementation, and full operation. The trajectory comprises cycles of dialogue and action, a gradually expanding set of participants, a gradually enlarging sphere of activity, and a movement from unaccustomed, innovative practice to stable, institutionalized relations.

There is an external dimension to the change process as well, an ancient tension in the history of education reform. On the one hand, study after study has reiterated that creating worthwhile change in schools takes considerable time and must be managed with great skill and persistence. On the other hand, there is the press for tangible results from outside interests whose support is essential to the overall effort. Among these interests are public and private funding sources; state, district, and university leaders; professional associations; and representatives from the larger public, such as parent groups and the business community. Those involved in changing their practices and their institutions testify to the hardship of simultaneously operating an institution and changing it. They face not only the problems of overload and stress but the challenge of bringing all the members along. Forming the vanguard is but the first step in convincing a much wider circle that both the new direction and the journey are worth pursuing. Those on the outside inevitably fix their gaze on the desired outcome, the bottom line, and demand results, usually more quickly than participants can produce or demonstrate them.

The standard-setting process must accommodate the developmental nature of the PDS. Standards should assist all the participants in managing the tensions of change. Standards should be developmental in several senses: The process of creating them should engage a range of participants in cycles of formulation, test, and revision; the standards themselves should undergo regular revision and refinement; the process of applying them should encourage school-based learning in response to feedback; and the standards should account for the developmental stage of the school at the time of application.

STANDARD SETTING AS A LEARNING SYSTEM

A central concern within the educational standard-setting movement is how to link national to local action. On the one hand, national standards such as those promulgated within the Goals 2000 legislation seek to raise expectations for learning across the country. The federal government supplies the stimulation via expert-produced standards and grants to states, while states supply a mix of assistance and regulation to localities. If standards are to have real significance locally, both commitment and learning are needed. Localities must initiate processes through which they scrutinize, adopt, and adapt standards, learning how to teach and reach them. Within this model, conflict between national and local agencies is not inherent, but there is plenty of room for it; whether it will work out is open to question (Cohen, 1995; Eisner, 1995). Is this the model for Professional Development Schools?

A useful principle here distinguishes regulatory from programmatic approaches to policy development (Elmore, 1983) — designing controls versus building capacity (Darling-Hammond, 1993). The relationship between an authorizing entity and a local respondent may be organized around compliance, with a set of rules or regulations that the center develops and the periphery implements; or, it may be organized around exchanges that aim to "improve and support the capacity of public organizations to deliver services" (Elmore, 1983, p. 346). Within this latter construction of national–local relations, standards serve not as rules that exact compliance but as guidelines that convey information. Expressed metaphorically, interchanges between national and local agencies resemble reflective dialogue between two professionals working on a problem, rather than the encounter between a traffic cop and a motorist caught speeding. The aim in the first instance is mutual learning around a central problem of practice, while in the second it is compliance with the law. The one image is as congenial as the other is forbidding, suggesting a misleading dichotomy or a false choice, so a closer look is needed. What exactly would a "programmatic" or "capacity-building" approach to PDS standards involve?

A number of national entities that represent the educating professions' interests in standards are already at work on this issue. NCATE is engaged in a project to develop PDS standards in the context of accreditation. The Holmes Group (1996) has recommended standards for PDSs in their most recent report. Such groups, together with others that supply experience and expertise (e.g., the National Center for Restructuring Education, Schools, and Teaching; the School Development Project), may join in the first stage to develop a set of national standards whose authority derives from the weight of professional judgment and the consensual process through which the standards are formulated, reviewed, revised, and eventually adopted.

The next stage in a capacity-building mode is most critical. National standards are offered to local institutions on a voluntary basis as the focus for dialogue and scrutiny. The national agency sets forth a general, provisional set of guidelines that may be put into practice in a variety of ways. The agency must be artful in supplying guidance that firmly indicates what is required, while granting enough latitude to encourage local use and adaptation to context. The agency undertakes to manage a learning system made up of many dispersed schools that are experimenting with the standards, and to stimulate local learning and facilitate the flow of information across sites. Participating schools use the standards both to gauge their own development and to refine the standards themselves. Initial standard setting is relatively decentralized, with learning flowing from school to school and from the schools to the national agency, rather than from the national to the local level. In the third stage, as expert consensus emerges based on experience, the national agency may progressively codify the standards, increasing their specificity and uniformity. This would occur much later in the process.

This is not the customary approach to standard setting, and Schön (1971) aptly drew the contrast. Writing about the development of governmental policy, he first described the conventional approach.

> There is a particular version of the center–periphery model, broadly and powerfully held at least in the United States, in which central formulates specifications for a new policy, makes funds available for its implementation, and solicits proposals from local agents for behavior conforming to the policy. Central then rewards certain proposers with funding, punishes others by withholding funds, and proceeds to monitor the behavior of local agents for conformity to proposal. Withdrawal of continued funding is the sanction invoked to enforce compliance. There is sometimes the further notion that the local agents will, after a time, secure their own resources to continue implementing the policy. (p. 147)

This "propose–dispose" model, Schön argued, is seriously flawed, not least in its inability to stimulate local commitment and learning. He then outlined his preferred alternative, policy as a learning system.

> Government cannot play the role of "experimenter for the nation," seeking first to identify the correct solution, then to train society at large in its adaptation. The opportunity for learning is primarily in discovered systems at the periphery, not in the nexus of official policies at the center. Central's role is to detect significant shifts at the periphery, to pay explicit attention to the emergence of ideas in good currency, and to derive themes of policy by induction. The movement of learning is as much from periphery to periphery, or from

periphery to center, as from center to periphery. Central comes to function as facilitator of society's learning, rather than as society's trainer. (pp. 177–178)

This latter approach places primary emphasis on learning, stimulation of development, and capacity building. It assumes that all the agents involved in standard setting must learn, including those who set the standards and those who "implement" them in schools. The aim of the standard-setting enterprise, then, is to support the development of strong Professional Development Schools throughout the country, linking them together in a network around the standards that schools shape and that shape the schools.

Standard setting as a learning system is a conceptual approach that might be carried out via a number of models. For example, the evaluation of complex organizations is the mission of state inspectorates in many nations, among which the most prominent has been Her Majesty's Inspectorate (HMI) in Great Britain. Another model is the regional accreditation of secondary schools in the United States, or the national accreditation of schools of education by NCATE. Within the medical field there are well-established standards for teaching hospitals, including specific standards for internships and specialist residencies. In addition to these accreditation and review processes are those that result in awards for excellence, including, for example, the Malcolm Baldrige National Quality Award issued by the U.S. Commerce Department's Bureau of Standards to outstanding American firms.

Each of these models bears a close look, but another variant, the School Quality Review, may fit particularly well with the conceptual approach advocated here. This model was initiated in New York State some years ago, based on interest in HMI. It combines self-study and the formulation of local mission and goals with reference to external standards and goals of various kinds (see Ancess, 1994, for a description). Review teams visit a school, examine mission and goals statements and other aspects of school functioning, observe classes directly, and interview members of the school community. Their report back to the school serves as a stimulus for continued development. This model could be adapted to include such other features as progressive refinement of the external standards and cross-school sharing of ideas and approaches.

SCOPE, UNIT, AND TYPE OF STANDARDS

The general model to be used is the central choice for standard setting, but there are several others as well, including the scope or range of the standards, the unit of analysis, and the type of standards to be employed.

Scope

Questions of scope deal with institutional functions. The core functions may be considered those that are shared by the university and the school, primarily the field-based aspects of professional education, and also the inquiry-oriented activity. Restricting the scope of standard setting to those functions may not be simple, however. At issue is the idea of exemplary practice, which may be defined school-wide and also within particular areas of instruction. One ideal is to apprentice novices to master practitioners working in professional school cultures, who convey best practice through precept, guidance, and example. Arguably, the quality of instruction in a PDS and the quality of the school itself are critical learning resources for professional education and so should be included within the scope of standards. School-wide features, such as the character of decision making, the stance toward inclusion, the presence of practices such as tracking and the use of labels to sort children, relationships with parents and community, and the extent of collegial interaction among educators, are relevant to professional internships. The character of instruction in the classroom is equally pertinent. Do teachers reflect contemporary standards of mathematics and science, for example, around such precepts as teaching for conceptual understanding, creating a learning community, fostering active learning, setting high expectations for all learners, responding sensitively to individual learners, and capitalizing on students' social and cultural diversity?

Such expansive standards encompassing all aspects of "the good school" are likely to be controversial and to provoke conflict between the school and the university. PDSs operate in a gray zone of authority, partially oriented to the district's school board and administration, partially to the university. PDS standards that influence all aspects of schooling potentially challenge the school board's authority in favor of the university's. Conflicts also will emerge between university faculty imbued with the latest reform ideas and school faculty engaged in traditional practice (for example, see Kagan, 1993). Quality standards then might target professional education and inquiry, overall school functioning, and instructional practice. Within the PDS these cannot be neatly separated, but dangers are evident in tackling the whole and all its parts.

Nevertheless, the first scope issue for standard setters to address is the idea of exemplary practice. A misleading conception here is that the teachers in a PDS must be paragons, master teachers all, capable of initiating novice teachers into reform- and research-based practice. The quality of instruction in a PDS is a crucial matter, but a realistic conception of best practice suited to the PDS has two aspects: a school-wide commitment to inquiry and continuous improvement (Little, 1982), where educators are engaged in regular study of their practice and in efforts to make improvements; and the use of professional standards of various kinds as points of reference for improvement. Standards, for example, might include those of the NBPTS, Goals 2000, various professional associations, and the state/district. The standard to which a PDS faculty commits itself, then, is a steady striving for excellence gauged against the best professional thinking that is available.

The second principle regarding scope is to begin conservatively with a concentration on aspects of the PDS mission, that is, to prepare educators, that are most clearly shared—the organization, resources, conduct, and results of PDS-based professional education. The focus of standards-based dialogue should be on this function of the PDS as a starting point for trust building and the progressive deepening of the collaboration. Gradually, broader concerns for the school community and the character of instruction can emerge out of such dialogue. Likewise, other aspects of the PDS mission, such as the conduct of collaborative inquiry and the professional development of faculty, should be worked into the standards conversation, as the joint faculties develop the capacity to undertake more complex forms of collaboration.

Unit

Another issue concerns the unit to which PDS standards apply. The school is the obvious target, but schools are members of larger organizations and contain subunits within them. NCATE accreditation, for example, consists of both unit and program standards, the former referring to the school of education as a whole, the latter to individual program areas within the school (e.g., education of teachers, counselors, administrators).

Within the PDS, various subunits exist, including most obviously the departments within a high school, or such areas as social services, special education, or interdisciplinary teams within elementary or middle schools. Research indicates significant variation across departments within the same high school (see, for example, McLaughlin & Talbert, 1993; Siskin, 1991). Teaching interns in the mathematics department may be socialized into a highly professional, collegial work culture, while those in the same school's social studies department may encounter an isolated, divided faculty. The quality of professional internships, then, may vary considerably within as well as between schools, a matter of concern for PDS standards. Uneven practices within schools are an important issue for standards.

Likewise, a PDS operates within a partnership between district and university that may itself be subject to standards. As part of a PDS review, examiners may ask about the degree of commitment from the university and the extent of its involvement in terms of core faculty, resource exchanges, and integration of the PDS into the school of education's overall operation. These are all matters that partnership agreements may cover, but they also are integral to the functioning of the PDS. The larger intention of the PDS movement — to reform university-based teacher education — comes into play here, but as a subsidiary concern.

Initially, no formal differentiation of standards should be made. A single set of standards for the school should be developed, with appropriate reference both to the standards and practices within subunits of the school and to the ways that the partnership supports the PDS. Some schools, for example, build in regular cycles of review around particular areas of the curriculum (e.g., reading, math, science), and such continuous improvement processes could be a feature of a school review, so that the entire curriculum is not reviewed all at once, but over time. School standards, then, would specify that such area-by-area reviews be a regular feature of the school.

Type

A third important issue concerns the type of standard that is employed to evaluate the PDS. The most common typology distinguishes among input, process, and outcome standards, with a major shift under way generally in our society from input to a combination of process and outcome standards. The shift is reflected in greater attention to results, outcomes, or performances as a basis for linking individual assessment to judgments of institutional effectiveness, and in the quality movement in American business that emphasizes process measures as a basis for quality improvements. At the same time, however, there are serious questions about the resources devoted to PDSs, calling for attention to inputs.

For example, external examiners might want to know about the arrangements for supervising interns and inservice teachers. How many interns are placed in a PDS? How often are they observed and by whom? What opportunities are provided for guided practice and self-study of teaching via videotape, supervisory conferences, and other means? These are input questions, directing attention to the resources supplied to the PDS by the partner institutions. Examiners also might ask about the governance arrangements in place, look into the quality of supervision, and inquire how intern teaching is related conceptually and practically to other learning within the professional studies. They also might determine whether those in supervisory or evaluative roles have been prepared properly for their responsibilities. These are all aspects of school process that require close scrutiny.

Finally, standards also might cover the learning that results from PDS experiences. Several approaches are available. One choice is to examine the learning itself as demonstrated by conventional tests, performance assessments, direct observation, and other means. Another alternative is to examine the processes that the school uses to evaluate student learning, sampling the learning itself, a procedure that actually substitutes a process for an outcome standard. Another variable here is institutional versus "client" or "customer" assessments. Schools may gather evidence of learning and evaluations of graduates from faculty, from students themselves, or from employers. These choices all concern ways of gauging institutional outputs, typically judged against program goals or objectives.

If PDSs trace a path from initial exploration between interested parties to initiation, expanded implementation, and eventually mature operation, then the standards applied to an institutional assessment should take into account the stage of development. The most likely prospect is that a PDS would not volunteer for external review until it had reached a certain level of maturity, with the foundation laid in terms of governance agreements that included resource exchanges, initial experience with joint activity, and the general sense of a venture well launched. It may be wise to formalize this process by establishing some threshold conditions that schools must meet before applying for review.

The spirit of this approach parallels development within the accreditation field generally. The major shift under way, complicating traditional accreditation procedures, is much greater attention to the assessment of outcomes both as an institutional process and as a basis for judging institutional effectiveness directly. In his wide-ranging treatment of accreditation issues, Ewell (1992) noted several critical choices for institutional reviews, including validating quality (directly) or the quality assurance process, and certifying quality versus stimulating improvement. As part of the quality revolution sweeping American business, he noted a number of implications for institutional review.

> First, the content of information moves from a comparison of institutional goals, resources, and processes with implied fixed standards to include a comparison of obtained results with established goals. Second, the primary role of evidence is to indicate progress rather than to certify attainment, and patterns of indicators are intended to be used in combination to suggest effectiveness rather than to establish piecemeal the degree to which individual standards are met. Third, provided evidence should indicate a concern with the institution's "customers" (students, employers, and community) as well as its own members. Finally, the primary case to be made is less the fact that the institution meets minimum fixed criteria than the fact that it has the capacity, the will, and the culture to continuously improve. (pp. 11–12)

As with the School Quality Review, this description indicates that the ultimate aim of external standard setting should be to establish a culture of review and ongoing improvement based on evidence. This aspiration fits well with the capacity-building approach and the goal of stimulating PDS development nationwide.

THE CONTENT OF PDS STANDARDS

Standard setting for the PDS should stress self-study and improvement, concentrating on the shared work of school and university: professional education and inquiry. Exemplary practice should be identified, with improvement processes that are inquiry-oriented and standards-based, utilizing the best guidance available. External standards should be developed gradually, based on local learning, with a variety of established standards for such subprocesses as curriculum content, performance outcomes, teaching, and professional development. The standards should include reference to resources or inputs, processes, and outcomes. Threshold conditions should be established as a baseline for external reviews. The overall process should be treated as a learning experience both locally and nationally. Local feedback should stimulate development, as the national agency speeds the flow of information about good practice in the PDS around the network and continually modifies the standards in light of what is learned from local innovators.

A starting point is needed, however, to establish the content areas or categories within which to develop more detailed guidance. In addition to a set of prerequisites or threshold conditions, four broad domains organize the standards: (1) mission and goals; (2) quality assurance processes; (3) the school as learning community; and (4) learning and development outcomes.

Threshold Conditions

The purpose of prerequisites is to protect those engaged in standard setting and PDS development from premature evaluation. The aim is not to create cumbersome barriers but to ensure that groundwork has been laid locally and collaboration has commenced so that meaningful activity within the school may be assessed. Prerequisites function as a kind of standard, a form of guidance about what must be established first, before operational standards may be applied.

First are *governance arrangements*. The PDS should be able to document that working agreements are in place regarding decision making in the PDS and participation in the process. Rights, responsibilities, rules, and roles should be specified, not to the ultimate degree, but with enough detail to supply guidance. Parties to the agreement may include representatives of the district, the school principal and teachers, the teachers' union, and the university. Governance arrangements may specify decision-making committees and their composition, strategic planning processes, policy development, dispute resolution procedures, and others. Although many PDSs begin quite informally based on individual contacts among faculty of the cooperating organizations, institutionalization of the PDS requires increasing formality in governance.

Second, *resource commitments by each partner and exchanges* should be firmly established and documented, particularly around professional education and inquiry. Resources include time, funds, personnel, and materials, and they may be supplied externally or located internally, based on restructuring. For example, at Holt High School, a PDS affiliated with Michigan State University, the faculty worked out a plan to revise the school schedule to make Wednesday mornings available for PDS planning and professional development. Students now arrive after lunch on Wednesdays, and faculty work on professional matters in that regularly scheduled time period. Schools across the country are becoming inventive in locating time for professional activity. A PDS already has potential resources available in the form of interns, graduate students, and university faculty and staff. Such personnel may be deployed in a variety of ways to support the learning of all participants. Resource exchanges of various kinds can support the PDS mission, and plans for this should be formally articulated (see, for example, Theobald, 1991; and the cases in Darling-Hammond, 1994). Since external standards against which to judge resource adequacy are not yet available, standard setters will want to begin developing more detailed guidance on this as experience accumulates across schools.

A third threshold condition establishes the *meaningful involvement of key participants*. Such assurances cover the extent of school faculty involvement and the university's commitment; they include not only graduate students and support staff, but regular, tenured faculty from both the school of education and the liberal arts and sciences departments. On both school and university sides, these are tough-minded conditions. On the school side, some PDSs engage only a small subset of the total faculty and so cannot be considered a school-wide commitment in any sense. Although the standard may not be full participation, and there will be many degrees of involvement in PDS-related work, substantial participation of school faculty is a requirement that should be documented.

Likewise, on the university side the early experiments suggest heavy involvement by graduate students and staff, some engagement on the part of young, untenured faculty, little regular participation by senior faculty in education, and almost no involvement by liberal arts and sciences faculty. Prerequisite standards here should signal the firm intention that tenured faculty of the university engage in PDS activity on some regular basis. Universities can work out many arrangements, including rotating assignments, but this must be a resource commitment for the PDS enterprise. Again, no external standard is available to specify level and degree of participation so this must be codified gradually and inductively.

PDS Mission and Goals

Self-study typically begins with the institutional mission and goals as a basis for assessing progress. For the PDS, the mission concentrates primarily on the shared work of professional education and inquiry, although this may overlap with broader school planning activity. Mission and goals are not standards, but they are integral to the standard-setting process. Guidance to schools may supply specifications about the content and character of the mission statement and supporting goals, together with criteria for evaluating this aspect of the PDS.

The scope of the mission is an important consideration. As a minimal expectation, the mission should encompass the education of novice educators; the continuing education of school staff, particularly around PDS-related responsibilities; and the conduct of improvement-oriented, collaborative inquiry, especially teacher research on their own practices. Within this mix the question arises whether the PDS should be a site not only for the education of teachers but for guidance counselors, administrators, social workers, school nurses, and other personnel. What seems prudent at present is not to require such a range but to explicitly encourage many PDSs to experiment with multiple internships and their coordination. The balance here lies between the productive use of the PDS as a professional education site and the danger of overwhelming a school with an overly complex agenda, particularly at the start. Planning cycles may be multiyear to encourage long-cycle goal setting according to strategic plans that indicate how a PDS progressively will pursue its mission.

Reviewers also will establish criteria of various kinds for the mission and goals. For example, are they sufficiently specific in supplying operational guidance? Are they thorough in addressing key aspects of the PDS agenda? Do they account for central aspects of school context? Do they identify and address school problems in a forthright manner? Do the goals evolve from year to year to reflect development and to respond to changing conditions? Central guidance on the mission and goals, then, takes the form of specifications for these statements and criteria for their evaluation.

An emergent issue in many PDSs today is coordination among initiatives. The school may include a general improvement committee, often in response to state or district policy; a PDS coordinating or planning committee; and several other governing bodies associated with such reforms as the Accelerated Schools Program or the Coalition of Essential Schools. School leadership in such cases is responsible for "coordinating the coordinators" to avoid the ill effects of fragmentation. School examiners will want to cover this aspect of school functioning as they scrutinize the mission statement in relation to the school as a whole.

Quality Assurance Processes

This category for standards responds to the commitment of a PDS to engage in processes of continuous improvement. Standards warrant that a school have methods in place for tracking progress toward program goals and objectives. The origin of this commitment is the total quality management (TQM) movement, which emphasizes regular use of quantitative indicators to gauge ongoing quality of production processes with an eye to continuous improvement. Although the specific practices of TQM need not become part of PDS standard setting, the general principle is worth observing.

Central guidance on quality assurance processes would specify a set of content categories, together with criteria or principles for judging the adequacy of responses in each. The general approach is to specify the critical processes within a PDS that must be managed well if the mission and goals are to be fulfilled, then examine them based on evidence that can be presented via documentation and site visits. For the PDS, there are three core areas where quality assurance standards are important: learning professional practice; continuing professional development; and conducting improvement-oriented inquiry. Each of these areas requires a more fine-grained breakdown for standards, derived from research and consensus of relevant professional bodies.

Learning professional practice, for example, might include categories such as these:

- Co-planning and revising the curriculum of professional study;
- Evaluating progress of interns and making formative and summative decisions about them;
- Placing interns with teachers to ensure a good match;
- Preparing school-based practitioners for new roles such as mentor and master teacher;
- Co-supervising interns and practice teachers;
- Creating shared understandings among school–university faculty about central program themes and commitments;

- Studying professional pedagogy and supervision in order to make improvements;
- Coordinating the various aspects of the professional studies to ensure continuity and reinforcement of learning experiences.

For each such category, principles based on research and professional judgment would be established. For example, the Learning from Mentors research project of the National Center for Research on Teachers' Learning has developed the following principles of good practice for mentor teachers:

- For mentoring to be effective, it must be connected to a vision of good teaching.
- For mentoring to be effective, it must be informed by an understanding of learning to teach.
- Mentoring is more than a social role; it is also a professional practice.
- Mentors need time to mentor and opportunities to learn to mentor.

These and related principles covering other specific contexts could be explored, for they illustrate what quality assurance standards might consist of in particular aspects of professional education.

Likewise, an illustrative set of categories for improvement-oriented inquiry might be:

- Developing a mutual inquiry agenda among school and university faculty that identifies significant questions and issues;
- Sharing inquiry results within a community of practice;
- Enhancing the inquiry skills of school-based practitioners;
- Using the results of inquiry to guide educational improvement;
- Scrutinizing inquiry results according to methodological standards of good practice;
- Translating inquiry results into tools and practices for use in schools and classrooms.

The expectation is that PDSs will seek the best professional guidance in creating their standards, with regard both to school-wide processes and to subprocesses around central aspects of school mission and function. External standards or principles of good practice are available as a reference point in at least some areas. For example, the National Staff Development Council has established a set of principles for continuing professional development that can serve as a starting point in this area, together with review of available research findings on effective professional development practices.

The general approach, then, is to develop a set of principles and criteria for best practice in these three core areas, based on careful reviews of the available research and consultation with relevant professional bodies that have developed principles of good practice. These standards become the basis for local dialogue and development that review teams may examine.

The School as Learning Community

In addition to quality assurance processes organized around the core of the PDS mission, an external review team would want to examine the whole school as a context. The primary concern is the PDS mission—its resources, processes, and outcomes—but some attention to the school as a learning community is needed. There is a subtle but important distinction here, however. PDS standards are not the same as school accreditation standards. They should not encompass all aspects of school functioning at a close level of detail. At the same time, the whole school serves as an important context for the professional learning that is provided there. It would make little sense to warrant a PDS that attended relatively well to core mission issues, but otherwise was a dysfunctional school. Consequently, PDS standard setting must take account of overall school quality in terms of its impact on the core PDS mission, although in practice this will be a difficult balance to maintain and a tension for standard setters to consider.

A school review team might want to examine four broad areas of school functioning as an overall context for PDS activity. First, *school climate* includes attention to such basic issues as safety, security, and discipline, and the quality of relationships among adults and children. Next, *professional community* includes collegial interactions; school-embedded opportunities to learn; joint planning and work on curriculum, assessment, and instruction; teacher leadership; access to outside resources and perspectives; and other activities. Third, *school–community relations* encompass ways that the school engages parents in support of children's learning and development, coordinates services to children with special needs, draws on community resources for learning, and provides other services. Finally, the *school program* is a broad category that includes attention to the schoolwide curriculum and extracurriculum, the structural regularities of the school around time use and scheduling, student grouping practices, and related matters.

To reiterate, while these broad areas of school functioning are not a primary concern for PDS standards, they are a context that influences the

PDS mission and so must be examined. Problem identification and solving in these areas are important aspects of an effective school, and the standards process should have means to explore how a PDS goes about improving itself in basic terms.

Learning and Development Outcomes

Finally, each PDS should be able to demonstrate what results it is achieving and how it goes about examining them. The core question, from a public perspective, which as yet has no firm answer, asks what evidence exists that PDS experiences produce first-rate beginning teachers. It is vitally important to the future of the PDS movement to begin collecting data in response to this fundamental question, and the standard-setting process should serve as stimulus.

Here is another developmental issue, because good measures of learning to teach are only beginning to emerge. An important commitment of PDSs must be to create methods for gauging what teachers learn and to apply them within the context of the teacher preparation program, including experiences in PDSs. Performance assessment is one promising avenue to explore, and individual schools will want to experiment with a variety of methods tailored to program goals and objectives. The external review team, then, will ask a three-part question: What should novice teachers learn? Why is this the most important learning within the limited scope of preservice preparation? How is success in promoting the desired learning among students determined?

This approach frames outcome assessment as relative to locally determined mission and goals. External standards, however, would specify at least in broad outline the content categories of professional learning. Here, the continuum linking standards of the Interstate New Teachers Assessment and Support Consortium (INTASC) to those of the NBPTS is the logical starting point. The expectation is that PDSs would examine these standards, adapting them to the local context, together with relevant state licensure standards, then develop measures of learning to teach within this external–internal framework. The assessment practices created by the INTASC project and the NBPTS also constitute a starting point for methods that may be employed within the teacher education program and the PDS internship.

CONCLUSION

Standard setting for Professional Development Schools should be conceived as an opportunity to stimulate the growth of these new institutions and to promote the necessary changes in the partner institutions. If managed well, the standard-setting process can serve the learning and change process, and this is the proper aspiration for the PDS. The balancing act is to introduce external standards of various kinds grounded in professional consensus and empirical results that local schools may use flexibly to develop their own practices. In this spirit, standard setting may become a positive force in the growth of the Professional Development Schools.

REFERENCES

Ancess, J. (1994, April). *School learning from the school quality review: The Highland Elementary School one year after their SQR.* Paper presented at the annual meeting of the American Educational Research Association, New Orleans.

Ball, D. (1996, March). Teacher learning and the mathematics reforms: What do we think we know and what do we need to learn? *Phi Delta Kappan, 77*(7), 500–508.

Cohen, D. (1995). What standards for national standards? *Phi Delta Kappan, 76*(10), 751–757.

Darling-Hammond, L. (1993). Reframing the school reform agenda: Developing capacity for school transformation. *Phi Delta Kappan, 74*(10), 752–761.

Darling-Hammond, L. (Ed.). (1994). *Professional development schools: Schools for developing a profession.* New York: Teachers College Press.

Eisner, E. (1995). Standards for American schools: Help or hindrance? *Phi Delta Kappan, 76*(10), 758–764.

Elmore, R. (1983). Complexity and control: What legislators and administrators can do about implementing public policy. In L. S. Shulman & G. Sykes (Eds.), *Handbook of teaching and policy* (pp. 342–369). New York: Longman.

Ewell, P. (1992). Outcomes assessment, institutional effectiveness, and accreditation: A conceptual exploration. In *Accreditation, assessment, and institutional effectiveness* (pp. 1–17). Washington, DC: Council on Postsecondary Accreditation.

Goodlad, J. (1990). *Teachers for our nation's schools.* San Francisco: Jossey-Bass.

Goodlad, J. (1994). *Educational renewal: Better schools, better teachers.* San Francisco: Jossey-Bass.

Holmes Group. (1996). *Tomorrow's schools of education.* East Lansing, MI: Author.

Kagan, S. (1993). *Laura and Jim and what they taught me about the gap between educational theory and practice.* Albany: State University of New York Press.

Little, J. W. (1982). Norms of collegiality and experimentation: Workplace conditions of school success. *American Educational Research Journal, 19*(3), 325–340.

McLaughlin, M., & Talbert, J. (1993). *Contexts that matter for teaching and learning. Strategic opportunities for meeting the nation's education goals.* Palo

Alto, CA: Stanford University, Center for Research on the Context of Secondary School Teaching.

Sarason, S. (1982). *The culture of the school and the problem of change* (2nd ed.). Boston: Allyn & Bacon.

Schlechty, P. (1990). *Reform in teacher education: A sociological view.* Washington, DC: American Association of Colleges for Teacher Education.

Schön, D. (1971). *Beyond the stable state.* New York: Norton.

Siskin, L. (1991). Departments as different worlds: Subject subcultures in secondary schools. *Educational Administration Quarterly, 27*(2), 134-160.

Theobald, N. D. (1991). Staffing, financing, and governing professional development schools. *Educational Evaluation and Policy Analysis, 13*(1), 87-101.

Part III

Stories from the Field

The Stories of Insiders

ROBERTA TRACHTMAN

During the past 15 years, reformers repeatedly have called for school restructuring and the reinvention of teacher education. While advocates usually focus on either one or the other reform stream, all consistently suggest that school-based teachers are the linchpin to change. According to many, teachers are both the cause of school failure and the only hope for its salvation. Not surprisingly, then, states and localities have attempted to mandate change by passing dozens of new school policies directed toward improving schools by improving teacher quality and the professionalization of teachers.

By locating the problem and the promise of school renewal within teachers, the recruitment and retention of quality educators became headline news in the 1980s. States sought to improve teaching and teachers through screens and magnets (Sykes, 1983). Legislators tried to increase the "supply side" of the teacher pool through the provision of scholarships, forgivable student loans, and alternative certification routes. In addition, they sought to screen out less able candidates by imposing admission and exit tests.

For the most part, the states' efforts to reform teacher education did little to alter the practice of teaching, since the laws changed neither the ways that new teachers came to understand their roles nor how they were inducted and socialized into the profession. By supporting programs like Teach for America and other quick routes into teaching, the states (and corporate leaders) continued to reinforce a prevailing belief that almost anyone could teach (Darling-Hammond, 1994).

While the reform-by-mandate army appeared on all fronts, other voices began to emerge. Most notable among them were the Holmes Group deans and professors who called for the creation of Professional Development Schools in order to redesign teacher preparation, induction, and continuous teacher development.

At the American Federation of Teachers (AFT), Marsha Levine (one of this book's editors) responded to the call for PDSs by creating a national task force of AFT-elected officers, education research and policy experts, teachers, and university representatives. Supported with funding from the Exxon Education Foundation, the task force developed a theoretical framework for creating new institutions that would be collaboratively planned and implemented by the teachers' union, the school district, and the university in local areas. After 2 years of work, and with additional support from Exxon, the AFT recruited three pilot sites to move PDS theory into practice. Two of the PDS pilots were created at urban high schools, one in the northeast and the other in the midwest. The third site was a very large, urban elementary school in the far west. In spring 1991, after a year of planning, each site received a 2-year grant to develop its PDS.

As participants in the AFT Professional Development Schools began to plan for their work in late spring 1990, Marsha asked me to join the project as its documenter. In this role, I would attempt to record for "the field" (nonproject members) the ways that participants in these three PDS sites initiated their work, encountered and solved problems, and created new school forms. As we began to collect and analyze the data, we soon realized that the documentation process also could be used as an instrument for reflection among the PDS insiders. We believed that the data would provide participants with an opportunity to examine what was happening and with a basis upon which to make mid-course corrections, recognize needs, and address obstacles.

While for 2 years I sought to make meaningful connections with participants by attending all cross-site meetings and by speaking with them at length by phone, at best I was able to move from being a dispassionate outsider to being a friendly, neighborly outsider (Savage, 1988). I listened to the participants and recorded their stories, but I was only a part of their retrospective reflections; I was off site and out of sight for the real action, for the practice-in-action. While I worked hard to create a useful document, the stories I reported were distant and decontextualized. Given my outsider status, the year-long data collection process, and the decision to weave the stories from the three sites into a set of generic themes, this work did not substantially affect the participants in their daily struggles.

During the first 2 years of the project, it appeared as though I was the only one systematically engaged in a process of inquiry. While PDS members declared themselves dedicated to the goal of inquiring about their practices, participants were too busy doing the work to find time to reflect on it. The experiences of these participants mirrored much of what was happening at other PDS sites: The processes of reflection and analysis continued to take a backseat to action (see Teitel, 1995, for a full discussion of this dilemma).

As we approached the final project year, we decided to change the documentation process by asking the sites to take over this effort and tell their own stories. We asked them to write the insiders' story about what it was like to build a Professional Development School. We invited participants to a cross-site meeting to discuss how the work might be done. By the end of the meeting, a school-based teacher had volunteered to take on the task at one site; a university-based teacher had taken it on at a second site; and an outsider was invited to work with participants at the third site, where participants did not want to write their own story.

The stories that follow are not intended to represent all PDS sites, nor are they included as exemplars of good practice. Instead, we ask readers to think about them in two ways. As Walton (1992) suggested in his discussion of case studies, these stories are "instances": They are situationally grounded, limited views of social life. At the same time, as Wasley (1994) described, these school change stories are also "tales of contemporary pilgrims set out on a shared journey toward better schooling" (p. xvii). Because we hoped that these stories would reflect the perspectives and values of participants, we did not bind the chroniclers to a predetermined set of questions or to other narrow prescriptions. Instead, we asked them to tell their stories by raising the voices of participants (McDonald, 1986). As we brainstormed an array of approaches for doing this work, we anticipated that each story would be different in important ways. We hoped that each would somehow reflect the PDS and its context, knowing how complicated it would be for the writers to move between their roles as participants and authors.

We soon discovered that not all participant voices would be represented equally in the tales. Some members had little to say when they were asked to contribute their perspectives. Others worried about "coming clean" about their experiences, given their anticipated continued employment in these schools. Some, in fact, insisted that we keep their individual and site identities hidden. We have honored their requests, but acknowledge that not all participants preferred anonymity (see Shulman's, 1990, discussion of such dilemmas).

In their work on narratives, Tappan and Brown (1989) wrote that "the telling of a story is not the rendering of facts, but rather the putting together of a plot that imposes meanings on the events reported" (cited in Gitlin, 1990, p. 46). We would like to propose some ideas that may help readers examine meanings suggested by the PDS storytellers. They should not be confused with law-like generalizations. Instead, as Carter (1993) suggested in her discussion of the place of story in teaching and teacher education, these organizers are "explanatory propositions" (p. 10). These ideas may help make sense of the "dilemmas and problematics" inherent in the creation of PDSs.

CHANGING THE CORE

For the most part, during the 1980s school reformers avoided the hard issues associated with learning and teaching (Louis & Miles, 1990). As school-based management and shared decision-making advocates worked to change the governance and authority structures in schools, initiatives aimed at curricular and pedagogical change slipped out of sight. With the states, the business community, parents, administrators, and teachers demanding to know, "Who's in charge?" the core concerns of schooling— teaching and learning—were cast aside.

In stark contrast to myriad structural and organizational change efforts initiated during the past decade, inventing PDSs required participants to change their core practices and beliefs about teachers and students (see Chapter 1). As the PDSs developed, participants found themselves in simultaneous pursuit of school improvement and teacher development. Unlike others who were pursuing these goals in parallel fashion, Professional Development School members learned that the goals were inextricably linked.

These stories highlight some of the complexities involved in translating theory into practice. By describing what it takes to make change happen, the authors reveal how hard it is to do more than just think good thoughts.

INVENTION—PLANNING FOR THE CREATION OF NEW SETTINGS

General Challenges

The theoretical literature describing the creation of new settings offers some important lenses through which to examine the school invention tales that follow. First, we know that the creation of new settings challenges the sacred beliefs and taken-for-granted behaviors of organization members (Sarason, 1972). Further, since new organizations take resources away from existing initiatives, they are watched closely; their visibility and high-profile status raise the stakes by which nonparticipants measure their wins and losses. Second, because people and places have long histories, participants in new organizations need to pay close attention to the time before the beginning (Sarason, 1972). For each PDS, this refers to the time during which participants at the school or university site may have developed problematic or supportive beliefs about themselves, their work, and their prospective cross-institutional partner. Third, as Stinchcombe (1965) suggested, inventing new roles, developing new relationships, and creating an organizational culture have high costs in time, worry, conflict, and temporary inefficiency. This is because the new organization must go from having no beliefs to new beliefs, from no rules to new rules, and from no culture to new culture (Pettigrew, 1979). Fourth, especially in the beginning, new organizations rely heavily on social relations among near or complete strangers. In new settings, the actions and attitudes of each member are particularly visible, since people have yet to develop routinized roles and responsibilities. Fifth, as Schein (1985) wrote, each new organization faces problems related to external adaptation and internal integration. Consequently, the new institution must struggle simultaneously with its own growth and its effects on the rest of the ecosystem to which it belongs. Finally, according to Selznick (1957), how the organization evolves depends largely on its early decisions regarding where its resources are and upon whom it is dependent.

Challenges for the Schools

During the planning year, participants in these three PDSs learned the importance of continuously examining their intellectual and conceptual understandings. While participants articulated a shared mission and considerable agreement regarding project objectives, their activities and processes in the planning year revealed "conceptual blips" on the Professional Development School screen. As they worked to define new roles for teachers, they discovered an array of dilemmas (including sacred school and teacher norms) that discouraged collegiality and connectedness. They discovered that earlier experiences had not prepared them for working in new ways with other school and university members. Further, they learned that current institutional resources did not provide for teacher activity outside the classroom and across traditional role boundaries. School and university participants were not excused from fulfilling their regular role obligations during the planning year. Their work lives were complicated further by their efforts to connect the PDS to the rest of the school and university community; consequently, they spent countless hours sharing their plans with colleagues, hoping to gain support for the concepts and assumptions undergirding their work. Most significantly, they learned that the redesign of teachers' work would require forging new bonds with building administrators. As they worked toward redefining teacher and administrator influence, they discovered that not all school and university administrators wanted (or knew how) to play a role in the creation of this new organization.

At times during the invention process, school-based participants were distracted by exogenous shocks in the form of unsigned contracts, school calendar realignments, and unanticipated budget shortfalls. In other instances, local site, district, and university support for the project appeared to wane, leaving participants unsure about the short- and long-term future of their efforts. During the invention process, the university participants struggled to convince their underresourced departments to support a more expensive field-based model of teacher education. Further, bound by traditional publish or perish obligations, university-based faculty felt considerable tension as they spent more time at school sites, collaborating with practitioners in ways that did not necessarily lead to articles for refereed journals.

The Professional Development School's local context affected the planning process in important ways. As resources grew tighter at the school and university, some began to suggest that the PDS was a luxury they could ill afford. For some, the new initiative posed unacceptable opportunity costs in terms of time, space, money, and staff. By the end of the planning year, several participants had lost their jobs. Unlike other school and university improvement efforts, the development of the PDS required approval, support, and cooperation from the larger school community. Participants learned that the creation of new settings with new norms required lengthy meetings, ongoing discussion, and new kinds of intra- and interorganizational connections. They learned that they needed more time than they had budgeted for planning the creation of a new organization.

ESTABLISHING COUNTERCULTURAL SETTINGS

The PDS is countercultural. It asks participants to let go of important beliefs, significant allegiances, and deeply ingrained practices. For example, participating elementary and secondary school teachers already had multiple group memberships and allegiances when they decided to become part of the PDS. They might have seen themselves primarily as members of particular departments or grade levels, as teachers of special students, or as union leaders. Yet, the Professional Development School asked them to become members of a different group. For some, membership in the PDS meant that they had to give up their other allegiances when it came time to allocating scarce resources. This shift in allegiance at the school sites increased teachers' role strains and made their work in the PDS more "costly."

As a group, the experienced school and university teachers in these

PDSs had already learned how to work well independently. However, the PDS demanded that they collaborate with school- and university-based others as part of their daily work lives. As participants tried to reinvent themselves in this new way, they had little time and few resources to develop the skills and knowledge needed for collegiality, inquiry, and a problem-based orientation to learning and teaching. Unused to receiving and giving feedback to peers, they often kept silent, waiting for inevitable conflicts to pass. Interestingly, some teachers summarily dismissed the value of the PDS because of its implicit indictment of long-standing practices and beliefs. For these teachers, the PDS seemed to suggest that their careers as teachers represented little more than a history of malpractice.

At first, teachers' beliefs continued to reflect their overarching commitment to self and students rather than to the workplace or to the development of others (Huberman, 1990; Lortie, 1975; Prawat, 1991). Teachers found that PDS activities took them away from their students. For many, this out-of-classroom work filled them with guilt (see Hargreaves, 1995, for a compelling examination of the ways in which school reform initiatives intensify teachers' work). They were not ready to consider teachers' job enlargement as a legitimate way to improve student learning.

Individuals and institutions voluntarily choose to work together only when they have reason to believe that their engagement will serve each of them well. In cross-institutional relationships, participants seek reciprocity and fair rates of return on their investments. PDS school-based teachers spoke warmly about their new collegial relationships with university colleagues, their new roles as learners, and their new understandings about the ways that children think and grow. Like other mid-career teachers engaged in the redesign of their work (see Ebmeier & Weaver Hart, 1992), participants enjoyed the unique opportunities for personal and professional growth related to the PDS.

Through their PDS work, teachers developed important leadership roles. As they began to participate in activities at the school building, district, state, and national level, they developed group process, conflict management, and power skills. As mentors to new colleagues, as peer coaches, and as collaborative developers of new curricula, they developed new kinds of interpersonal and human relations skills. Finally, as they began to work regularly with other professionals (teacher colleagues, administrators, and university teachers), they tapped into previously unexplored reservoirs of personal power.

Some student teachers seemed to value especially the group experiences and the climate of trust provided in the PDS. In a few instances, school and university teachers worked collaboratively to design opportunities for themselves and their student teachers to teach and learn together. However, for the most part, the university teacher education programs in which PDS student teachers were enrolled did not differ markedly from traditional approaches. Given the limited participation of university-based faculty and administrators, the clinical supervision of student teachers remained dependent on the preferred practices of individual college-based supervisors. Ironically, while theorists had proposed the redesign of teacher education as one of the four most critical goals of the PDS, the paradigm of teacher education remained relatively unchanged in the early years of PDS invention.

As the writers suggest, after the initial 3 years of work, the Professional Development School remained an important project, rather than an integral part of the school and university. Its "project" status was reflected in the limited participation of school and university members and the ways in which nonparticipants described the PDS. The PDS stood apart from the larger school and university communities. Participants traced this distancing to the ways in which the initiative started, to how it had been promoted, to the secrecy and mystification that surrounded membership, and to the long-standing organizational norms that made it difficult to do cross-institutional, countercultural work. Riots, student walkouts, and citywide violence made it even harder for participants to focus attention on their work. State initiatives, including alternative routes to teacher certification and proposed reductions in university budgets, raised concerns from members of both institutions about the returns on their investments of time, energy, and resources.

I conclude by restating the obvious: Inventing and building a PDS is very difficult work. While the theory is powerful, the practice is often exhausting and overwhelming. By writing about their work, the PDS authors have learned a great deal about themselves. We hope that their stories help readers to think about their own Professional Development School experiences and the work that lies ahead.

REFERENCES

Carter, K. (1993). The place of story in the study of teaching and teacher education. *Educational Researcher, 22*(1), 5–12, 18.

Darling-Hammond, L. (1994). Who will speak for the children? How "Teach for America" hurts urban schools and students. *Phi Delta Kappan, 76*(1), 21–34.

Ebmeier, H., & Weaver Hart, A. (1992). The effects of a career-ladder program on school organizational process. *Educational Evaluation and Policy Analysis, 14*(34), 261–281.

Gitlin, A. D. (1990). Educative research, voice and school change. *Harvard Educational Review, 60*(4), 43–66.

Hargreaves, A. (1995). *Changing teachers, changing times.* New York: Teachers College Press.

Huberman, M. (1990, April). *The social context of instruction in schools.* Paper presented at the annual meeting of the American Educational Research Association, Boston.

Lortie, D. (1975). *Schoolteacher: A sociological study.* Chicago: University of Chicago Press.

Louis, K. S., & Miles, M. B. (1990). *Improving urban high schools.* New York: Teachers College Press.

McDonald, J. P. (1986). Raising the teacher's voice and the ironic role of theory. *Harvard Educational Review, 56*(4), 355–378.

Pettigrew, A. M. (1979). On studying organizational cultures. *Administrative Science Quarterly, 24,* 570–581.

Prawat, R. S. (1991). Conversations with self and settings: A framework for thinking about teacher empowerment. *American Educational Research Journal, 28*(4), 737–757.

Sarason, S. (1972). *The creation of new settings and the future societies.* San Francisco: Jossey-Bass.

Savage, D. (1988). Can ethnographic narrative be a neighborly act? *Anthropology & Education Quarterly, 19,* 3–19.

Schein, E. H. (1985). *Organizational culture and leadership: A dynamic view.* San Francisco: Jossey-Bass.

Selznick, P. (1957). *Leadership in administration.* Evanson, IL: Harper & Row.

Shulman, J. H. (1990). Now you see them, now you don't: Anonymity versus visibility in case studies of teachers. *Educational Researcher, 19*(6), 11–15.

Sykes, G. (1983). Public policy and the problem of teacher quality: The need for screens and magnets. In L. S. Shulman & G. Sykes (Eds.), *Handbook of teaching and policy* (pp. 97–125). New York: Longman.

Stinchcombe, A. L. (1965). Social structure and organizations. In J. G. March (Ed.), *Handbook of organizations* (pp. 142–193). Chicago: Rand McNally.

Tappan, M., & Brown, L. (1989). Stories told and lessons learned: Toward a narrative approach to moral development and moral education. *Harvard Educational Review, 59*(2), 182–205.

Teitel, L. (1995). *NCATE PDS standards project literature review.* Washington, DC: National Council of Teacher Accreditation.

Walton, J. (1992). Making the theoretical case. In C. C. Ragin & H. S. Becker (Eds.), *What is a case? Exploring the foundations of social inquiry* (pp. 121–137). Cambridge: Cambridge University Press.

Wasley, P. A. (1994). *Stirring the chalkdust: Tales of teachers changing classroom practice.* New York: Teachers College Press.

Chapter 9

The Thomas Paine Professional Development School

JEAN A. KING

HOW THE PDS CAME TO BE

If any one person can be credited with the origin of the Professional Development School at Thomas Paine High School (see Figure 9.1) in a midwest city, it is Lois Allen, president of the Metropolitan Federation of Teachers (MFT) and long-time supporter of professional development activities for Metropolitan teachers. Allen served on a national task force that initially brought practitioners and researchers together to formulate the PDS concept. The task force commissioned papers on various aspects of the concept that were presented as a document, including recommendations for the structure and design of a Professional Development School. When the Exxon Foundation funded the implementation of the concept outlined in the task force report by creating three such schools nationally, Allen believed strongly that one of these three should be in a Metropolitan high school. Several factors supported her belief: the political desirability of this particular project, which promoted collaboration between schools and universities and professional development across teachers' lifetimes; an opportunity to build visibly on the long-standing University of Midstate tradition of and reputation for developing educational practice for the nation; some political standing in the national organization that caused people to believe the project would be planted in fertile soil; the highly pragmatic fact that Linda Kellogg, an MFT associate teaching in the MFT/College of St. Sebastian master's degree program, was available to write the grant proposal; and a likely site for the proposed PDS.

Making Professional Development Schools Work: Politics, Practice, and Policy. Copyright © 1997 by Teachers College, Columbia University. All rights reserved. ISBN 0-8077-3633-3 (pbk.), ISBN 0-8077-3634-1 (cloth). Prior to photocopying items for classroom use, please contact the Copyright Clearance Center, Customer Service, 222 Rosewood Dr., Danvers, MA 01923, USA, tel. (508) 750-8400.

Thomas Paine High School

Lois Allen approached Metropolitan School District Superintendent William Sicoli to discuss which of the several high schools might apply to become a PDS. Few in Metropolitan would have identified Thomas Paine High School as the likely site, and another high school actively sought support. But Thomas Paine was known to be a school in need and, of all the high schools, the one most deserving special attention. Once the pride of its white, blue-collar neighborhood, Paine's reputation after desegregation in the 1960s had sunk to that of the worst high school in the city, a reputation supported by declining student enrollment, attendance and behavior problems, and test scores continually the lowest of all high schools. Although a small group of teachers remained at Paine year after year, few others sought to join them, viewing placement at Paine as a temporary stop until an opening occurred at a more desirable school. Paine was the only Metropolitan high school at that time without a magnet program to attract academically motivated students. Instead, its functional "magnet" was a special education program that drew emotionally and behaviorally disordered (EBD) students from around the city, creating special challenges for the entire faculty.

The choice was actually not as bold as it might have seemed. As Allen and the superintendent knew, Paine already contained the seeds of dramatic change: Principal Rita Mease and a cadre of reform-minded teachers were determined to improve the school. Mease's leadership style, described as "supportive" and "invitational," encouraged teachers in the building to break with tradition in order to better serve Paine's students. "Rita was the administrator who said, 'You have a new idea. Go try it.' She'd get things to happen." As one teacher put it:

> Rita was very clear in the message: "You are here to change, and I will support your change. Don't be limited by what you have done in the past. If you want to try something different, think about it. Don't tell me it can't be done; tell me what you want to do first."

Her success-oriented style led eventually to a feature story in the *Metropolitan Post*. During Mease's tenure, numerous initiatives sparked Paine's faculty and staff into action. They included a continuing partnership with Metropolitan City Bank (MCB) that provided, among other things, MCB mentors for Paine students, summer jobs in the bank and college scholarships for a small number of students, and a program to recognize student achievement publicly; a grant from a local foundation that assisted the Paine school community in organizing for site-based decision making; and the initiation of teacher and student teams for some Paine staff. By providing professional development opportunities for Paine teachers, access to the latest research, and the potential of additional staff, the PDS proposal would be a further initiative to develop the changes Mease actively sought.

She was not alone in seeking these changes. Six Paine teachers had enrolled as a cohort in the MFT-sponsored master's degree program with the College of St. Sebastian. Together, these teachers were studying the process of education reform and change in the context of their practice at Paine, taught in part by Linda Kellogg, a knowledgeable instructor with extensive background in school change and a special interest in the ideas of Theodore Sizer. The Paine cohort was a group of committed urban professionals. As one of them stated, "Why would you teach somewhere where anybody could teach? At Paine, we're needed." For these teachers, the ideas from their graduate studies were motivating. One teacher, recalling the experience, wrote:

> I can remember feeling like I had crawled out of a cave into light. The problems at Paine had seemed so unbearable, hopeless, and impossible, yet here were other schools trying to make a difference. . . . The assignments I wrote for class were my dreams of what could happen. . . . And then Linda and Lois came to Paine, and, as they say, the rest is history.

Given the support of a dynamic principal and a core group of committed teachers, the selection of Paine as the PDS site made sense. A majority of the Paine faculty voted to support the proposal's development in spring 1990 after a challenging faculty meeting. In retrospect, this support may have come for fairly personal reasons, that is, seeing the PDS as a way to "get more adult bodies" into the building, to reduce the student–teacher ratio, and, for many, "to make my own life easier." But with the support of the faculty, the MFT had one-half of the collaboration in place.

The University of Midstate

The choice of the College of Education at the University of Midstate as the other half of the partnership also made sense. The College's dean had been extremely active in the American Association of Colleges for Teacher Education (AACTE) in the previous few years, serving in a leadership role for a year and working locally to change certification in the College from undergraduate to postbaccalaureate programs. The University of Midstate was the only teacher preparation institution in the area that belonged to the

Holmes Group, owing to its status as a research university and its commitment to teacher education based on both disciplinary and pedagogical knowledge. While preparing only a small number of teachers for the state, the College's programs sought to be model versions of what teacher preparation should be.

So when Lois Allen approached Don Lund, the associate dean charged with teacher education in the College, he did not hesitate in agreeing to participate, recognizing the long-term potential of this collaboration. "We brainstormed what the content could be. It was all these issues out on the table, all these possibilities, and they [Allen and Kellogg] took every one of them and put them into the proposal." The problem, however, was timing. With the proposal due in just 21 days as faculty were leaving for the summer, Lund had virtually no time for the consultation that is the hallmark of the traditional collegial process. As he later remembered, "No faculty had any time to put any input into it at all. . . . It just seemed a way to connect in ways that we hadn't before, that this was the right thing to do from my perspective. Difficult, but the right thing to do." The long-term effect that this would have on the project was significant.

The Professional Development School

The MFT received notice of the proposal's success in July 1990 and then began a year-long planning effort in preparation for implementation of the PDS in 1991–92. During the planning year, Linda Kellogg served as project director, facilitating discussion between Paine and College faculty. Don Lund assigned George Swenson, a long-time faculty member and head of the College's Student Teaching Office, to serve as liaison from the College. At Paine, 10 teachers expressed interest in the planning, as did the representative from Paine's business partner, Metropolitan City Bank.

Plan they did. During the year, numerous meetings of a PDS Steering Committee explored ways in which Paine and College faculty could work together to change both institutions and to prepare teachers to teach effectively in an inner-city environment. Three professional visits outside the area—the Holmes Group annual meeting in Washington, DC; a trip to New York City to visit schools implementing the Coalition of Essential Schools model; and attendance at AFT's QUEST in Washington, DC—all paid for by the local union, led to continuing discussions of how the Paine Professional Development School might function. The active support of Principal Mease and Dean Lund was evidenced by their attendance at both the Holmes Group and PDS project meetings, as well as at several locally held sessions.

During the third trimester, a Paine social studies teacher was released an hour a day to devote time to planning the PDS, and the Steering Committee decided that, rather than hire an outside project manager, two co-coordinators—one a Paine teacher (Susan Travers) and one a College faculty member (George Swenson)—would direct the PDS in the coming year. Knowing the importance of leadership training for Travers, Lund successfully nominated her for a well-known educational leadership training program in the state, ensuring that she would study with a group of Midstate's educational leaders, both principals and teachers, examining contemporary issues in leading change. In addition, Linda Kellogg, who directed the year-long planning effort, began her doctoral work in the College, serving as a teaching assistant to George Swenson and working with secondary education students. When John Goodlad visited the school in May 1991 to meet with PDS faculty, there could be no doubt that PDS ideas were thick in the air.

From the beginning, however, it seemed at times an almost overwhelming challenge to create a unified professional community from two highly disparate faculties already running at full tilt. At both Paine and the College, a sizable number of people expanded neither their philosophies nor their professional efforts to include the PDS. This is not to say, however, that people were not working hard. Problems stemmed in part from the fact that people were engaged in parallel change efforts, rather than one unified endeavor, a by-product of Rita Mease's open style that allowed Paine teachers to choose where to place their emphases. So, for instance, the group developing the PDS was different from the group developing the site council for the school, leading one day to simultaneous meetings at opposite ends of the media center. Given that their intentions overlapped to a wide extent, the PDS table noted the irony of the dual meetings, but the committees were never merged. One person later defended this separation: "There were still so many things going on that they needed to be distinct."

Other Paine teachers chose to put their efforts more directly into teaming and classroom instruction or into program development (e.g., the International Baccalaureate program introduced that year to attract academically oriented students to the school), all clearly related to the long-term goals of the PDS, but not to its immediate planning. As one person put it, "I want to be very much involved with this [PDS], but [my programmatic leadership] has to be my primary responsibility if that program is going to succeed." For probationary teachers, many of whom would lose their jobs over the summer due to layoffs, teacher transfers, and minority hiring preference, day-to-day functioning took precedence over long-term thinking.

For College faculty, the development of the PDS may have seemed a timely effort, but two important factors worked against their involvement.

First, teacher education faculty already were busily engaged in what they viewed as meaningful collaborations with schools other than Paine and saw little reason to commit themselves to an untried and challenging endeavor. Several held the belief that Paine was a bad site for a PDS, both because of its overall reputation and because of the perceived level of professional practice in the school. As one faculty member explained,

> My notion was if they [PDS planners] could have shut Paine down, had hiring of staff by both the College and Metropolitan, and took some time off to restructure their program to truly make it a labora- tory kind of school, it could have worked a lot more effectively. . . . If you had more teachers who really wanted to be there and were re- ally competent to be there, the university would have been more ex- cited to be there.

Second, in the words of Don Lund, "the process that had to be used in putting the proposal together was a major detriment to getting faculty on board because they had no awareness of this; it was done by a dean." The project's origin with the MFT — outside the College, rather than from within the several programs that prepared teachers — and its visible support by the Dean's Office were extremely problematic for some faculty. The PDS "was viewed as a Dean's Office project," an "arranged marriage"; "there wasn't ownership of the program by the College." In addition, faculty questioned the extent to which service projects like the PDS would be rewarded in the College's research-oriented reward system. In retrospect, given these constraints, what is fairly surprising is the willingness with which faculty from a number of licensure areas attended PDS meetings and engaged in serious planning.

Plans for the initiation of the PDS were finalized over the summer of 1991. A 2-day retreat off site led to a public commitment of effort and the refinement of three overarching PDS goals: to support student academic and social learning; to support the professional education of teachers; and to support inquiry directed at the improvement of practice. The year of planning was completed.

TWO YEARS OF PDS IMPLEMENTATION

Year One

Thus began the implementation of the Thomas Paine PDS. Over the course of the first year, 27 practicum students and six student teachers worked at Paine. A unified staff development plan, created in conjunction with the district head of staff development, provided support for PDS teachers to attend professional meetings related to school climate and restructuring. George Swenson actively sought to involve College faculty by inviting them, one at a time, to visit with various departments (e.g., science, second languages). He saw his role as "developing partnerships and programs," and, to the extent possible, he tried to meet the needs of specific teachers. Travers and Swenson prepared a successful grant to the Midstate Department of Education to establish a mentoring program for new teachers, and three highly experienced PDS teachers served as faculty mentors during the year.

PDS faculty from both the school and university sites attended professional meetings outside of the area — the Coalition of Essential Schools' Fall Forum in Chicago and a meeting of the PDS sites in Washington, DC — as well as a conference on assessment and reform, sponsored by the Panasonic Foundation. Susan Travers participated in off-site leadership training sessions and developed a change project in conjunction with a professor in the College's Department of Recreation who served as a consultant on experiential education to the student leadership program. During the spring, the PDS funded an extra hour of daily planning time for the three members of the Essential Schools team, time later labeled as one of the most important supports of the change process: "There was a lot of trust that if they gave us that time, we would use it."

While much good happened during the year, there were also problems that affected the process. A crisis of enormous consequence to the PDS during its first year of operation was the serious and debilitating illness of Paine's principal, Rita Mease. Mease was unable to work for long periods of time and, when she did return to the building, was often too weak to remain a full day. A supportive Paine staff rallied around her, pitching in to keep the school functioning. However, the absence of the enthusiastic and smiling principal, who walked the hallways speaking words of encouragement to students and staff alike, was a major loss. Without her support and leadership, all change efforts felt less secure. As one PDS teacher put it, "We didn't have someone who could say, 'The PDS is important.'" Mease's transfer to a junior high school in the spring of 1992 and the assignment of a long-time administrator due to retire in October 1992 as temporary principal left the PDS without the active and long-term support of its building administrator.

While a second 2-day summer PDS retreat "broke down the barriers" for those who attended, 1992–93 brought Paine's PDS faculty — and especially co-coordinator Susan Travers — face to face with almost continuous tensions and continuing challenges. Because of district policy related to layoffs, many probationary faculty were removed from the building, resulting in last-minute hiring of numerous teachers and the need to orient them to Paine. In a district where building leadership could have a dramatic effect on educational practice, the question of who would become Paine's principal occupied people's minds during the fall trimester. At the same time, few people from the university actively sought to participate in the PDS. The College co-coordinator became occupied with matters on campus and spent less time in the building than he had during the first year. In the midst of their strenuous teaching schedules, PDS teachers had the feeling that College faculty might be reluctant to place students at Paine and worried that, although the mentorship program for new faculty at Paine was successful, the PDS might not thrive. "There's been no feedback on our pioneering efforts and no assistance from the university," said a teacher. Another noted, however, that "the noninvolvement had a positive side. The good side of it was that we really had to evolve our own things. There were no answers, other than what we wanted to try."

Those who developed the quarterly reports about the project, required by the funders, sensed that nothing they wrote could please the Washington-based director, who repeatedly asked pointed questions about what progress was being made.

Year Two

Two crises in the fall of 1992 pointed to the leadership role Susan Travers necessarily had assumed in the absence of a permanent building principal and more involved College faculty. In response to public pressure, a Metropolitan School Board member proposed a policy early in the school year to dramatically limit staff development in the district. Metropolitan teachers were to be in classrooms teaching, not out of classrooms learning during school hours. As one Paine teacher summarized this view, "Teachers at the K–12 level cannot afford to be out of their classrooms [because] too much disruption takes place." This meant that Paine lost its "banked" days, that is, release days created by keeping track of the time that students were in school longer than was required by law. These banked staff development days were to provide critical time for meeting, planning, and reflective dialogue essential to the development of the PDS, and their loss was a severe setback for the project.

To his credit, the acting principal was willing to battle the bureaucracy, and he and Travers requested a variance from the School Board to reinstate the days. The first hurdle, the district Variance Committee, comprising teachers, parents, and community representatives, was easily passed. By contrast, the formal hearing by the full Board was in retrospect a grueling nightmare—an hour of intense grilling, public posturing, and an eventual favorable vote, supported in part by a Paine parent who served on the Board. Few teachers in the building understood Travers's stressful experience that regained the lost days; for Travers, it was a lesson in district politics never to be forgotten.

The second crisis again found Travers fighting to preserve Paine's status as a PDS. Over the course of the 1992–93 school year, College faculty, led by George Swenson, were working to restructure the fieldwork portion of the College's teacher education program. The efforts had little to do with Paine directly; given the budgetary demise of the College's Student Teaching Office, Swenson and other teacher educators needed a new structural mechanism to ensure good placements and effective supervision of College practicum students and student teachers. The notion of "district centers," that is, school districts that would agree to a long-term relationship to develop highly competent teachers in specific schools to work with groups of College students, emerged, with Metropolitan a likely first site.

However, at a meeting in December, the question arose as to whether the Metropolitan PDS should be exclusively at Thomas Paine or whether the concept should be spread to multiple sites. Perhaps the new PDS model should consist of a constellation of departments, rather than a single school. Those present—including Swenson, MFT President Lois Allen, and the head of the joint MFT/MPS Teaching Support program—cited troublesome issues at Paine, such as too many programs that diffused focus and too few departments with experienced staff. Some staff and parents questioned the amount of teacher turnover, presumably dissatisfied staff moving to better school sites.

Fortunately, two teachers attending the meeting with Travers spoke in support of the PDS efforts at Paine. After all, the project was in its second year of implementation, and from what they knew about school change, that was hardly a fair trial of a complex, new idea. Certain efforts, like the mentorship program, were in place, and the process was evolving. There were many exemplary teachers at Paine. To expand the PDS program beyond Paine at that point, with Exxon funding still available, would send a strange message both to the external funders and to the PDS teachers who had struggled to establish a professional community around teacher education and education reform. One of the teachers later reported that Travers "stuck to her guns," refusing to even allow the possibility of Paine's not being the single professional development site. But, as was the case with the Board appearance, Travers again felt responsible as the protector of the PDS in the face of external threats.

Accomplishments

If that was the fall's bad news, there was a great deal of good news to report throughout the year. For the second year, a sizable number of College students — 23 practicum students and three student teachers — worked in the school. The entire cohort of science education students spent a quarter at Paine. Perhaps most important, however, was the naming of Jim Hissop as principal in December 1992. The political machinations that led to his appointment were not fully known to Paine faculty, but once Superintendent Sicoli appointed Hissop, who had served as one of Paine's assistant principals since August, the building experienced immediate administrative relief. Teachers who worked with him believed he would provide needed support not only for the PDS, but for every program at Paine.

> I really credit Jim Hissop with bringing some focus to all the stuff going on in that building. . . . He knew what to observe, what was happening. . . . Jim can see the big picture. He can put all of the parts together in a way that makes sense, not just to him, but to all of us.

Specific activities supported the continuing development of the PDS. The mentorship program targeted postbaccalaureate and first-year teachers for professional support. In an important precedent, long call reserve (substitute) teacher dollars were used to hire two teaching interns to release PDS faculty for professional development work during the school day. In the words of one teacher, the internship "is so crucial to the success of this program. . . . It frees us, but at the same time we are not harming students because they have their teacher. It's not like bringing someone in temporarily for a week or a day here and there."

The internship arrangement benefited both groups: The interns taught two classes of their own, then worked with PDS teachers' classes, experiencing a variety of students and teaching styles; the PDS teachers had continuing opportunities to spend time on, for example, mentoring and development of Paine's career ladder continuum. In addition, a postbaccalaureate student was hired as a full-time teacher, making visible the notion of developing professional practice.

Other activities addressed the challenges of making Thomas Paine a better school. Through the North Central Association's Outcomes Accreditation (OA) process, Paine faculty, led by a faculty colleague, identified five "target goal areas" for study and intervention: language arts, mathematics, critical thinking, respect, and self-esteem. A research assistant from the College supported the OA effort, and at one meeting in the winter,

College staff facilitated discussions of each target area. A committee of extremely committed teachers took on the troublesome problem of attendance, seeking to understand why a third of the student population was absent on any given day. With Hissop's guidance, a staff group planned for integrating Paine's special education program into the ongoing functions of the school the following year, seeking inclusion, rather than segregation, to the greatest extent possible. Modeling the change process, Hissop also planned, with the help of management at MCB, to restructure the administrative team to better support faculty in new roles.

So, by June 1993, there was again a feeling of forward movement within the PDS. George Swenson's term as co-coordinator ended, and Deborah Prince, a faculty member who had served as administrator of the College's collaborative research center, replaced him. With Hissop and Prince in place, the leadership vacuum that had made Susan Travers feel alone in the face of PDS conflicts and challenges was filled, and the three could model a collaborative leadership team. The addition of Assistant Principal Laura Laughlin, a highly experienced administrator, to this team gave the PDS vital administrative support.

The core group of PDS faculty at Paine reported a number of positive outcomes as the third year of the grant ended. Some were programmatic: "As a school, I think our increased enrollment and school-wide teaming would not have happened without the participation of the PDS." Some were personal: "Working with the project has forced me to be more outspoken, have confidence, [and] have a broader range of thinking." Some spoke of professional change in general terms.

> For me, [the PDS is a process of] becoming, an affirmation that what I'm doing is correct, that I really did learn something. It's encouraging. I don't want to stay stagnant. I want to try other things. Students are changing, and I want to be changing, too.

> The PDS gave us the expectation that we can reform our teaching. There is consensus around certain ideas now.

> The PDS has refined that sense of reflection and made me realize the need to document what it is I do and how effective that teaching practice is for my students. . . . I believe all teachers have that sense of starting over — this is the way I did it this year, but next year I can make this even better.

Others pointed to the increased awareness and discussion of the fabric of teaching — curriculum, instruction, and student learning — that affected their professional development at Paine.

If there hadn't been a PDS, I wouldn't be the person or the teacher that I am today because, first of all, it exposed me to other ways of thinking and teaching and classroom management [through seminars, conferences, and visits to other schools].

I have had to become much more conscious of what I do in the classroom and why I do what I do. . . . Involvement with the PDS has required me to struggle to reach a consciously competent level.

Among PDS faculty, there was now an increased focus on Paine students and making changes that would positively affect them. "People are trying to justify the changes [on the basis that] it's good for students here." There was also a newfound professional assertiveness, still being developed, that said, "We are professionals — we believe this method will help our students and our school, and we insist on doing it."

For College faculty involved at Paine during the initial 3 years of the PDS, there were also reported benefits. Faculty noted:

It's a real interaction between the university and the schools. . . . Any experience that is tied to reality is better than an experience that is abstract and academic.

In many ways it [the PDS] . . . forces people like ourselves who can easily hole up here [at the university] to go and really recognize the challenges that are there. You need to be constantly thinking about that to ground what we're doing in some reality.

The results after 2 years of PDS implementation reflected favorably on the efforts of those involved. In part, the PDS served to connect change activities into a more coherent whole: "One of the real strengths probably is that it [the PDS] has been a unifying element of all the stuff going on at Paine; it has been a way of drawing all this into focus." In part, it is testimony to the potential impact of a single person's [Travers's] efforts, an individual who reportedly "never let it [the PDS] die, even when it was dead." Faculty involved in the PDS, from both Paine and the College, spoke repeatedly of Travers's role in the change process, with comments such as, "Susan Travers's presence at Paine was necessary for this to happen. . . . She's taken the time and initiative and has networked with people to see that things happen. She also was very personally supportive. She always took time to listen to me."

In part, it is setting a vision and never losing it, despite naysayers, setbacks, and confrontations. In the words of one PDS teacher,

I am most proud that we are continuing after the hard first years where payoffs seemed few. . . . The major effect on me has been to allow a vision of 5 to 10 years in the future to seem attainable rather than a fantasy. I have hope.

PROFESSIONAL COMMUNITY AMONG THOMAS PAINE FACULTY

As Darwin might have predicted, the evolution of professionalism within Paine's faculty over the 3 years was — from the perspective of those most committed to the PDS — painfully slow. The original cadre of teachers enrolled in the MFT/St. Sebastian master's degree program roughly doubled in size by absorbing other faculty committed to professional development, teacher education, and fairly radical school change. For this PDS group, the collaborative experience was a highly positive one. Said one participant, "There is a core of teachers at Paine who have now become very willing to work in this program and are very anxious for success. . . . We can see how it benefits the school." Perhaps even more important, another PDS colleague noted the continuing nature of this work: "We now realize more fully that we will always be changing and keep progressing."

Evidence of faculty experiences with their PDS colleagues speaks powerfully to the extent of their mutual collegiality. One of the interns highlighted the "incredible amount of support and encouragement from those individuals who were active in PDS," adding, "For lack of a concrete term, I would have to say that there was 'positive energy' in the school and among the staff." A teacher of 20 years reported, "We achieved true collegiality among our own staff who were involved in the PDS." Another pointed to a "cooperative atmosphere here," where PDS teachers routinely discuss pedagogy, share instructional ideas and materials, and, for those on teams, plan collaboratively. Breaking down traditional barriers, PDS teachers invite other teachers and practicum students into their rooms to observe, reportedly feeling cheated that they have so little common time to reflect on these experiences together. "If there is anything that has improved my teaching in these past 2 years, it has been having people come in [to my classroom]. . . . Some days don't go well at all, but that's the way it is." To a person, the PDS teachers who reflected for the case study wrote comments like, "I have developed more collegial, rather than just personal, relationships with other staff members."

The true potential of the PDS at Paine is evident in comments that document the effects of such collegiality. In the words of one PDS teacher, "We have had to learn to trust our colleagues. . . . We are much stronger in collaboration than as lone operators." There is the clear sense, after 3 years, that others are joining the group of PDS teachers. "People [at Paine] have developed the concept of 'why not' rather than 'why,' which is great to see. This has even expanded to include some teachers who were very resistant to change before. . . . People are willing to risk saying something to the negative teachers, to confront people openly in meetings. . . . The PDS said it's okay to engage in change activities."

Some PDS teachers also spoke of the interdependence of their professional activities: "We learned that we didn't just make decisions that affected ourselves, but [that] our choices affected students and teachers all along the continuum."

One of the questions facing the PDS teachers in the coming years is how to build on the existing collaboration and how to move other teachers to an appreciation of interdependent practice. As one PDS participant noted, "I am still hoping there is something that will somehow transform our staff into a group of learners."

For the 12 or so teachers who actively participated in the PDS, the results were highly positive. But other Paine High School faculty chose not to participate. Some veterans felt no need or desire for participation. In their opinion, they were good teachers in the traditional sense: They closed their doors, taught well, and engaged in professional activities they personally valued, regardless of whether these activities related to the stated goals of the PDS, the site goals, or the development of a profession. For these individuals, collegiality, as in past years, may have included routine discussions of school business (e.g., homecoming events, assemblies, and trimester grade due dates) or personal news, but not PDS activities related to teaching, learning, and improved practice in a collective sense.

Reasons for nonparticipation in PDS activities varied: "You have to change the culture of a school. [For many at Paine] there is no feeling that we need to do this." Some teachers were simply too busy with personal or non-PDS professional activities (e.g., time-consuming extracurricular activities or work for professional organizations outside the school) to add one more professional commitment. Some, typically based on past experience, were unwilling to commit once again to an unproven collaboration with the College, harboring "the suspicion that university people never walk into a 'real' school and have no real understanding of what I do all day — yet think they have all the answers about education — and that . . . their work is more important than mine."

Others questioned the leadership role of "Principal Travers" and her PDS colleagues, with some labeling PDS participants as "them" and "they," and a "very select group of people [who] get more privileges, better students, more supplies, in-building substitutes." But it was not merely jealousy that led to this perception. As one PDS supporter noted, "There is some animosity toward Susan. Decisions are made, but we never quite know where they come from. . . . Some people saw her as taking advantage of a situation. . . . She did her own thing to further her own work."

Holding this attitude, one highly regarded Paine teacher reportedly refused to read any memos that contained the term PDS, tossing them instead into the office trash. (It is heartening to report that this person has since become active in PDS activities and an outspoken supporter of the collaboration.) Given the early stages of the collaboration and valuing the competence of many such teachers, the PDS faculty patiently accepted them as eventual targets for PDS conversion — or as individuals who might eventually be encouraged to move to another school.

PROFESSIONAL COMMUNITY AMONG PAINE AND THE COLLEGE FACULTY

If the PDS faced challenges in involving members of the Paine faculty, it faced seemingly greater difficulties in reaching out to members of the College faculty, people who didn't necessarily restructure their work lives to include Thomas Paine. This was the other "us" and "them" that caused continuing tension. In interviews, PDS teachers recognized the importance of their involvement in teacher preparation.

> Whatever I was doing in my classroom, I wanted people to stand on my shoulders and reach out . . . I don't think I would have had quite the courage to make as many changes and as far-reaching ones as I had if I didn't think that someone is going to use this. It is not just for me. . . . If we can be a laboratory for good education, everyone is going to benefit.

One spoke of the importance of connecting with colleagues outside of Paine.

> We needed to have a large enough community of people interested in education that you get a professional camaraderie about you. [So] you have enough thinkers and changers and doers that you don't feel isolated. Paine is a small school. . . . We needed to feel that we were part of a bigger community, whether it was the university, whether it was the union, whether it was connection with other schools.

Teachers also recognized that this coming together would take time: "For this relationship to be truly meaningful . . . it must be built slowly — one on one — until we get a critical mass at each institution feeling really valued by the other."

In their written reflections, Paine's PDS teachers discussed common biases and attitudes on each side of the PDS collaboration. "I think we all had to tear down walls of prejudice relating to each other's institution. I think that we had to bring down some personal walls relating to values." "People at both the university and Paine are so consumed by their present responsibilities and ways of doing things that they have difficulty 'adding on' to their job." The challenge of the future, noted Lois Allen, is "to restructure ways of doing their jobs so that the work of the PDS is not an add-on," but rather an integral part of ongoing, day-to-day activities. To the extent that faculty on either side viewed PDS activities as additions, rather than different ways of doing things, the relative success of faculty involvement after 3 years was somewhat surprising. By the summer of 1993, several PDS faculty spoke favorably about the involvement of College faculty in the PDS. Said one, "Instead of 'us' [Paine] and 'them' [the College], we became partners."

However, if progress has been made, everyone was also clear that much more needed to happen as the PDS moved forward. For example, "There has to be a lot more involvement with university staff." As one College faculty member summarized, "The connection's getting better, but it's certainly not ideal. There are very few university faculty who really care about it as much as they should ideally care about it."

Not surprisingly, Paine teachers reported fairly stereotypical attitudes toward their College colleagues to begin with, sensing that the "people there just have to be more aware of what the day-to-day business [at Paine] is." College faculty "need to see a real school." For some teachers, another attitude related to a traditional role differentiation: "I had to tear down a feeling that the university people are automatically more knowledgeable and are the 'experts.' We have a great deal to learn from each other." One PDS teacher in particular expressed high expectations for the College faculty—and extreme disappointment at the results.

> I wanted to find a burning enthusiasm for pedagogy . . . emanating from the university . . . I wanted them to come in and really say, "Look, study such and such says that if you try this . . . ," and I would go out, try it, and see if it fits. . . . I have become disillusioned, and I don't believe that the people at the university are on fire for teaching or for education. . . . They have their own agendas, and that is what they want to do.

In part, teachers blamed College faculty for attitudes of distrust. As one PDS teacher commented, "I think that many professors would have preferred to develop a PDS with a school that had the best teachers and programs of excellence already in place. Why set yourself or your student teachers up for failure?" Others noted, "The university [faculty] must trust us before they'll commit to shared vision and work," and "I do believe that more could be done with the university if they would give us more of a chance," that is, if they would be more open. Some were understanding of the College faculty's perceived attitude, as suggested by one comment: "People are caught up in what they're doing at the university. They need to see it's [the PDS's work] valuable to themselves."

On the other side, College faculty reported some initial distrust from the Paine faculty, that is, the attitude that "we don't need the university here; we're fine on our own."

What led to the successful involvement of College faculty? The importance of "face-to-face meetings" was clear. "Every time you get university and Paine people together, it's a step forward. It's that straightforward." One person, commenting on the two summer retreats, noted that they were helpful "because they brought people together who could make things work. Each summer brought yet a little more progress." He continued, "It is a cliché to suggest that we created 'a level playing field,' but I think that is exactly what happened. In other words, power was shared; no one was perceived better than another."

The long-term success of the continuing collaboration may well depend on the PDS's ability to attract and integrate more College faculty. In part, this continues to be a problem of finding time: "One of the major problems is that both groups of us don't have time. It's hard for us to carve out time." Another reported hindrance is the lack of incentives for College faculty. More basic is the evolving definition of the work of the PDS.

> For a while the PDS program for me has been ill-defined in terms of what it wants to do. I think that has to do with the two cultures, the school culture and the university culture, which aren't so easily aligned as we might think. We have different value systems, which makes for some ambiguity. . . . The Professional Development School has to ask why it is out there. Why is this a Professional Development School?

As the PDS began its third year of implementation, the extent to which more College faculty would become involved was not clear. One Paine teacher said, "At first it was difficult to see how the PDS would fit in with Paine. Paine is going to go on. The PDS might be here; it might be gone. . . . If there was a commitment from the university, I would go 100 percent. But if they continue the way they have been, I would say I wouldn't bet on it."

Events in the next years would determine whether that was a bet worth taking.

THE FUTURE OF THE PAINE PROFESSIONAL DEVELOPMENT SCHOOL

In reflecting on the future of the PDS, a teacher made the following comment: "This has been like a hike up a cliff, and we're getting near the top. But now we see that hilltop over there, so we can't stop and rest." Having attained one level of collegiality and commitment to improved practice, PDS collaborators both at Paine and at the College were already moving on. In October 1993 the Paine Leadership Council voted to make the PDS school-wide, so that faculty would no longer opt to become PDS teachers. By definition, employment at Paine makes staff an integral part of the PDS, although exactly what that would mean in practice would evolve over the course of the next several years. In written reflections and interviews during the summer of 1993, PDS participants had clear ideas about what was needed as we moved forward, including — and certainly not limited to — the following:

We need to keep it [PDS] in the forefront of people's minds.

My main concern would be for continuity. There needs to be that focus, and whatever means are necessary to keep that focus should be taken.

Some restraints have to be put on to adding more new ideas. . . . At one point that was okay, but then too many things happened. [We need to] take what we have now and perfect it and make it really work.

We really need to talk about school and education, for example, how to serve special needs students, self-esteem issues, etc.

As the PDS went school-wide, maintaining consistency and high-quality instruction for College students became more difficult. The challenge remained of creating and funding meaningful incentives and rewards at both institutions to support participation. There was no doubt that enormous sources of potential conflict also remained, for example, the continuing challenge of how to involve more College personnel in PDS work, issues of diversity and interdisciplinary studies at both sites, and the effects of scheduling that tie up certain Paine students during much of the day. However, the Professional Development School had the ways and means to address these challenges, building on the professional community within Paine's faculty and between Paine and College faculty. In June 1993 one individual wrote, "I have not really wavered from the beginning of this project in believing that it could be a success." As we continued our work together, we sought to validate the truth of that statement for both students and teachers.

AFTERWORD

Seemingly against all odds, the Professional Development School at Thomas Paine is thriving. A sizable number of College students from a variety of academic areas now come to Paine for their practicum experiences, and there is a competitive selection process for those who wish to student teach in the building. The most visible example of collaboration comes from the mathematics education program, all of whose new teacher education students (more than 30 in 1995–96) begin the school year with 2 full weeks of classes and observation on site, and several of whom remain at Paine throughout the year. Paine and College faculty engage in ongoing dialogue about teacher education, and an increasing number of Paine teachers make presentations to classes on campus.

The Professional Development School also is expanding connections beyond traditional teacher education departments. A doctoral student in counseling currently holds an internship in the building, and this year for the first time the school hosted student teachers in special education. Planning is under way for an interprofessional education program, connecting pre- and inservice experiences in special education, social work, and counseling. Numerous research projects, both action-oriented and more formal, connect faculty with university collaborators around school change issues.

Several structures foster and sustain PDS activities.

- Weekly brown bag lunches during both lunch hours, with snacks provided by the PDS, continue to provide a time and place for interactive discussion.
- A regular meeting of the PDS co-coordinators with the assistant principal charged with responsibility for the PDS assists with the coordination of activities.
- Periodic meetings (once a year) of the PDS's steering committee, a group of key actors in the College, district, and teachers' union, provide political and resource support for continuing development of the PDS.

• Paine's teacher residency program has become a model for the state, where policy makers are debating how this idea can be implemented statewide.

In the program, certified teachers with no previous teaching experience teach a reduced schedule at Paine (typically three classes, one of which might be co-taught with one of the building's mentors) and spend the rest of their day in professional development activities. In 1995–96, Paine had seven residents, up from five the previous year. Activities include a one-hour weekly seminar (with optional credit), work on a professional development plan, an action research project, and experiences in a variety of other teachers' classes; qualified teachers can sign up for an hour of release time periodically, working with the resident who will take their class for that hour. By the end of the year, each resident creates a personal teaching portfolio, an item that previous residents report was an invaluable tool during job interviews. An annual PDS conference brings together a group of educators in the state to discuss issues related to the professional development of teachers. New in 1995–96 was a monthly PDS after-school forum, creating time for teachers to connect around issues related to ongoing change in the building. Thomas Paine remains a school bootstrapping its way to excellence, and the activities associated with its status as a Professional Development School contribute to this long-term change effort. The district's commitment of $1 million for a major physical renovation during the next 3 years will provide a fitting physical parallel to the continuing renovation of educational practice in the building.

The names of all institutions discussed in this chapter are pseudonyms. I wish to thank the teachers of the high school and the faculty of the university who are discussed in this case study for their willingness to be interviewed and for their comments on earlier drafts of this chapter. I owe special thanks to Linda Trevorrow and Louise Sundin for their thoughtful ideas and to Daniel Weiss for his continuing assistance.

FIGURE 9.1
The Thomas Paine High School Professional Development School

Demographic Profile
1990

SCHOOL

Students

    Highest student turnover rates in school district*

    730 students in a building that could house 2,000**

    Lowest attendance rate of high schools in the district*

    Race/ethnicity

        49.5% African American

        42.0% white

        4.0% Asian

        3.0% Native American

        1.5% Hispanic

Achievement Indicators

    Standardized test scores: Below district in reading and math

    Ranked at the bottom of the district academically*

Instructional Program

    Five instructional teams in which teachers and students are joined

    Houses district-wide program for severely emotionally and

        behaviorally disabled students

    School–business partnership with local bank

Faculty, Administrators, and Staff

    Three principals between 1990 and 1993

    40 teaching and support staff members

    Shared decision-making council

    Almost all white

District

    12% teachers of color

    All schools are schools of choice

Community

    Working class white

    Poor working class African American

COLLEGE OF EDUCATION

Holmes Group member

    Relatively few students of color

    Began moving secondary teacher education to postbaccalaureate

        program in 1985

    Created a center for applied research for educational improvement in

        1988

---

*   As of 1996, these rankings were no longer true

** As of 1996, enrollment was up to 1,000

Chapter 10

The Thomas Jefferson Professional Development School

RITA LANCY

THE CULTURE AND CONTEXT

In 1988 Thomas Jefferson High School, along with all other secondary schools in the Center City City School District in a northeast industrial city, became a school of choice. (The names of all institutions and individuals discussed in this chapter are pseudonyms.) The school of choice concept was, and continues to be, an effort to have students "buy into" a particular school and/or program. It also serves as a tool to ensure full integration as well as racial balance. There are a number of magnet schools in the district as well as three comprehensive high schools that each house separate magnet programs. Jefferson was a comprehensive high school that included a law and government magnet program.

Coupled with a complete reorganization of schools was a historic teacher contract that became part of something often referred to as "the Center City Reform Movement." Apart from highly publicized teacher salary raises, the contract also instituted a career ladder for teachers and site-based management, known as school-based planning. Thus, Jefferson became a comprehensive high school in an era of optimism and goodwill on the part of everyone in the district.

Then, during the 1988–89 school year, teachers began to look around and wonder what had really changed. True, many of them had been assigned to new buildings, the student population had been shifted, and school-based planning teams were beginning to take shape, but something else was missing. As time passed, some teachers began to question the reform movement and its true purpose. Toward the end of the school year,

Making Professional Development Schools Work: Politics, Practice, and Policy. Copyright © 1997 by Teachers College, Columbia University. All rights reserved. ISBN 0-8077-3633-3 (pbk.), ISBN 0-8077-3634-1 (cloth). Prior to photocopying items for classroom use, please contact the Copyright Clearance Center, Customer Service, 222 Rosewood Dr., Danvers, MA 01923, USA, tel. (508) 750-8400.

teachers thought that maybe much of the change had been one of space rather than practice.

In the spring of 1988, William Land, a science teacher who had been assigned to Jefferson as part of the reorganization, attended a meeting about Professional Development Schools sponsored by the Ford Foundation. At a time when talk about change seemed all around, he asked, "Why not a Professional Development School at Thomas Jefferson High School?" When Land returned from the initial meeting, he, special education teacher Sharon Ross, and State University professor Wilson Brittingham began to pursue the question in earnest. They contacted the quadrant superintendent, Dr. Fisher, who told the team that he would support programs such as a Professional Development School until "they failed." He added that the team could take 3 days to write a proposal to be presented to the Jefferson administration and the school-based planning team. At the conclusion of the initial presentations, the team began to consider possible funding sources.

At about the same time, Wilson Brittingham at State University learned about the existence of a national grant for the creation of Professional Development Schools at the secondary level. The team contacted Center City Teacher Association (CCTA) President Alan Ogle, who directed Land to the national project director in Washington, DC. While pursuing questions about possible funding, Land learned that another team, headed by Renee Diez at the central office, had been preparing an application for the creation of a Professional Development School at Lincoln High School. Initially, there was some friction between the teams regarding the location of the PDS site. According to Land, central office personnel wanted the Professional Development School at Lincoln to serve as "sort of an image maker" for a floundering high school. He saw efforts to place the PDS at Lincoln, without much input from faculty, as a management decision to implement change according to the old top-down model, and believed that the program should be placed at Jefferson in recognition of the teacher-driven initiatives that already had occurred in the building.

Ross was attracted to the PDS model because she wanted to take part in a student education model sensitive to the needs of special education students, regardless of its ultimate location. It was believed that Lincoln High School was a better choice simply because it was a larger building and could accommodate a new program more easily. Furthermore, the school was in the process of restaffing, and the possibility of turf battles between teachers and existing programs was greatly reduced. Eventually, Land contacted CCTA President Ogle, who recommended an open call for applications from all interested city high schools. Superintendent Paul Jones and

Ogle agreed that a panel should be established to review applications from the city high schools. At the conclusion of the application process, the panel would recommend a site for the Center City City School District PDS program. Everyone agreed that this process would ensure a fair and open application process.

Ultimately, the grant was awarded to Thomas Jefferson High School, where a new principal, along with the teachers' union representative and Superintendent Jones, signed the proposal with the intent that all would support the Professional Development School vision. In addition to State University, the Professional Development School included Lakeland University and a project facilitator. Now, the planning could begin in earnest.

In spring 1990, an invitation was sent out to all at Thomas Jefferson High School to help form a design team to build a vision for the Professional Development School. Everyone was welcome. However, by the time the summer arrived, 3 years had passed since the historic teacher contract of 1987. Patience with reform was beginning to weaken, and members of various constituencies were asking for results. Teachers found themselves in the middle of stalled contract talks, frustrated by high expectations from the community and no real sense at all that much had changed. Therefore, when the call to build a Professional Development School was sent out, Jefferson teachers were somewhat jaded, waiting to see what the next contract would bring. According to Land, those who did come forward were risk-takers ready to continue the reform movement and invigorated by the prospect of education reform on the national level.

Land felt that even though the environment was tentative, the original design team was energized by the PDS vision. Eventually, a small group of teachers met with representatives from Lakeland University and State University as well as a central office administrator to build a vision for the Thomas Jefferson High Professional Development School. However, the initial team trying to conceptualize a Jefferson Professional Development School would soon confront a school culture advocating "law and order," and union representatives unable or unwilling to look past traditional labor controversies. In the words of William Land, "In fact, we met at local restaurants and at people's houses so we wouldn't offend our union colleagues, even though we were planning with grant money. Eventually, we did lose one math teacher to the union's 'work to rule' response to stalled contract talks."

Why then did a team of educators continue to work on a vision at a time when dissatisfaction with reform was once again on the rise? Reasons seemed as varied as the people involved. In the midst of all the talk about reform, teachers continued to feel isolated. The euphoria over the reform movement of 1987-88 was slowly replaced by a feeling of discontent. The reform of 1988 had not really affected most of the teachers at Thomas Jefferson High School. True, some organizational changes had been made but, overall, the school culture continued to support the grouping of teachers according to discipline, with a schedule that allowed no flexibility for teachers. The teachers who worked on the design team of the Professional Development School were those who had believed in and been affected by the reform movement and generally were ready to "seize the moment" in order to bring about real change.

Members of the team who were on the faculty of Lakeland University and State University had shown a long-standing commitment to teacher education and saw the professional development concept, in the words of Wilson Brittingham, as a "vehicle to better prepare student teachers for their ever changing roles." Furthermore, Brittingham, along with many of the teachers on the team, felt that he wanted to actively take part in any change process rather than watch it pass by him. Don Harshman from Lakeland University also felt attracted to the Professional Development School because of his continuing goal of developing "structures where educators at the primary, secondary, and tertiary level share responsibility for the education of students at all three levels."

FROM THEORY TO PRACTICE

Early Struggles

Early in the implementation process, the questions of leadership, power, and style became extremely important. Thomas Jefferson High School continued to be a top-down organization with an authoritarian, outspoken principal who enjoyed the support of many of the more traditional teachers and staff members. When members of the professional development team became vocal, many outside the team perceived them to be agitators. In addition, there was a concern about the leadership style of William Land, the project facilitator. Some of the Jefferson staff outside the original design team felt that his personality did not lend itself to compromise. Therefore, other members of the professional development team were encouraged to take a more active leadership role. The rationale was that non-PDS staff might then find the whole team more acceptable. At times, there was discussion among PDS team members about "how hard William should push," and when "to pull back and compromise." No one on the team really knew the leadership characteristics necessary to confront the administration in the building without alienating faculty outside the PDS team. Eventually, a dual system of leadership evolved. Whereas some staff members perceived Land to be somewhat radical, they recognized his partner, Sharon Ross, as more compromising and objective. On occasion, the team and/or the team leader asked her to defend a position to the leadership in the building. This was done on the premise that her approach would be more diplomatic and, therefore, less threatening. Ross herself noted, "I needed William to get people's attention; he would open the door for me so I could go in and be diplomatic."

While the questions of leadership and style were important, some conflicts became defining moments. Initially, the principal believed that a Professional Development School could exist at Jefferson as a separate entity that would not affect the rest of the building. At the administrative level, some seemed unable to comprehend that the PDS signaled the beginning of a second wave of the reform movement. At Jefferson, it would be the beginning of a renewed attempt at restructuring.

The first, and most bitterly fought, conflict of the summer of 1991 became the battle over the schedule. A vision of the Professional Development School team had been the delivery of collaborative as well as thematic instruction across subject areas. To accomplish this, teachers needed a common planning time, preferably at the end of the day. A rationale for the planning time at the end of the day was the issue of the university connection. The PDS team and college faculty expected student teachers to attend weekly seminars at Jefferson High School. Teachers felt that on those days student teachers, teachers, and professors could meet during the last period, before the beginning of the seminars, to discuss individual concerns. The request for a common planning time for PDS teachers was the first indication to the administration that a Professional Development School in the building would affect the building after all. The request also prompted negative reactions among other staff members in the building. When teachers asked to be released from the eighth period, they asked for something that traditionally was reserved as a special favor. Often, by the time students come to eighth-period classes they are restless and less attentive than they were earlier in the day. Therefore, teachers often find classes that meet during the last period of the day more challenging and consider anyone who "gets it off" to be lucky. When PDS teachers asked to have a common planning time for professional development during that period, staff outside the team saw it as a ploy to take something away from more senior teachers. The fiasco over the eighth-period planning time left Professional Development School teachers with a stigma that was not soon forgotten. The principal never supported the eighth-period common planning time and often stated in public how difficult things were in the building at the end of the day because PDS teachers were "off planning." By doing that, he was able to undermine the need for a common planning time, and by the time the 1992–93 school year arrived, PDS teachers no longer had the eighth-period planning time.

Another barrier undermining the implementation of the PDS program during the first year occurred at the university level. Don Harshman from Lakeland University wrote:

> At the university level, no effort was made to restructure the university program to accommodate the activities of the Professional Development School. During the '91–92 school year, when student teachers were placed at Jefferson, they received no credit for their involvement in the project and therefore were less likely to take it seriously.

At the building level this meant that even though everyone expected student teachers from Lakeland University to participate in weekly seminars, some did not attend. The inconsistency created ill feelings on the part of the PDS teachers. They felt that attendance at the seminars was crucial to the growth of student teachers as well as a necessary part of the Professional Development School idea. The absence of institutional support for a change in teacher education was also a concern for Renee Diez, the project director. The lack of a restructuring process at Lakeland University left Renee with the impression that "across institutions the lack of seriousness with which the student teaching experience is perceived makes it obvious that it is of little value to them."

Early Successes

In spite of the barriers, there were also accomplishments. The collaborative teams that formed were an overwhelming success. Based on Land and Ross's model, English and social studies teachers in the PDS began to team with special education teachers. Together, the two would blend their regular students with a group of Option 1 learning disabled students. Even though teachers who teamed did not self-elect their partners, combinations worked out well and helped enormously in the effort to build a sense of collegiality among PDS teachers. The overwhelming success of the collaborative teaching model was voiced repeatedly among all the PDS teachers. Social studies teacher Lisa Myers wrote that a critical incident in her PDS experiment occurred when "I found a partner I could work with. I could not have come this far without Nora." A vice principal at Thomas Jefferson High School, Nick Roberts, also wrote about the teachers' dedication to the collaborative model: "By the end of the '91–92 school year, the collaborative model was beginning to find acceptance from teachers outside the PDS." Furthermore, the collaborative model helped student teachers as well as veteran teachers experiment with new educational strategies.

Wilson Brittingham of State University wrote, "By the end of the '91–92 school year, teachers had arrived at a feeling of comfort with one another that content area boundaries began to disappear. Student teachers seemed to reflect this trust and were willing to take risks modeled after the teachers with whom they worked." Generally, student teachers liked the collaborative model but voiced concern over their training in one model when much of the "real world" operated in another. However, as the semester progressed, student teachers commented that upon successful completion in the collaborative teaching model, they had no desire to teach in isolation. These student teachers hoped to build collaborative relationships in their future teaching assignments.

Nevertheless, when informal follow-up information was collected, the data suggested that most of the student teachers were placed in traditional settings with little or no support. As new teachers, they were more concerned with job security than innovative teaching methods. Many spoke fondly of their student teaching experience when they had not been the only adult in the classroom. However, all former student teachers expressed gratitude for having found a job in a difficult employment market and were willing to accept demanding assignments. It seemed as though much enthusiasm and idealism were lost as soon as student teachers left the supportive environment of the Professional Development School. Overall, by spring 1992 team teaching had become the one success story in the Professional Development School that allowed teachers outside the PDS a look at an innovative teaching model.

Another early success was, and continues to be, development of a real sense of collegiality across institutions, specifically the school's relationship with State University. During conversations with PDS teachers, many mentioned the value they placed on Brittingham's contributions of relevant professional reading materials. One teacher commented, "I'd come to school in the morning and there on my desk would be an article about something I had recently talked or wondered about. It is such a wonderful resource." Wilson Brittingham was fortunate in that he had been able to gain the support of State University early on. In Brittingham's case the organization allowed him to spend one day a week at the school interacting with staff, student teachers, and students. This contact proved invaluable for numerous reasons.

- It allowed college personnel to observe, firsthand, challenges met daily by everyone in the building.
- It broke down barriers between the school and the college as the college faculty member was not perceived as an outsider.
- Most important, it validated the student teachers' clinical experience. Urban high schools are unique and often problematic. Having

the college faculty become part of the school showed student teachers the college's commitment to connect theory with practice. It gave the student teachers a real sense of the college's promise to no longer "hide behind theory," but commit and validate the university–school connection.

Don Harshman at Lakeland University experienced fewer successes with the collaborative model, due partly to the lack of institutional support, as well as to his changing role at the university. By the end of the planning year, Harshman had become the chair of the teacher education program in the College of Education. The change allowed him less time to devote to individual programs. Furthermore, he felt frustrated by a sense of "ongoing crisis at Thomas Jefferson High School," which, in his opinion, made it easy to neglect the teacher education aspect of the project.

STUDENTS IN THE JEFFERSON PDS

When students were asked about their experiences in the PDS program at the end of the first year of implementation, they reported that they liked the increased attention they received in the collaborative model as well as the blended classes. But, they indicated that they really did not feel part of any Professional Development School model. However, there were a few exceptions.

During the first year of implementation, some ninth graders were clustered so that there would be a core of students that would share PDS team teachers. All students in the cluster were identified as "at risk," which meant that they had exhibited behavior and accumulated a record indicating vulnerability to dropping out of school. Many were also working at least 2 to 3 years below grade level in core subjects. When these students entered Thomas Jefferson High School, their first reaction to learning that they had been clustered was that this had happened because of their past failures. Immediately, being in the Professional Development School became synonymous with the label "kids in trouble." Some students, early in the first year, wanted to get out of the cluster because they did not want to be stigmatized or associated with the label. As the year progressed, attitudes changed. Students appreciated the fact that in many cases teachers were willing to work through difficult periods, and responses to problems at school were not always automatic out-of-school suspensions. For some students, suspension levels dropped significantly, while overall the group's academic performance rose. Many students commented on their evaluation forms at the end of the year that they "had not done this well since elementary school." Even though the cluster had experienced some success, the group was dissolved at the end of the 1991–92 school year due to scheduling conflicts.

Special education students in blended classes liked the classes immediately. They felt liberated from the small, self-contained classrooms that everyone in the building knew to be "special ed rooms." During the first year of implementation, some of the students were observed to be more quiet, almost shy, in their blended classes. Even though these students were excited about being in a "regular class," they seemed less sure of themselves, almost afraid to be "found out." During the last year of implementation, it was observed that special education students who had been in blended classes the previous year were more outgoing and more sure of themselves; in many cases it seemed as though these students themselves had forgotten their "special ed" labels.

As noted above, by the second year of implementation, the cluster group had been dissolved, and teachers as a team did not share a common group of students. However, individual teams did retain about 40% of the regular/special ed students they had taught the previous year. During the final year of implementation, these students became more familiar with the PDS model and saw their own growth over the 2-year period. For example, in English class, where portfolio assignment was implemented, students compared writing done at the beginning of ninth grade with that done at the end of their sophomore year. Most could not believe how far they had come.

Overall, special education students as well as regular students liked the classes that were team taught and often included student teachers. They were happy to return for a second year, and those who had been with the team for 2 years expressed hope that they could continue for a third. The only group that initially did not like the Professional Development School was the original ninth-grade cluster for whom the PDS label stood for past failures.

PARENT INVOLVEMENT IN THE PDS

Whereas there had been much talk, and some planning, on the part of the PDS team about actively recruiting parents, the results of these efforts were mixed. In the summer of 1991, Vivian Ferdinand, an African American and active church member, joined the PDS team. At the time, the team considered co-sponsoring events with churches and other organizations that would help families learn about Jefferson and its PDS program. This plan was never carried out, for a variety of reasons. For example, due to scheduling disputes, the team never received a list of shared students until a few days before the opening of school. By that time it was too late to plan activities designed to build a group identity based on the Professional Development School.

Another problem was the makeup of the original group of shared students. As a cluster, these students represented a high-risk group that, in some cases, was extremely transient. Therefore, the initiation of parent/ guardian contacts needed time to develop and was best done on an individual basis. Individually, parents and guardians of the cluster students liked the increased attention their youngsters received. Since many of the children had been in trouble before, some parents commented on the less punitive and more nurturing personality of their children's teachers. They also liked the increased attention the students received in the classroom due to the teaming of teachers and the addition of student teachers. Parents understood that increased attention from adults often helped keep their children out of trouble. Overall, parents liked the parts of the PDS program that they saw as helpful for their children's success in school. One parent even volunteered to address a School Board study session, where she talked about the benefits of collaboration. However, whereas parents understood the effects of the changes at Jefferson, they were unfamiliar with the vision of the PDS school and did not understand that the PDS program at Jefferson led to the changes in their children's educational experience.

Building home–school connections with the parents of the special education students was easier. Traditionally, these parents had been forced to be more directly involved with their children's education due to stringent guidelines mandating their level of involvement. Special education teachers whose students were in the blended classes contacted parents individually during the summer. They explained the PDS vision of inclusion as well as the reasons for their children's placement in blended classes. The home contacts of special education teachers were possible because special education students were scheduled separately and therefore not part of the scheduling conflicts experienced by other teachers in the program. Again, parents reacted to the effects that inclusion would have on their children, rather than to the philosophy behind the PDS vision. In all cases, parents knew that students were in blended classes, but did not really understand, or know about, the PDS program at Jefferson. Overall, parents of special education students were better informed than parents of other students in the program, largely due to the stability of the special education population compared with the cluster group.

During the second year of implementation, the PDS team did not share a common group of students, which made it impossible to coordinate parents behind the efforts of the PDS team in any kind of organized fashion.

THE STUDENT TEACHER CONNECTION IN THE JEFFERSON PDS

The integration of student teachers into the collaborative teaching model had been perceived to be less problematic than it turned out. By the time the first student teachers arrived in the fall of 1991, everyone was enthusiastic about their coming. However, it soon became clear that few of the participants knew how to proceed or what to expect. At first, sponsor teachers were surprised to realize that student teachers were generally unclear about the reasons for their placement in the Professional Development School. Nor did they seem to know much about the ideas behind Professional Development Schools. PDS team members spent much time in the beginning of the experience familiarizing student teachers with the goals of the Professional Development School, as well as with the philosophy behind the collaborative teaching model. Once the student teachers were placed with teams of teachers, their reactions were as individual as the student teachers themselves. Louise Barnett and Amy Ewing expressed concerns about feeling "left out" early in their student teaching experience. As Ewing said in one meeting, "You guys know what you are doing, or going to say; I never know when it's okay for me to jump in, or when to keep quiet." Both student teachers expressed concerns about feeling like a "fifth wheel" at times. Everyone agreed that teams needed time to coalesce.

Sponsor teachers did not plan any specific team-building activities, but tried to reassure student teachers in formal as well as informal settings that their feelings were common and that time and open communication would be the key to their successful integration into the individual teams. By the end of their experience, all student teachers agreed that, after their initial period of adjustment, they did feel as though they were part of the team and even went on to say that the collaborative model reduced their anxiety level regarding evaluation. Often sponsor teachers worked in the room alongside the student teachers, minimizing the need for one formal evaluation that could determine the student teacher's fate. Feedback was ongoing, informal, and perceived as helpful rather than threatening.

Questions regarding where, when, and how to integrate student teachers led to one experience where student teachers, under the supervision of a collaborative team of experienced teachers, were teamed. Kathleen Smith was the product of a traditional Catholic high school and college education when she arrived at Thomas Jefferson High School as a graduate student. She felt that her educational background, as well as her upbringing in a suburban, upper-middle-class family, left her somewhat unprepared to teach a culturally diverse student population. For that reason she had requested to teach in an urban high school. When the PDS team suggested that she team teach with an older, more experienced student teacher from the special education department, Smith was unsure. Frankly, she told her sponsor teacher, she felt more comfortable alone in the classroom. However, eventually she was persuaded to team teach with the other student teacher. The collaborative team was supported by English teacher Ruby Long and special education teacher Sonia Ward.

Early in the experience, the sponsor teachers observed numerous generic discussions about methodology and content. Both student teachers met before each lesson to "talk it out." Then they would meet again after the lesson to talk about what actually had taken place in the classroom. At first, many of the discussions centered on the basics. For example, would it be more advantageous for classroom management to take attendance at the beginning or the end of the period, and what should be done if students refused to take notes from the overhead projector. However, somewhere in the middle of the experience, discussions became much more passionate and specific. For example, there were heated lunchtime conversations about the value of memorization. Then there was a debate over the validity of a test one of the student teachers wanted to give. When they could not agree on whether to give the test, they compromised. The test was given and the results were analyzed and used as a basis for further discussion among Long, Ward, and the student teachers.

Both sponsor teachers felt that the discussions forced the student teachers to verbalize their own beliefs about education that they had not even been aware of themselves. Unfortunately, most of the discussions were held between sponsor teachers and student teachers rather than the whole team. One reason for this was that topics for weekly seminars had been scheduled in advance and there never was enough time to address all the issues of concern to individual teams of teachers and student teachers. However, all teachers in the PDS were aware of the unique concept of teaming two student teachers, and even though there were no formal discussions, there were numerous informal conversations about their experiences. At the completion of their student teaching experience, both student teachers felt proud of their accomplishments and Smith even chose to write about her experience in her master's thesis at the university. Whereas she freely admitted that she was much more comfortable teaching the traditional twelfth-grade English class, she also felt that the team teaching experience made her more willing to experiment with new ideas within the more traditional teaching model.

If some student teachers found the collaborative teaching model difficult at first, all liked the support that the professional development group as a whole could provide. Many commented that it was easier to bring questions to other team members than to approach a sponsor teacher. Student teachers often perceived any problems they experienced as a sign of weakness and had an irrational fear that the admission of inadequacies, real or perceived, would affect their evaluation. Therefore, team members provided student teachers with a nonthreatening support group that could be used as a resource. For example, many student teachers found it difficult to remember exact procedures for filling out various attendance reports or disciplinary referrals. Rather than repeatedly ask the sponsor teachers, student teachers would approach other teachers on the team. Most often, questions and concerns brought to the attention of various group members dealt directly with issues of discipline and/or classroom management. It seemed as though student teachers felt quite comfortable addressing questions about content to their sponsor teachers, but felt less comfortable asking questions about the "nuts and bolts" of daily school life. When sponsor teachers talked about this phenomenon as a group, they came to the conclusion that student teachers felt most comfortable discussing "curriculum to be covered," and very uncomfortable dealing with issues of classroom management and methodology.

Finally, the professional development group made a conscious effort to familiarize student teachers with changes taking place in the field of education. The group stressed repeatedly that the role of teachers was changing and student teachers needed to be aware of the different roles teachers could take on. Overall, student teachers arrived in the building with a "mission to teach." They had little knowledge of, or interest in, the organizational structure of the school that could directly influence their ability to "just teach." For example, since all student teachers liked the collaborative teaching model, the group explained steps that needed to be taken in a school to ensure that groups of teachers could work together. Sponsor teachers explained their involvement with many committees to ensure that the collaborative teaching model would become a reality.

Also, student teachers were amazed to see many students wander the halls between classes and then report late to their classes, which directly interfered with the student teachers' ability to teach. PDS group members pointed out scheduling changes that could take place at the school to reduce hall traffic. Again, it was pointed out to student teachers that if they wanted to see changes at a school, they themselves needed to get involved to try to bring about those changes. Finally, PDS group members reminded student teachers that just because they thought something was a good idea, it would not necessarily be accepted, but that they needed the perseverance to fight for what they thought to be in the best interest of the students they taught. Most student teachers were surprised to learn about the other roles they might play in a school building. Many student teachers who had arrived at Jefferson just wanting to "teach English" or any other subject, began to understand that their roles might be much more complex than they had thought or even been led to believe at the college level.

THE 1992–93 SCHOOL YEAR

When the 1992–93 school year began, the PDS team planned to build on its accomplishments and continue to work on its goals. A new team member, Kathy Costa, had joined the group and planned to blend her special education students with regular mathematics students and their teacher. Other team members had expanded the number of classes in which they would team and overall PDS team members were hopeful. Over the summer, teachers had been informed that the eighth-period common planning time would no longer be possible for all team members but, as a compromise, the principal had agreed to free two teams of teachers during that time. Furthermore, it was agreed that individual teams of teachers would share a common planning period. After the struggle of the previous summer, team members decided to accept the proposal and show goodwill at the beginning of the new school year. School opened, there were student teachers in all core subjects, and teachers felt confident about the direction of the Jefferson PDS. While the PDS continued to be viewed as a program rather than a school-within-a-school, there had been enough interest in it during the previous spring to assume that more converts could be recruited that year who would share the PDS vision.

September 30, 1992 came to be known in the City school district as the "day of the shooting." On that day, one student shot another in a crowded hallway outside of the main office at Thomas Jefferson High School. Even though no one was seriously hurt, the incident served notice to the district that "something had to be done" at the school. Teacher Nora Klein felt that the shooting led to a toughening of attitudes on the part of everyone. Students became harder, fights more desperate and violent. Until that time, there seemed to have been an unspoken understanding by students that school was off limits for serious fights involving weapons. Now, many students felt that they needed "protection" in order to survive. For adults too, the shooting came as a defining moment. Suddenly, everyone realized that this incident had happened in a building whose guiding principle had been "control." Anyone who questioned the leadership's need for control saw the shooting as evidence of failure. Traditional staff members were shaken by the shooting because they had believed in and supported the leadership's ability to control. Other groups in the building saw the shooting as evidence of the principal's vulnerability and his inability to offer any real leadership or alternatives.

Another defining moment was the decision by the superintendent and his support staff to appoint a fact finding team that would look at curriculum, organizations, and accusations of racism at Thomas Jefferson High School. A group of concerned African Americans had charged various entities in the building with racism as well as with perpetuating a system that supported institutional racism.

Finally, the school-based planning team (site-based management) charged to lead on matters of instructional improvement and staff development ceased to function. The development of a 3-year improvement plan was bogged down in a series of confrontations ranging from fair representation to racism.

CONCLUSION

Changes in the School Structure

The 3 years covered by the Jefferson case study were years of turmoil and upheaval at the high school. Over the period, many different entities in the building worked to redefine the mission of the school, while others played the role of obstructionists opposed to any change. When the Professional Development School concept was introduced at Jefferson, the school was very much a traditional, comprehensive high school organized according to departments and governed by a clearly defined chain of command. Today, the school has been completely reorganized and been renamed the Thomas Jefferson Center for Learning. Students are now offered an array of programs from which they can choose a course of study. In the new Center for Learning, the traditional chain of command no longer exists, but questions and concerns regarding the decision-making process remain. Uncertainties about governance structures, new job descriptions, and the underlying issues of power linger. While there is an air of openness and attempts to create new governance structures continue, many still want to know, "Who is really in charge?" In this environment, the Professional Development School has taken much care to continue to help redefine roles of teachers and other adults, while helping to create a governance structure that will minimize the need for someone to be "in charge." Educators involved in the Professional Development School at Jefferson would like to develop a system that would motivate people to work together without the return of the old bureaucratic structure.

Changes in Teacher Roles

Initially, Professional Development School meetings provided teachers with opportunities to talk about their craft—the art of teaching—with adults from other disciplines as well as other institutions. The addition of university personnel, for some teachers, legitimized their participation in these conversations. After many years of teaching, some veteran teachers found it stimulating to talk about instruction with educators at all levels. As people became more comfortable with each other and trust among the participants grew, something important happened. College personnel began to listen to teachers' practical classroom knowledge, while teachers became more open-minded about theoretical information that the college provided. At the conclusion of the first year, conversations became less provincial and more cosmopolitan.

How did these conversations serve to help change the roles of teachers at Jefferson? Initially, teachers began to see themselves as professionals who could talk about their work with other people in the field. After the first year, when the student teachers arrived at Jefferson, veteran teachers once again changed roles. They changed from professionals who not only talked about their work, to those who also reached out to teach others. As teachers became more comfortable with the idea of working as equals with college personnel, their newfound self-confidence manifested itself in a willingness to take on many other roles. Eventually, teachers would become guest lecturers at area colleges, co-author various papers about educational issues, and serve as active participants in the overall transition of the old Thomas Jefferson High School.

How did these new roles of teachers as knowledgeable educators influence their place in the school community? As teachers changed roles, so did their standing in the school community. Colleagues' reactions ranged from indifference, curiosity, and hostility to sometimes grudging respect. As long as changing roles did not interfere with daily life at the school, colleagues seemed unconcerned. It was only when questions of turf and power were at stake that hostility became palpable. Many times, Professional Development School teachers were perceived to be more powerful because they were better read, spoke up more at meetings, and were seen to interact with educators outside the building. The perception of Professional Development School teachers as people who did more than "just teach" served to make them more visible, which in turn helped to make them noticeable when decision-making teams were formed. Their visibility and willingness to get involved served to increase their voices in and outside the school. However, by no means could it be said that Professional Development School teachers have the power to be the "masters of their own destiny." In other words, the governance structure at the school in many ways remains one where decisions are made at the administrative rather than the teacher level.

If the college connection helped change teachers' roles by fostering a sense of professionalism, another impetus that helped change teachers' roles was the team teaching concept. The presence of two professionals in the room concurrently did much to help teachers. For example, it broke down the walls of isolation that classroom teachers traditionally felt. Being alone in the room with a group of students never allows teachers the necessary feedback from other adults. Over the years, nagging questions about one's effectiveness, or ineffectiveness, are never answered. However, if not one but two teachers are in a room, a natural tendency to talk about the daily lessons develops. The stress level in regard to the other adult in the room is quickly reduced because soon each professional will "observe" the other on good, as well as bad, days. Once the initial barriers are removed, it becomes natural to have other adults in the room. Team teaching, in many cases, opens the door to other "visitors" in the classroom.

How does team teaching change the traditional role of a classroom teacher? Talking about his or her work allows the classroom teacher truly to become a "reflective practitioner," a professional who talks about his or her work. More important, by breaking down the walls of isolation, the classroom teacher removes the provinciality that he or she has been accused of for so long. Through having others in the room, ranging from partner to student teacher, to resource consultant, to other members of the school community, the role of the classroom teacher changes from the one "take charge" adult in the room to another learner/teacher in the classroom.

While the team teaching concept changes the role of the teacher inside the classroom, it also helps to broaden it outside the classroom. If one returns to the original thought that teachers' changing roles eventually might influence power relationships in a school, it is possible that team teaching helps change those relationships. For example, when the teacher is always the only adult in the classroom, certain things happen. As mentioned earlier, isolation can foster uncertainty in regard to one's effectiveness or ineffectiveness. Isolation also affects a teacher's use of time. If a teacher is always alone in the classroom, it becomes very difficult for that teacher to take part in meetings that may have an impact on his or her professional life. The ability to leave the classroom to take a phone call or to participate in meetings helps to ensure that items relevant to teachers remain on the agenda rather than be postponed indefinitely due to teachers' inability to come to the meetings.

Outlook for the Future

Originally, the question was posed, "Who's in charge at Jefferson and how does the Professional Development School's attempt to continue to redefine the roles of teachers influence the power relationships in the building?" At this point, there is no clearly defined single person who "runs Jefferson." Rather, there is a team of administrators and teachers trying to change the governance structure so that teachers have a greater voice in the daily operations of their programs. However, obstacles ranging from union-related issues to personality conflicts are posing numerous problems.

The roles of Professional Development School teachers have changed tremendously since the beginning of the project. Today, more teachers are visible, more self-assured, and more cosmopolitan in their professional lives. However, at the time of this writing, there is a sense that structural changes need to follow soon in order to sustain the impetus of the program. Many believe that there is no returning to the "good old days" when teachers delivered a prepackaged program to students who passively sat in rows and took notes. Teachers, by reaching out beyond the classroom, have let it be known that they want to be involved in other teaching/learning activities as well as in the decision-making process. They want to be thoughtful partners with other adults in schools, the community, and the university. While they do not yearn to be in charge of a school, they do want more autonomy over their own programs and professional lives.

As the people at the Thomas Jefferson Center for Learning search for a new way to govern themselves, Professional Development School teachers look for more freedom in the scheduling of students in their program. Furthermore, while they do not want to be in charge of student teaching, they would like more autonomy over the seminars that accompany student teaching. For example, rather than some, all seminars should be site-based so that the relationship between school and university becomes a true marriage rather than a dalliance. Finally, structures need to be built that constantly work to institutionalize the college–school connection so that, 10 years from now, schools and universities do not need to begin another journey on the road to getting to know each other.

FIGURE 10.1
The Thomas Jefferson High School Professional Development School

Demographic Profile

SCHOOL
Students
> 1,419 students
> Race/ethnicity
>> 53.8% African American
>> 36.5% white
>> 6.8% Puerto Rican
>> 2.3% Asian
>> 0.6% Native American

Achievement Indicators
> Standardized test scores: Below state norms for reading and math
> High middle school failure rates for entering students

Instructional Program
> Comprehensive high school
> Law and government magnet programs
> Collaborating teachers in blended classrooms (inclusion)

Faculty, Administrators, and Staff
> Three principals between 1990 and 1993
> School-based planning council

District
> All high schools are schools of choice
> Career ladder for teachers

Community
> 7.8% unemployed
> $21,000 per capita income

COLLEGES OF EDUCATION
> Two higher education partners with distinct missions and goals
> Student teachers from each college alternated semesters at the site

Chapter 11

The Oak Street Professional Development School

JON SNYDER WITH FRANCES GOLDMAN

This is a case study of a collaboration between Oak Street Elementary School in a southwestern urban school district, the local teachers' union, and Southwestern University (SWU) to develop a Professional Development School. (The names of all institutions and individuals discussed in this chapter are pseudonyms.) As with any relationship, the parties entered with differing perspectives, interests, histories, and goals. In relationships that survive over time, the differences become respected and, to some degree, understood. In some relationships, however, the differences do not complement each other, or the communication systems do not work, or the essential continuous tension of power and its uses within the relationship is destructive. In these cases, there is insufficient energy to push through the inevitable collisions and conflicts, and the choice is made to discontinue the relationship. This latter situation characterized the partnership that created the Oak Street PDS.

In June 1993, I was asked to help chronicle the discontinued Professional Development School. By that time, the Oak Street school and SWU were no longer interacting as institutions. As one university participant said, "At the end of a tumultuous 3 years participants were tired, frustrated, angry, and disappointed. Everyone was looking for a place to lay the blame."

My role, from the perspective of a dispassionate observer, was to record the account of the participants as they attempted to construct both the activities related to the PDS and their meaning. The project director, several school participants, and the university participants agreed that I would relate their personal stories, using their words whenever possible. My role was not to determine facts or establish the relative strengths of different perspectives, but to reflect, as sensitively and accurately as possible, multiple and often conflicting perspectives.

The participants agreed to respond to a series of questions generated by the national project director, which were used by most school participants as starting points for their reflections on the Professional Development School project. Thirteen of the 14 school participants turned in written reflections that may have been spurred by the prescribed questions, but did not follow a question and answer format. Three of the most active university participants also wrote comments, but did not use the project-generated questions as a starting point. One sent a dissertation based on the project, another the final report to the funding agency, another a paper co-written for an American Educational Research Association presentation. Another source was a transcription of a presentation made by two of the university participants to a conference of teacher educators. The different formats used by school and university participants to relate their perspectives serve to heighten the juncture between their perspectives.

By fall 1993, there were sufficient responses to begin to categorize and analyze the data. I formulated the categories that structure this chapter and prepared a draft to share with school and university participants. Each group discussed the draft and used it as an opportunity to reflect and clarify thinking. Their comments subsequently were incorporated into the chapter and, as appropriate, noted as responses to participant observations made earlier.

SITE SELECTION

In May 1990 the school district, the local union, and Southwestern University submitted a proposal to the National Teachers' Union seeking funding to plan and implement a Professional Development School. The Oak Street Elementary School was one of the three such collaborations selected to create restructured schools designed to provide field experiences for new teachers.

At the time of the selection, SWU had reservations about Oak Street, yet acquiesced to the union: "This was a union project. We were supposed to have had voice in site selection, but the school we had initially asked to work with, because we had a relationship with it based on previous student teaching placements, was rejected by the union for political reasons."

School staff members did not know that they were a negotiated second choice. They felt they were the "chosen," and in their eyes SWU, as the chooser, was the holder of power: "They interviewed us to see if we were good enough, and that set the tone."

The initial proposal discussing the role of the school added to the perception of power differential.

Teachers and the principal of this school have agreed to commit themselves to school-based management. This commitment includes specified interest in the development of curriculum and instructional materials, learning new instructional strategies, working collegially in teacher teams, supervising student teachers who are paired collegially (two student teachers in a classroom), and engaging in school site research.

Staff development, delivered by SWU participants, would improve the school. Knowledge was defined as residing in the college. This may have been as much a school perception at the initiation of the project as a university imposition. In retrospect, some school participants believed that they may not have grasped totally what was involved in becoming a PDS. One teacher recalled, "I don't think any teacher really understood what was involved in becoming a PDS school."

CONTEXTS

Oak Street Elementary School

The school members described their community as follows:

Oak Street Elementary School is located in a predominately Hispanic community on the periphery of [the city]. Most of the residents of this densely populated, low socioeconomic community live in over-crowded, substandard apartments or houses. Many have migrated here from impoverished and Latino countries.

The school is located in one of the highest crime areas of the city, state, and country. Gangs, drugs and violence have been on the increase. Due to the multiplicity of family needs (economical, physical, emotional, social and educational) the overwhelming majority of the children and their families in the school are considered at-risk.

Oak Street, with an enrollment of 1,300 plus students in prekindergarten through sixth grade, has been a four-track, year-round school for the past 13 years. Given the challenges from the Oak Street student population and surrounding community, the selection of the school may have exacerbated the notion that the PDS was to be more a school improvement effort than a simultaneous school and teacher education restructuring effort.

Southwestern University

SWU is a private institution offering both undergraduate and graduate degrees. It has several successful programs designed to increase the diversity of its undergraduates, but, like many other private institutions of higher education, it remains significantly "whiter and wealthier" than the community in which it resides. Teacher preparation at SWU is a 4-year undergraduate program serving fewer than 75 elementary teacher candidates each year. As explained in the original proposal:

> Since the fall of 1988 the teacher education program at SWU has been experimentally engaged in a collegial model for teacher preparation. Student teachers select partners and are assigned together to one classroom and a single supervising teacher. . . . The student teachers learn both generic teaching strategies and specific models of teaching in their methods class.

Like those of many other research universities, SWU's reward structures did little to support the time and effort needed to collaborate successfully in the world of schools.

District and City

The collaboration occurred during a tumultuous period for the district's public schools. One of the problems the collaborators had to deal with was labor–management conflict, involving proposed pay cuts and givebacks. One teacher said, "This past year the teachers' union took three strike votes. We spent many hours trying to protect the student teachers and their university credits in the event of a strike. To say that times were stressful would be an understatement."

Further, during the collaboration, the district changed superintendents and there were repeated legislative attempts to break up the district. In addition, the state was experiencing the worst economic conditions in its history. Much of the frustration about the economic downturn was focused on immigration patterns (e.g., the children in Oak Street) and on school funding. Although teachers were hesitant to mention it for fear of feeding media-driven stereotypes, a massive and violent uprising literally surrounded the school. One teacher reported, "In the course of our collaboration with SWU, we experienced a riot which actually took place in and around both the university and our elementary school. That took an emotional toll on everyone." Given the contextual turmoil, it is not surprising that neither the union nor the district galvanized resources and energy into the project. Still, neither union nor district got in the way.

School, union, and national project staff tended to question why they didn't do more with the provided flexibility, why permission was not sufficient. The university suggested that the lack of overt support, especially in a school environment as challenging as Oak Street's, hindered their work.

INITIAL PDS ACTIVITIES

The PDS attempted to overcome school-site confusion and the anticipated suspicion of the university with a specific process. As described in a jointly authored paper:

> Initiated by the university participants, individual interviews were conducted with school site and university project members by the doctoral student serving as participant-observer. Participants were asked to describe personal and curriculum goals for the project. A cumulative list was generated and recirculated to school site participants, who were asked to prioritize the list. . . . During an all-day meeting of all participants, results . . . [were] shared . . . and substantive conversation about those goals took place.

There was considerable variation among the teachers regarding priorities for the PDS. The group agreed that its goals should emphasize student achievement, critical thinking, and documentation of student achievement (e.g., assessment strategies). Using the process described above, school and university participants came to agree that the activities of the collaboration should consist of three elements: (1) models of teaching, (2) curriculum change (specifically thematic units), and (3) student teaching. This process and its outcomes became the impetus for SWU's subsequent efforts, while for a variety of reasons, these initial goals were less of a force for the school people as the project evolved.

For the most part, even in retrospect, all participants viewed these early efforts positively. One teacher asserted:

> We spent countless hours in meetings, building rapport and getting comfortable with each other. We heard interesting lectures aimed at improving student achievement, saw videotapes on the how and why

of creating new paradigms, read scholarly articles on teacher education and curriculum building, learned about networking with other
PDS sites. . . . This was an exciting time to be alive. I was teaching,
studying, attending meetings like crazy, and planning my head off,
and it was all great experience. I have never felt like such a vital part
of my profession.

Despite positive initial attitudes by teachers, there was an understanding that the reason for the planning and implementation of changes, which
occupied the first 2 years of the relationship, was that Oak Street needed
"fixing" and SWU was there to support those efforts. Joint decisions to
hold meetings at the university and to have them facilitated by a university
participant may have exacerbated this perception. In the long run, unidirec-
tional help is not a recipe for a strong relationship. The national project
documenter, summarizing the issue across all three sites, wrote, "University
professors confined their discussions to the ways in which the sites would
have to change and how they would help the sites in the process."

In response to this statement, one SWU participant wrote:

Since the setting of the project was the school site it seemed logical
that initial change was to take place at the field site. My perception
was that change was to be envisioned at the site level first, and that
changes in the teacher education program there would result in univer-
sity-wide changes. It is interesting how "traditional paradigms" assumed by others pigeonholed my intentions. I was not trying to "fix"
anything; I was trying to meet perceived philosophical expectations of
the national project.

THE SWU–OAK STREET PARTNERSHIP

The Professional Development School project had three major goals:
collaboratively restructuring the professional preparation of teachers; constructing a model for teaching as a profession; and restructuring the school.

School and university participants agree, as one SWU participant put
it bluntly, that the PDS "did not effect any change in teacher education at
SWU. This project really had no effect on it." In a sense, this story is
already known: The institutions discontinued the relationship and both
perceive their efforts as failures. University and school perceptions differed
on the outcomes and factors involved in all three areas. The following
discussion deals with participant perceptions about these factors.

SELECTION OF PARTICIPANTS AND PARTICIPANT TURNOVER

One of the few areas of retrospective agreement among all participants is that each became involved in the project to improve his or her classroom teaching. There was, however, never any agreement on how school-level participants became involved in the project. The school principal stated:

> The group that formed the school-within-a-school concept at Oak Street was almost self-selected. There were basic criteria to be met and if the person wanted to join—that was it.

The college perspective was much different.

> Participants in a project of this dimension must self-select membership. The teachers in this project were somewhat coerced to join by the administrator. In contrast, the university members chose membership, but ultimately resented the time investment and disinterest of the school-based faculty and the university community.

Teacher recollections of the process were idiosyncratic and suggest that confusion might best describe what occurred: "It all happened so quickly. I always wondered why I was never asked to be in the PDS. I was bilingual, I was permanent. I guess after a while I figured I just didn't fit in. Who knows?"

There were also the inevitable comings and goings of school staff who were selected, which "were frustrating and divisive," said one teacher. The net result, according to an SWU participant, was that "we had almost 50 percent new people. They didn't understand the goals or the philosophy. So we saw the momentum take a nosedive." Frequent changes in membership created problems. As new teachers entered, they felt disadvantaged. "Time is limited to bring 'novices' up to date," said one participant.

One university participant responded:

> It is interesting how the flavor of learning models and writing units [the enabling activities selected by original school participants] changed after the first year and became "something the university had pushed on the school membership." In actuality, it feels as though it was the original teacher membership who imposed it "in absentia." If the first year teachers who stayed in the project had been willing to discuss membership formally with potential newcomers, goals from the first year could have been shared before membership commitment. In-

stead, there were members who did not understand what had come before and had difficulty grasping what they had signed on for.

Routines, Schedules, and Calendars

The university believed that day-to-day differences hindered the establishment of a lasting relationship: "School routines actually supported inaction. Recess schedules, mentoring responsibilities, other projects—all affected the school-based faculty. The university faculty had anticipated total intensity of effort to develop the PDS."

There was also Oak Street's four tracks and year-round schedule.

Probably the first surprise for the university-based educators was to discover that all of the school-based participants did not work during the same calendar period, and would not attend meetings together. During the initial planning for the project we were not informed that the school folks were on different tracks. There was no effort to change the schedule for these teachers. Also, classrooms were spread out across the campus. The consequence of this was very little interaction among participants except at project meeting time.

Lack of Time

Lack of time, as always, also inhibited the relationship, as a teacher observed.

Realistically, there just aren't enough hours in a day to plan lessons, gather materials, teach, advise student teachers, deal with children's special problems, meet with their parents, attend PDS meetings and take on a myriad of PDS assignments. Your energy wanes after a while. Then your will weakens and you start feeling frustrated and defensive about all the things you haven't done. You forget all the good things that you have accomplished.

School-Level Suspicion of "Outsiders"

Most "external" projects arouse suspicion of the outsiders by school personnel. This one, although less external than others, was no different. One teacher recalled an attitude of "Who was trying to run our lives now? Who were these SWU people, and what did they really want?" Those who collaborate with the outsiders are often suspect also, partially because their recognition breaks the equity culture of teaching. Confusion about who was involved and why they were selected fed the suspicion and, according to teachers, resulted in overt antagonism.

> Many teachers were angry that they had not been included. They wanted to know what we were getting that they were not getting. I found it emotionally draining and unnerving to live in this atmosphere. I felt as if I was being whispered about and judged.

Oak Street's union chapter chair provided a perspective distanced from the immediacy of the participants' pain.

> I believe that when you take a small group of teachers at any school, single them out as being exceptional (whether it is the case or not), and then provide them with extra resources not available to the average teacher you run the risk of alienating other teachers at that school. I do not think that it is a good idea to do this, especially if you intend on calling the school a Professional Development School.

The university responded that it had been cornered into the situation of working with a "small group of teachers," with little to say in the matter.

> Fifty percent of the school faculty were emergency credentialed teachers. As a consequence the principal singled out the more experienced credentialed teachers to participate. Though there were many other projects operating at the school site, none were dependent on experience — such as this one. It was the advice of the union vice president and the national project director that the project be conceived as a school-within-a-school. This was not a university-made decision.

University participants responded that they "were surprised that the project teachers and principal seemed to lack the self-confidence to communicate about the project to their school colleagues," and that "though we assured the PDS faculty that professionalism, good teaching, and an improved school culture were contagious and ultimately would serve the whole school faculty, we were unable to convince them."

Relations Between the Project and the Whole School

School personnel wanted to maintain peaceful relations with the school as a whole. They did, after all, "live" there. SWU worried that "whole school" concerns were undermining the project that they felt had been defined by others as a school-within-a-school. School participants felt that the clean distinction between the whole school and the PDS project exhibited a limited understanding of their world and it did not sit well with them.

> There was no patience or understanding of the administrator's role in the school. For example, if my time for the PDS was infringed upon by other responsibilities, I was told point blank, "That's your problem." [Administrator]

> It was the position of the university that we should have whatever we wanted in order to make the PDS work, and that we should not be concerned about the rest of the school. The university only cared about their PDS. [Teacher]

The university responded strongly to that comment: "The university participants never felt that the PDS was 'theirs'; in fact, most of the time the university-based educators did not feel that the school participants accepted and treated them as equal project participants."

Conflicts Regarding Student Teachers

One of the primary interests of college-based teacher educators is their students.

> School- and university-based educators have similar client commitments. The school-based educators are committed to children and their families; university-based educators are committed to the education of student teachers. The university commitment is to provide the very best clinical practice for student teachers. [University participant]

Teachers also felt a commitment to student teachers and teacher education and that it was beneficial. Said one, "I also learned to look at my strengths as a teacher. I had become so concerned about my weaknesses, that it took my student teachers to help me see what I was doing as a teacher of students, as well as a master teacher, that was right and valuable. That was very empowering."

One SWU participant responded, "There was a small group committed to working with students. They were the same few who always were trying to take on the bulk of the work." For the most part, however, university participants felt that the school was committed neither to student teachers nor to preservice teacher education.

> The school-based educators had meager experience working with student teachers. By the end of the first year three of the five supervising

teachers dropped out. During the second and third years of the project four teachers worked with student teachers; several of the qualified teachers declined. The important point is that the project teachers (despite your quotes) were reluctant to work with student teachers.

Significant conflicts centered on student teacher issues hindered the relationship. One set of conflicts involved schedule differences and communication patterns.

When the student teachers arrived, time management became exceedingly frustrating. Typically, they had to leave by noon each day, with few exceptions, in order to attend classes. To compensate for their lack of time, my partner and I generally offered up lunch to meet with my trainees. But how do you critique today's lessons, preview tomorrow's and plan next week's in the space of an already jam-packed lunch period? [Teacher]

I was approached to take a pair of student teachers. I really didn't have a clue as to how the SWU teacher preparation program operated and what my responsibilities were to be. I had expected that, as a new member, I would receive some prior training. [Teacher]

Underlying these organization issues, however, was a consistent sense on the part of school personnel that the university did not value their knowledge, expertise, and time. A PDS teacher who supervised SWU student teachers at another school wrote:

Discovered that all five students were very good. I couldn't resist discussing their progress with other teachers at Oak Street. One brought up a good point: Why weren't trainees of such caliber sent to the Oak Street–SWU PDS? Such students would obviously require less of our time and contribute more to the quality of our programs, freeing us to work on other PDS goals. When we asked SWU about this, they responded that there were so many factors involved in student teacher placement, it was virtually impossible to place everyone exactly as desired. We discovered that the "top" students were regularly sent to another site and Oak Street received whomever!

University participants felt that teacher concern on this issue exhibited a lack of understanding of their world. First, they felt that asking PDS teachers to supervise student teachers at other schools "certainly belies the idea that PDS teachers were not valued and that no opportunity for input was available." Secondly, "We never sought to place inferior preservice teachers at Oak Street." As the university responded:

Schools of Education have yet to devise a system whereby the success of student teachers can be predicted prior to student teaching. PDS teachers were invited to participate in the entrance interviews so that they could select student teachers for their site. One PDS teacher participated and one signed up to participate but did not show up.

Another constraint was the discrepancy between SWU students and Oak Street students — especially around the sensitive (and politically charged) topic of bilingual education.

It didn't make sense to me that at an inner-city bilingual school we were training monolingual teachers. [Oak Street teacher]

I was the only bilingual primary grade teacher in the group. The SWU professor supervising the student teachers seemed disinterested in my contributions. Then the next student teacher walked out on me saying she didn't know she had to teach Spanish in a bilingual program. I felt a failure. [SWU participant]

Again, the university responded that it was being held responsible for a situation beyond its control.

Of the 11 participating teachers at the beginning of the project, only three teachers were bilingual and one of the three taught special education. At the university we typically have no more than 3–4 bilingual student teachers each school year. This was known at the beginning of the project.

The matter of the different backgrounds of SWU student teachers and the Oak Street population was one of the few instances where university people saw greater value in the project than did school participants. Regarding their other inner-city placements, university participants felt that "this was an eye opener for several of them [student teachers] to see kids that came to school without breakfast or without socks on, but whose parents really cared. They did see these great kids at the school and I think it changed some of their prejudices."

The issue for the teachers was more than the world of difference between SWU students and Oak Street students (and teachers). At issue also was the appropriateness of the preparation SWU students were receiving for the student population at Oak Street, specifically the need to adjust "prepackaged models" to the specific strengths, interests, and needs of the second language learners at Oak Street. A cooperating teacher recalls using a specific model of teaching.

> I had to adapt the model because so many students had recently transferred into English reading and were not yet comfortable or strong enough on the comprehension level to handle all of the necessary reading alone. She [the university supervisor] was extremely unhappy with my session because it was not faithful to the model. She was not interested in hearing why the model would not have worked as written. She did not seem interested in the fact that the lesson was successful. She was not interested in my concerns as a professional educator. Her feeling was that student teachers needed to see the models, as written, in action. My philosophy was that student teachers had to learn how to use the models to help improve instruction based on their student population, and if that required modification, so be it.

A university participant, in response to this comment, pointed out that student teachers are asked to learn various models of teaching, such as sheltered instruction, whereby limited English proficient students learn content as well as English, and the whole language approach to reading and writing. Student teachers are expected to "demonstrate them correctly before they begin to modify or adapt."

In the end, however, the bottom line for school participants was not one of these specific instances of concrete problems, but rather an intangible belief that they were not respected by the university.

> As the PDS teachers became more sophisticated they felt less and less like partners and more like underlings under the auspices of the University and its needs. The teachers had no input into the budget, no control over the student teacher assignments even to the point of no input into the grades issues. [Administrator]

Some university participants, however, sensed a subtext of teacher resentment.

> We saw that teachers needed help and they weren't getting it, so we tried to intervene and give them the support and technical assistance that we thought was lacking at the school site. This was not okay. Clearly the university had overstepped its bounds in terms of project balance and we got that response from them. In a sense we lost the

trust of the project at that point and it was very difficult earning it back. I don't know that we ever did earn it back. I think that the power that we had—maybe influence is a better word—was pretty much based on the amount of respect we could win from the teachers. When we mistakenly overstepped our bounds a little bit, we lost some of that respect, and also lost some of our input into decision-making.

One SWU participant attributed the termination of the partnership to technical and administrative issues rather than any disrespect on the part of university participants for school personnel and school culture. The technical problem was a lack of a clear governance plan for their work together—an institutional contract delineating rights and obligations. Roles and responsibilities never were clearly defined, so that many things never got done, and when things did, people's feelings were hurt—the university "overstepped its bounds." More significantly, teachers felt "left out" of some of the decision-making, particularly with respect to student teacher selection.

In the third year of the project the school was "restructured" into four semi-autonomous mini-schools called Corredores de Enseñadas. Each mini-school (including the PDS) had a corredor director. The university saw this person as the site coordinator for the project; the school people, as the administrator of the corredor whose primary duty was the operation of the corredor, not the PDS. The university-based principal investigator, believing a governance plan with responsibility clearly assigned to the corredor director was in place, relinquished the leadership role in the project that she had played the first 2 years. She explained:

The concept of a director for the PDS appeared to be a means to release university faculty from organizational responsibilities, and a way to help the school faculty assume responsibility. . . . With the director in place, I stopped facilitating meetings. The director took charge of meetings, and an agenda pertaining to school and corredor business occupied the meeting time. As a consequence there was little need for the university members to be present. The director and teachers began to formulate "new" project goals (without the university faculty members). . . . Except for keeping track of the budget, the director assumed all responsibilities for the project. . . . When responsibility for what was to be accomplished at the meetings became the director's responsibility . . . the university faculty lost PDS membership.

It may be that as the project evolved, school people wished to change the goals and enabling activities that the university felt they had agreed upon at the initiation of the relationship. The school people felt they were growing and thus the nature of the relationship needed to change. University participants felt left out of the decision to make changes.

A second major problem from the university perspective was the lack of building-level administrative support. University faculty felt that while school administration demonstrated enthusiasm for the project, it neither possessed the expertise nor exerted the pressure necessary for the PDS to succeed.

When the efforts of all the participants were acknowledged, and when emotions were calmed, both parties in the relationship believed that they, acting in good faith, did everything they could. A university participant stated, "We kept thinking this was just part of the process, this was the resistance that you would get in any change project and that we needed to try a little harder and hang in there and be there more. That was why we stayed there. We were really committed to making it work."

Both parties concluded that the relationship simply was not worth continuing. In the end, the principal summarized the school perspective: "The PDS staff felt the university had abandoned them — and I guess that's true." In response, and addressing the SWU perspective on "whole school" tensions, a university participant wrote:

> I truly believe that everyone on this project began with a feeling of equity and respect for the other participants. . . . There is a professional cultural difference at play here. At universities, people who teach together hardly ever agree, so it seems. Part of the stimulation is the debate. This does not mean these colleagues do not respect each other. At schools, there is an emphasis on maintaining good feelings and the status quo. A good school is usually seen as one where everyone gets along. Questioning, challenging, debate is not necessarily seen as essential or productive. The university wanted more challenge and initiative from teachers to maintain their respect, while teachers wanted more agreement, praise, and harmony to portray a feeling of respect. In the beginning it seemed that each side needed less and got more. While at the end, in exhaustion and disappointment, they needed more and got less. It is true that each group did come to disrespect each other at the end of the project. However, this was due to the perception that each was not holding up its end of the professional bargain, rather than because the partner was from a university or elementary school.

A MODEL OF THE TEACHING PROFESSION

A second major goal of the project was to construct a professional model of teaching. University participants believed the project failed in this regard, while school participants believe they made significant strides in positive directions. Different definitions of "professional" played a major role in creating the discrepancy in perspectives. The university believed that a profession of teaching required instructional leadership and educational leadership.

From teachers' traditional perspective, acquisition of instructional competence was a vehicle to becoming "better teachers" or "the best teachers they could be," rather than a means to acquiring a more professional image, greater decision-making power, governing influence, or moving up the career ladder. This view represents a focus on instructional, rather than educational leadership.

Another SWU participant stated, "Teachers' concerns were of personal/individual nature, but not necessarily focused on instruction. In the main the concerns had to do with time commitment to the project and expectations concerning improving student achievement." According to this perspective, the teachers' emphasis on the personal prevented them from "enhancing their professional role perception, and improving their stature within the project." The project, this reasoning argues, failed to build a model because the school participants did not grapple with issues beyond the personal/individual and thus never created the environment to enact instructional change.

School participants never overtly expressed their conceptual frame of a "profession of teaching." Their comments, however, reflect a very different definition, containing four commitments: (1) to the client — their students and families; (2) to use best knowledge and practices available; (3) to build new knowledge and new practice; and (4) to prepare and support quality educators (Darling-Hammond & Snyder, 1992). University participants felt that these commitments also were their commitments to their student teachers. One wrote, "Perhaps the most difficult part of a school–university partnership is in how to maintain and expand levels of commitment to populations other than your own, while respecting the commitment others perceive for themselves."

Commitment to the Client

A commitment to children and their families was both the rationale for entering the project and the heart of the positive outcomes described by school participants.

And best of all — I see it happening before me at this moment — the first day of the new school year — the emphasis is on the child and his/

her curriculum. The constant question is, "How can we improve instruction to guarantee a positive outcome for the student?" [School ad-
ministrator]

A major issue for the school participants in the project, also indicative
of a professional commitment to the client, was the effect on children and
their families of the time the teachers spent away from school improving
themselves. Participants felt pressure from the traditional perception that
one is "teaching" only when working directly with children; participants
also had it thrown at them by nonparticipating teachers. One teacher participant phrased it as follows:

> We tend to underplay the value of just plain teaching, cramming more
> and more activities into our schedules. This makes us look like high-
> powered professionals, until our teaching suffers. The so-called benefi-
> ciaries of all these efforts — the children — end up the real losers.

A teacher who criticized the project during its first 2 years and then
entered it in the third provides a compelling case that a professional model
of teaching requires time for teachers to develop, away from children. She
also provides evidence that the project was successful in this regard.

> Everyone complained of PDS teachers being called away from the
> classroom too often, disrupting the students' learning. All along the
> teachers were going to inservices, supposedly to become better teach-
> ers, to learn different methods or to better their methods. We didn't
> understand that. Now I kind of wish I had taken time out for the inser-
> vices even if it meant time away from my students. All those teachers
> seem to have such better teaching techniques than I or at least they be-
> gan to look at teaching differently. I need that.

Commitment to Use Best Knowledge and Practices Available

Commitment to one's clients means commitment to providing them
with the best services currently known. While the university thought this
definition limiting, the teachers defined best services as improved instructional practices. Again, this is why they entered the project and it is their
indicator of success.

> I for one didn't think of the acquisition of power or changing school
> roles. I wanted to improve my professional practice and effectiveness.

I learned a great deal from participating in the PDS. I not only learned several models of instruction and came to understand reasons to use them. I also refined my understanding of thematic instruction. Developing curriculum that was integrated, thematic, and differentiated in content and in methods of delivery became so easy for me and for my teaching partner that we modeled it for student teachers in a workshop session.

Commitment to Build New Knowledge and Practice

Because knowledge is not static and practice must be improving constantly, teachers felt that a professional must be engaged continually in inventing new knowledge and practice to meet the needs of children and their families. School participants felt the project succeeded in this respect.

I learned to look at my paradigms about the structure of the school day, my expectation of my students and myself, and the ways time could be made available to me, and the ways student teaching programs are structured. I realized that almost any change was possible.

I learned more about the field of curriculum and teaching than I have ever known. I've also become aware of how much more there is to learn.

Commitment to Prepare and Support Personnel

Both university and school participants agreed that eventually a professional teacher must assume responsibility beyond the classroom. The university felt that such responsibility should take the form of school-wide governance and decision making. The school participants felt a greater responsibility for the preparation of teachers "who would then be able to enter the profession with viable skills."

One of the issues teachers faced in this regard was how to transcend the traditional image of the teacher as a repository of knowledge and redefine it as a professional learner. How, in other words, can one be both a learner and a teacher? Eventually, teachers arrived at the position that assuming a role beyond the classroom makes it easier to be both. "Working with student teachers has taught me some vital facts: I am still a learner and I will always be a learner."

The different definitions of a professional and the concomitant different judgments about the success of the project shed further light on the termination of the school–university relationship. They exacerbated the school perception that the university did not respect school people. Teacher concerns, for instance, were defined by some university participants as personal/individual in nature, while university concerns were professional. Those value-laden labels were not lost on school participants. SWU believed they had given their students and their time to the school participants and wondered what could be a more valid representation of their respect.

The different attitudes toward success also provide an avenue for exploring the university concern about a governance structure and how that issue played into the respect factor as well. In effect, early in the project, there was an implicit governance structure. The school people, through their initial definition of their needs and the enabling activities, essentially bought into the traditional hierarchy that the university defines knowledge, defines "good teaching," and provides inservice training. The university, feeling positioned by an agenda defined by teachers at the initiation of the project, thought they were doing what the school people themselves had requested, and wondered why they were being blamed for doing what they were asked to do.

> The university participants in the project did not prioritize goals or suggest activities on how to reach them. The teachers themselves said they wanted to learn teaching strategies that would foster more inquiry-based thinking. It was at that point that they asked us about models of teaching because they had seen the student teachers practicing them the previous year.

The university examples of school failure are presented in terms of how the school failed to do what it had asked the university to help them do. While school participants felt that they greatly improved their practice, university participants noted that teachers were not using the models of teaching and curriculum units.

> At the conclusion of year two, teachers were desperately avoiding participating in new instructional techniques and collegial interactions. Models of teaching were used by only a few teachers; room environments had changed in only cosmetic ways.

The issue of the primacy of the teachers' initial choices provides deeper insight into some of the tensions that developed between the participants. First, as one SWU participant noted, "we were dealing with a group of people who really didn't know where they wanted to go" at the inception of the project. Thus, school people felt it perfectly appropriate to change their minds once their work with SWU began and they developed a more grounded sense of direction. Second, asking the questions is as much a position of power as answering them — especially given the traditional status hierarchy between higher education and schools. The college participants, understandably, had a definite sense of the kinds of teachers and school environment they wanted for their student teachers. Teacher responses may have been a result of trying to divine what they thought the right answers were. Finally, how a question is asked plays a major role in the nature of the answer. For instance, university staff recalled that "participants were asked to describe personal and curriculum goals for the project." It may be that the teachers' initial choices were a product of how they heard the questions asked.

As the project progressed, school teachers believed their practice grew and that the changes challenged their initial definition of knowledge residing external to themselves. Why, they wondered, was fidelity to a model of teaching more important than student learning? Once the knowledge and methods for transmitting knowledge were challenged, the implicit governance structure became explicit. The school participants then rejected it because they felt that it was not guided by the needs of their students. In short, school participants felt that the university's definition of professional was driven by a "knowledge base," while they felt that professionals should be driven by their clients. Since teachers have the knowledge of the client, their knowledge should count. When they perceived that it did not, their sense of the university's disrespect for them grew. When they came to believe that the university did not even care about their students, the relationship was over.

While SWU participants did not seem to doubt the professed commitments of the teachers, they did question whether the school people actually did anything.

> In a profession, commitment must be acted upon so that the profession becomes a reflection of that sense of commitment. I believe that the teachers in this project have individual and collective commitment about many beliefs relating to education. The teachers' quotes support their commitment, but to what extent was that commitment acted upon to build a new model?

RESTRUCTURING

The third goal of the project was to "restructure" the school — specifically to transform Oak Street into a site-based management school. School personnel recollect this as a major impetus from the beginning; conversely, the university, again citing the original goal-setting and prioritizing process, recollected: "At the beginning of the project neither teachers nor principal were interested in school-based management."

By the end of the project, the school felt that it was successfully engaged in restructuring. The university participants "agreed that the school was engaged in the process of restructuring, but that it still maintained a nondemocratic, bureaucratic structure." One university participant responded that perhaps expectations had been unrealistically high.

> Internal restructuring requires lots of change by lots of people. It requires a great sense of commitment to stay with it. Both teachers and principals must work hard to break out of preconceived role definitions. It is time consuming, energy sapping work, but it happens in an atmosphere of shared culture. A school–university partnership is an external restructuring project in that you are trying to bring together people from two different cultures and before you can restructure, you must build a shared culture. While you are trying to restructure, you are also trying to culture build. How much can you ask teachers to do all at once?

School participants did not feel they had access to restructuring teacher education, but wrote that the first stage of their successful school restructuring was an increase in communication and collegiality among the members of the entire school. This was difficult initially as there were charges of elitism and numerous "again's?" when PDS teachers were out of their classrooms. One teacher who entered the project in its third year noted succinctly, "There were lots of bitter moments." By the end of the third year, however, school participants unanimously spoke of increased collegiality.

> Initially teachers seemed isolated, protective of their turf, unwilling to cooperate. . . . As we worked on real issues, defined curriculum as the focus of change, learned new methodologies, the rapport within the PDS group grew. I began to feel accepted and began to feel that I could become more of a risk taker. I shed some of my baggage of fear of change and uneasiness when observed. Along with this growth in self-knowledge and confidence came a measure of independence.

> We had learned how long it took to be able to trust each other, and built that into weekly faculty lunch meetings just to talk about fears and concerns about restructuring. We had included enough of the school that the concept of organizing into curriculum-focused tracks

came with ease. Our principal had participated as a learner with us and had learned to trust teachers, take criticism or suggestions, and had facilitated school-based management.

The university participants were equally certain that the school was not restructuring successfully into a democratic, nonbureaucratic institution. The difference in perspective is perhaps shown most clearly in the discrepancy regarding a restructured administrative role.

> With complete immodesty, I feel that I personally have made the greatest changes of all. Think about it—from benevolent dictator (my description of school administrators) to a member of the group! Talk about changing paradigms! Me—give up authority! Why? I'm the fall guy—let me call the shots! Did I ever really feel that way? I'm afraid I did! But what is happening now is a miracle of accomplishment and JOY! Teachers now create their own collegial teams, determine their academic focus, develop their instructional units, hire their peers and teaching assistants, manage their own budget, plan their inservices and in general are in charge of and responsible for their professional life! [School administrator]

> Teacher–administrator interaction improved, yet it was not consonant with the restructuring movement. Significant decisions that affected the health of the project were retained by the administrator. University faculty either did not have the power, or chose not to exert it, to stop the perpetuation of blatant top-down administrative decision-making. Teachers appeared to hold university members responsible for their inability to achieve professional stature and empowerment. [University participant]

The core of the discrepancy between university and administrative perceptions about administrative restructuring might be understood as an inability to negotiate the tensions of power relations between the university and site administration. Who was going to have the power to empower the teachers? Was the school administration going to set the tone of the restructuring effort in a blatant top-down model or would the university? When the teachers, perhaps because of their previous history with site administration, followed what the university defined as the administrator's course of action, the university felt it had lost its appropriate role in the partnership.

In addition, the university's perception of failure is related to its definition of a professional as an instructional and educational leader. Because teachers maintained their focus on instructional leadership, the university felt the school could not really restructure.

> We learned that in order for teachers to be successful in the restructuring process, they need to transition their professional role perception. They cannot perceive themselves as in the role of teachers 20 years ago. They have to see themselves in the light of professionalism, in the light of teachers who can carry on school change in a professional manner. I think they did understand it, but one of the big stumbling blocks was that we weren't successful in actualizing it for them. That is the hump we never got over.

Another repeat theme is the conflict between the needs of the project and the whole school. Restructuring of the whole school may have drained energy from the Professional Development School.

> The site was entering into a schoolwide restructuring plan before the PDS model was completed. This usurped the administrator's time and ability to provide assistance and support to the PDS. [University participant]

> As a result of the changes engendered by restructuring, again the needs of the whole school became a focus for many of us, and our PDS efforts became diffused. [Teacher]

The tension is that the project was construed as school restructuring. The university perception of the core problem during the first 2 years was that teachers remained trapped in personal concerns. As the school broke into corridors, the teachers became closer to the educational leaders that the university seemed to envision. When the school began restructuring, however, it no longer fit the university's needs as it had prior to the reconfiguration into corridors. A university participant provides a rich rendering of the university dilemma.

> At the end of year two, the administrator came up with the idea that it would really be helpful to the project if the entire school entered restructuring. At that point we were working with about ten teachers. She came up with this idea that she called "corridors" in which each track would have a separate curriculum purpose. Over time each of these corridors would develop an essence of autonomy in running itself, and so it would essentially become four schools-within-a-school. What she didn't perceive is what that was going to do to our project.

Instead of being able to focus on developing this relationship with the university and how we are going to work with student teachers now the teachers felt in competition with the three other tracks at the school. How was our track going to look in comparison with the other tracks? The second major issue from the university standpoint was that there was some confusion and cloudiness about whether all of the teachers on the PDS corredor would be members of the Professional Development School. As university people we have very very definite ideas about the quality of the people who work with our student teachers. It really did not matter that we wanted teachers on that track who were competent. We were overruled, and teachers were allowed to self-select into the track and become members of the Professional Development School. We didn't have the kind of governance plan that could allow us to have a little bit more voice in saying who these teachers would be. So we lost our voice.

As with the different perceptions of the professionalization of teaching, the university felt that as the project evolved, the lack of an explicit governance structure resulted in loss of its voice. Once again, the examples that staff provided were seen by school participants as, "You did not do it our way, so you failed." For instance, as noted earlier, school participants praised the growth of professional collegiality over the 3 years of the project. The university felt otherwise.

Although teachers stated in written surveys that collegial relationships and exchange had become more open, there was little observation of enduring change in this area. Peer coaching, peer observation, and peer demonstration were not organized or participated in on a regular basis. Teachers remained mostly isolated from each other.

While the university felt there was no governance structure through which to make changes collaboratively, school people felt that what they chose initially was what the university wanted. As the project evolved, they began choosing what the university did not want. They believed that their growth rendered the initial roles and responsibilities inherent in their choices no longer appropriate. School participants felt that rather than the university losing its voice, they had found their own—and the university could not adjust to this change.

Ultimately, I think any process, such as the one entered upon between SWU and Oak Street, can only succeed if growth and change is expected from all participants. I think the ultimate termination of the

PDS project grew from the perception on Oak Street's part that as we grew and changed, SWU had no intention of changing. As a consequence, as we became more fully accomplished educators, viewing ourselves as full partners with the SWU personnel in the preparation of future educators, SWU never grew to see us as more than an extension of the 20-year-old students in their college classrooms. The SWU participants had a very clear idea of how they wanted their students, the Oak Street teachers, to turn out, how they wanted us to use our newly acquired knowledge. When we grew in our own directions, when we started to come into our own, I think SWU was unprepared for what they had wrought. We had refined our values, and they did not, in all ways, match SWU's. Our teaching styles, while reflective of our new learning, were still uniquely our own. Perhaps, most unnerving to SWU, was that although we were not college academics, but merely classroom teachers, we dared to consider ourselves as peers with the college faculty and expected to be heard and respected.

CONCLUSION

A school–university collaboration demands different roles of both school and university participants, and neither part in this relationship could find itself in these roles, nor did the two parts find effective structures and processes to work together on inventing such roles. School–university collaboration literature is rife with examples of the differences between the two cultures. In theory, those differences provide the potential power of such collaboration. In this instance, however, the two parties never found a way to talk about those differences so that they were not able to use them constructively. The negotiation of evolving power relationships was a particularly virulent unresolved conflict, which festered into an open wound. Neither the university nor the school could find the answers to its questions in the relationship.

Still, from an outsider's perspective, the relationship was not a failure. University participants presented their accounts of the work at national and state conferences, completed a dissertation on the subject, and published a chapter in a collection of case studies of Professional Development Schools (Darling-Hammond, 1994). In this way, the SWU experience of the partnership has been shared with a larger audience and has helped build significant theoretical and practical knowledge. I also believe that the professional knowledge the participants built and shared through their internal discussions shaped their thinking and reshaped the growth of the teacher education program. One university participant reminisced:

I do know that there were moments of greatness in this project. . . .
We all suffered some bruised feelings, but as adults I feel that we're
able to look beyond these for the contributions which can be made to
educational practice and literature. . . . I have personally never participated in anything in which I learned more.

I also believe that the partnership supported and continues to support
Oak Street's growth. Perhaps the most fitting closure is the testimony of a
school participant who remained with the project from beginning to end:
"Whatever approach we choose, whatever twists and turns the road takes
ahead, one thing is certain — we can never go back to where we were before."

FIGURE 11.1
The Oak Street Elementary School Professional Development School
Demographic Profile

SCHOOL
Students
    1,400 students
    Race/ethnicity
        99.0% Hispanic
        1.0% African American and Asian
    87.0% enter the school as non-native speakers of English
Instructional Program
    Prekindergarten–sixth grade
    Year-round schedule for faculty, staff, and students
    Only 75% of faculty and students are present at any given time
Faculty, Administrators, and Staff
    Same principal for more than a decade
    Large percentage of faculty are emergency-credential bilingual or
        probationary teachers
Community
    Predominantly Hispanic
    Low socioeconomic community
    High percentage of illiteracy among adult population

COLLEGE OF EDUCATION
    Prepares fewer than 75 elementary teacher candidates each year
    Four-year undergraduate program
    Pairs student teachers for their year-long clinical experiences
    Relatively few students of color

REFERENCES

Darling-Hammond, L. (1994). *Professional development schools: Schools for developing a profession*. New York: Teachers College Press.

Darling-Hammond, L., & Snyder, J. (1992). Framing accountability: Creating learner-centered schools. In A. Lieberman (Ed.), *The changing contexts of teaching* (pp. 11–36). Chicago: University of Chicago Press.

Index

About the Contributors

Kathy Beasley teaches second and third grade at Averill Elementary School in Lansing, Michigan. She and Carole Shank, her friend and co-author, share a 2-year looping configuration. She has been involved in several collaborative research projects, is a member of the Investigating Mathematics Teaching group, and is a doctoral student in the Teacher Education Program at Michigan State University. She teaches a class for student teachers.

Katherine Boles co-teaches a third-grade class with Vivian Troen at the Edward Devotion School in Brookline, Massachusetts. She received her Ed.D. from the Harvard Graduate School of Education in 1991 and currently serves on its faculty.

Richard W. Clark is a senior associate with the Center for Educational Renewal at the University of Washington and the Institute for Educational Inquiry in Seattle. He works with Professional Development Schools in the 34 universities, 100 districts, and 400 schools that constitute the Network for Educational Renewal.

Deborah Corbin taught at Averill Elementary School in Lansing, Michigan, from 1991–1994. She was a co-teacher with the second- and third-grade team and worked with Carole Shank and Kathy Beasley. Deborah is now a reading specialist at Post Oak Elementary School in Lansing. She is a participant in the Investigating Mathematics Teaching group and a doctoral student in the Teacher Education Program at Michigan State University.

Sharon Feiman-Nemser is a professor of teacher education at Michigan State University, where she directs a new, 5-year, field-based teacher education program. For more than 20 years, she has been studying and writing about teacher learning and teacher education. Most recently, she directed a cross-cultural study of mentoring for the National Center for Research on Teacher Learning. She greatly values her ongoing PDS collaboration.

John Fischetti is Associate Professor of Secondary Education at the University of Louisville. His work is focused around Professional Development Schools, high school restructuring, and curriculum design for student engagement.

Frances Goldman is a bilingual elementary school teacher in the Los Angeles Unified School District and serves as a school-based teacher educator.

Jean A. King is an associate professor in the Department of Educational Policy and Administration at the University of Minnesota. She served as Director of its Center for Applied Research and Educational Improvement, where she implemented a collaborative approach to research and program evaluation with 40 member school districts.

Rita Lancy has taught English in the Rochester City Schools since 1979. She has been active in the Professional Development Schools Project since 1990. Currently, Ms. Lancy is also involved with the New York State Quality Review Program and has had the opportunity to work as a member of a review team throughout New York State.

Marsha Levine is an education consultant in Washington, DC. She is the director of the Professional Development Schools Standards Project for the National Council for Accreditation of Teacher Education and is the editor of *Professional Practice Schools: Linking Teacher Education and School Reform.*

Nona Lyons is Associate Professor of Human Development at the University of Southern Maine. Her current research includes a project on the uses of portfolios in teacher education; a study of the school experiences of adolescent girls; and work on the ethical and intellectual dimensions of teachers' work and development, for which she received a Spencer Fellowship. Lyons is a 1996–97 Visiting Research Scholar at the Wellesley College Center for Research on Women.

Maurine Miller has been an educator for thirty years. She has taught every elementary grade, as well as at the university level. Currently, she is the Instructional Resource Teacher at Lincoln Elementary School in Madison, Wisconsin, a Professional Development School that collaborates with the University of Wisconsin–Madison. Maurine provides the university supervision for a cohort of student teachers each year, as well as support for the staff and students at the school.

Margaret L. Plecki is an assistant professor in Educational Leadership and Policy Studies at the University of Washington, Seattle. She specializes in school finance, educational policy evaluation, and the economics of education. She is particularly interested in the examination of the relationship between resource allocation and school improvement.

Carole Shank has taught at Averill Elementary School in Lansing, Michigan, for 27 years. She has been a member of the Professional Development Management Team for 5 years and is a participant in the Investigating Mathematics Teaching group at Michigan State University.

Jon Snyder is Director of Teacher Education at the University of California at Santa Barbara and a faculty member in the Educational Leadership and Organizations program. He is engaged in work focusing on how school–university partnerships enhance learning for teachers.

Beth Stroble is Associate Dean for Programs at the School of Education, University of Louisville, and an associate professor in the Department of Secondary Education. Her recent projects include a Summer Portfolio Institute for teachers and children.

Gary Sykes is a professor in the Departments of Educational Administration and Teacher Education at the College of Education, Michigan State University. He specializes in educational policy directed toward teaching, teacher education, and the professionalization of the education workforce.

Lee Teitel is an associate professor and the associate dean for Community, University, and School Partnerships at the University of Massachusetts at Boston. He co-facilitates the Massachusetts PDS Steering Committee and is a member of the PDS steering committee at the National Center for Restructuring Education, Schools and Teaching (NCREST). His work focuses on PDS start-up and institutionalization issues, new leadership roles in PDSs for teachers and principals, and the impact that PDSs have on the transformation of teacher education.

Roberta Trachtman teaches in the Teacher Education Program at the New School for Social Research in New York City. Her research focuses on the connections between school reform and the preparation of teachers and administrators. Most recently, she conducted research for NCATE's project to develop standards for Professional Development Schools.

Vivian Troen is a third-grade teacher at the Edward Devotion School in Brookline, Massachusetts, and project director of the Learning/Teaching Collaborative, a teacher-initiated Professional Development School. She is also on the faculty at Wheelock College, Boston.

Kenneth Zeichner is Hoefs-Bascom Professor of Teacher Education at the University of Wisconsin–Madison. His recent publications include *Reflective Teaching and Culture and Teaching* (with Dan Liston). He is currently Vice President of Division K (Teaching and Teacher Education) of the American Educational Research Association.